Can War Be Just in the 21st Century?

Can War Be Just
in the 21st Century?

Ethicists Engage the Tradition

edited by

TOBIAS WINRIGHT AND LAURIE JOHNSTON

ORBIS BOOKS

Maryknoll, New York 10545

Founded in 1970, Orbis Books endeavors to publish works that enlighten the mind, nourish the spirit, and challenge the conscience. The publishing arm of the Maryknoll Fathers and Brothers, Orbis seeks to explore the global dimensions of the Christian faith and mission, to invite dialogue with diverse cultures and religious traditions, and to serve the cause of reconciliation and peace. The books published reflect the views of their authors and do not represent the official position of the Maryknoll Society. To learn more about Maryknoll and Orbis Books, please visit our website at www.maryknollsociety.org.

Copyright © 2015 by Tobias Winright and Laurie Johnston
Published by Orbis Books, Maryknoll, NY 10545-0302.
Manufactured in the United States of America

Library of Congress Cataloging-in-Publication Data

Can war be just in the 21st century? : ethicists engage the tradition / edited by Tobias Winright and Laurie Johnston.
       pages cm
    Includes bibliographical references and index.
    ISBN 978-1-62698-158-4 (pbk.)
    1. War—Religious aspects—Christianity. 2. Just war doctrine. 3. War—Moral and ethical aspects. I. Winright, Tobias L., editor.
BT736.2.C265 2015
241'.6242—dc23

                                                    2015025469

*We dedicate this volume to Stanley Hauerwas.
We, too, pray for an end to war, and we also dedicate
this volume to all of war's victims.*

Contents

Foreword

STANLEY HAUERWAS

I often find myself in strange places. I do so because I am asked by good people to give a lecture here or there, and the here or the there is often somewhere I have never known existed. But "place" is not only a geographic term. It can also indicate an idea or set of ideas that seem strange because the ideas may not have been imagined by the one confronted by the ideas. That is the strange place I find myself by writing this Foreword. What am I doing, a person on record in support of Christian nonviolence, writing a Foreword to commend a book that in general assumes a just war perspective? This seems to be a very strange place for me to be.

The answer to the question about why I am writing a Foreword to a book dominated by the just war perspective turns out to be quite simple. I am doing what Tobias Winright asked me to do. I try to do what friends ask me to do, and Tobias is a longtime friend. I have always admired his intellectual and moral integrity, both of which are well on display in the Introduction he provides to this book as well as in his essay on cluster bombs. We may not agree about the status of just war as an expression of Christian charity, but I should like to think that Tobias asking me to write this Foreword is an indication that what we share outweighs our disagreements.

Friendship matters, but I do not want to leave the impression I am only writing this Foreword because Tobias asked me to do so. I am more than ready to write commending this book because I think this book represents an important development in just war thinking. Mike Baxter, a fellow pacifist, often asks, When has anyone who represents a just war position said "no" to any of the wars the United States has fought since World War II? By pressing that question Baxter is trying to force representatives of just war thinking to say when they have to "take a loss" because of their just war convictions. Which is why I think this book is so significant. Every chapter in *Can War Be Just in the 21st Century?* engages Baxter's challenge, showing clearly that a just war perspective may well mean that there are strategies and behaviors you cannot undertake as an adherent of just war.

The range of topics addressed as well as the honest analysis the writers employ is extremely impressive. I know of no other book by just warriors or by people committed to nonviolence that takes on such difficult questions. For example, "humanitarian intervention" sounds like a good idea, but as has become increasingly clear such interventions are filled with moral ambiguities. The chapters in this book on the kind of conflicts that occur in some countries in Africa are prime examples of such ambiguities. What does "legitimate authority" mean in countries where there has been little or no effective government? In such circumstances the existence of militias makes it very difficult to distinguish combatant from noncombatant. It is by no means clear how just war reasoning is possible in contexts where it is not clear a government exists. It is to the great credit of the authors of these essays that they refuse to evade these difficult questions.

Questions concerning torture, the use of drones and cluster bombs, and the place of women in combat are also addressed in this book. That these topics are taken up is extremely important. They are important because they put front and center questions of how the United States should, if we are a just war country, conduct itself. The consideration of these kinds of issues helps make clear that it is far too late to ask if this or that conflict is just or unjust once a war has begun. What is crucial is the kind of necessary reflection these essays represent before a war is begun. Only then can Americans make the claim that just war is an operative moral position for the war-making policies of the United States.

For some time I have tried to press a question to my just war brothers and sisters that I think is quite important. The question is, If a war is not just what is it? To continue to call a war a war when the war is judged unjust still gives the conflict moral legitimation. The writers of the essays in this book I think are not unsympathetic with my question. They are not only sympathetic with the question, but they understand why the question is important. That being the case, it turns out, therefore, that it is not so strange for me to commend this book.

So I am honored to write this Foreword. This is an important book. In truth it is the kind of work in which those committed to nonviolence should be engaged. So it is with real enthusiasm I commend this book. May it be the beginning of the kind of work that just warriors and pacifists can share and in the process may we discover that we are friends.

Introduction

TOBIAS WINRIGHT

"We must begin asking ourselves whether as things stand, with new weapons that cause destruction that goes well beyond the groups involved in the fight, it is still licit to allow that a 'just war' might exist."[1] These were the words of Cardinal Joseph Ratzinger, now Pope Emeritus Benedict XVI, in response to a question in 2003 about whether the United States–led war against Iraq fits "within the canons of the 'just war.'" After the horrendous terrorist attacks on September 11, 2001, the wars in Afghanistan and Iraq—and the Global War on Terror (GWOT) which they came to be called (including Operation Enduring Freedom, Operation Iraqi Freedom, and Operation New Dawn) prior to its current appellation Global Counter-Insurgency (global COIN)—were pitched by President George W. Bush to the American people and the rest of the world as just wars.[2] The just war tradition (JWT) was also invoked by President Barack H. Obama in his Nobel Peace speech in 2009.[3] For many people in the United States and elsewhere, however, "just war" may seem like a misnomer or even an oxymoron. They query whether there is *just* war, or if it is instead only just *war*. Indeed, for a growing number of Christians, including Catholics, the answer to the question "Is there such a thing as a just war?" is a booming "No!"[4]

Some doubt that just war ever truly existed, and many pacifist Christians, who believe that following Jesus Christ's teachings and example entails a life of nonviolent peacemaking, regard just war as a distortion, dilution, or even a violation of the gospel. Others, who may or may not be pacifists, point out the magnitude of devastation and myriad lives lost in modern wars and, especially, the wars of the past century, as evidence of the impossibility of

---

1. http://www.30giorni.it.

2. Chris J. Dolan, *In War We Trust: The Bush Doctrine and the Pursuit of Just War* (London: Ashgate Publishing, 2005), 2, 22; Alia Brahimi, *Jihad and Just War in the War on Terror* (Oxford: Oxford University Press, 2010), 2, 17.

3. Barack H. Obama, "A Just and Lasting Peace," December 10, 2009, http://www.nobelprize.org.

4. Tony Magliano, "Challenging the Just War Theory," *National Catholic Reporter,* September 1, 2014, http://ncronline.org.

just war today. War is now total, they note. It does not distinguish between combatants and noncombatants. Entire populations are regarded as culpable for or complicit in their nations' wars, and citizens are thus targeted, injured, and killed as much as—or now, more often than—members of the military. Even if today's wars are not on the scale of the First or Second World War, there are bloody civil wars, terrorist attacks, revolutions, and asymmetrical conflicts that seem resistant to, or utterly at odds with, just war principles that were formulated centuries ago when kings and lords commanded their soldiers to face and fight one another with swords and spears on a battle-field. If the invention of crossbows and gunpowder complicated things for just war theory once upon a time, how much more is it the case now with submarines, dirty bombs, fighter jets, drones, robots, waterboarding, cluster munitions, cyber-combat, improvised explosive devices (IEDs), and nuclear warheads!

Cardinal Ratzinger's question about the applicability of the JWT in these early years of the twenty-first century, therefore, is not merely a rhetorical one. Nor is he the first from Rome to ask it. An unsigned editorial, "Modern War and Christian Conscience," appeared in 1991 in the Jesuit periodical *La Civiltà Cattolica*, highlighting the same concerns about total and indiscriminate warfare in today's world.[5] Indeed, the editorial went even further and called for the abandonment of the just war tradition.[6] This present volume, *Can War Be Just in the 21st Century? Ethicists Engage the Tradition*, takes Ratzinger's question and these concerns seriously by engaging the tradition and addressing new technologies and weapons, current problems and issues, neglected voices and perspectives.

Its twelve contributors, including my coeditor Laurie Johnston and myself, are theological ethicists. Our task as ethicists is to ask the "ought" questions. Is the way things *are* the way things *ought* to be? What ought we do? What kind of people ought we to be? These are prescriptive, norma-tive questions regarding human and/or Christian character and choices, as individuals and as a community. Because war is a human activity—as foggy,

---

5. Editorial, "Coscienza cristiana e guerra moderna," *La Civiltà Cattolica* 142 (1991): 3-16. This is an anonymously written piece attracting wide attention, and an English translation, "Mod-ern War and Christian Conscience," by William Shannon; it appears in *Origins* 21 (December 19, 1991): 450-55. The quote is taken from the latter version (451). While possessing no official magisterial authority, such editorials in this Jesuit magazine published in Rome rarely contradict the pope's position. Indeed, the Vatican Secretariat of State reviews each issue prior to publica-tion. See Tim McCarthy, "Was Magazine's Opinion on Just War Just That?" *National Catholic Reporter*, August 16, 1991, 14.

6. Shannon, in *Origins* 21, 453.

violent, and horrible as it is—it is to be evaluated as such, that is, by whether it is moral or immoral.

War is not *a*moral. It is not like a tornado or a volcanic eruption; nor is war something that simply "breaks out," like a fire. Even if it resembles an inferno, Michael Walzer, who is a secular political theorist and preeminent just war theorist, notes that it is "more like arson than accident: war has human agents as well as human victims."[7] For Christians, therefore, war either is *always* immoral (pacifism) or is *sometimes* immoral (JWT). With the latter, war also is *sometimes* morally justifiable, and when it is, it ought to be fought justly—Methodist ethicist Paul Ramsey preferred referring to it as "justified war" rather than "just war."[8] Furthermore, as Saint Pope John Paul II emphasized in January 2003, shortly before the United States invaded Iraq, "War is not always inevitable."[9] Indeed, it can be prevented before it starts; it can be stopped after embarking upon it. A "no" can be said *before* going to war and to particular conduct *during* war—and this "no" can come from the lips not only of pacifists but also of Christians and others who subscribe to the JWT.

Admittedly, rarely have such negative judgments been issued by just war ethicists, let alone by most other Christians, citizens, politicians, and generals who adhere neither to just war theory nor to pacifism. As Catholic moral theologian Patrick T. McCormick has lamented, the actual "default position" of the "vast majority of American Catholics and Christians" is that they "approach the moral analysis of every call to arms with a strong presumption in favor of war."[10] Although some of the language or principles of just war—usually only the criterion of just cause—might be used, especially by the governing authorities, "by and large people do not know the just war tradition," according to Daniel M. Bell, Jr., a United Methodist theologian who teaches at Lutheran Theological Southern Seminary and at the US Army's Command and General Staff College at Fort Leavenworth.[11] Instead, most persons support, *carte blanche* (with a "blank check"), all of their nation's wars. They uncritically wave their flags and "support the troops." For many

---

7. Michael Walzer, *Just and Unjust Wars: A Moral Argument with Historical Illustrations*, 2nd ed. (New York: Basic Books, 1992), 31.

8. Paul Ramsey, *War and the Christian Conscience: How Shall Modern War Be Conducted Justly?* (Durham, NC: Duke University Press, 1961), 15.

9. John Paul II, "Address of His Holiness Pope John Paul II to the Diplomatic Corps," January 13, 2003, http://w2.vatican.va.

10. Patrick T. McCormick, "Violence: Religion, Terror, War," *Theological Studies* 67, no. 1 (March 2006): 159.

11. Daniel M. Bell, Jr., *Just War as Christian Discipleship: Recentering the Tradition in the Church Rather Than the State* (Grand Rapids, MI: Brazos Press, 2009), 14.

of them, this attitude isn't their fault; they may not have been educated about the ethics of war. But for many others, the underlying assumption is that ethics doesn't apply to war. If anything, "our" side is assumed to be "right," and what is important is that we *win*, doing whatever is "necessary" to achieve victory, rather than that we win *rightly*. They often bring up the "war is hell" phrase from Union Army General William Tecumseh Sherman, who believed that no limits should be expected or imposed on the wrongly attacked or aggrieved nation in its military response against an offending party. As Walzer describes Sherman's perspective, "Nor is he the only general to think that if his cause is just he cannot be blamed for the death and destruction he spreads around him—for war is hell."[12] This, I would add, seems to be the stance of too many Americans, including Catholics.

In addition, although Bush, Obama, and other political leaders might utter the words of just war, a number of theologians, ethicists, and others suspect that it is only a manipulative smokescreen used to "justify" wars of "national interest," where moral considerations really do not have a claim and, simply put, might makes right. A school of thought known as "realism," often associated with Machiavelli, holds that the criteria of the JWT are inapplicable during war except when they serve the nation's interest.[13] This is just war theory "without teeth," in which the rules are not firmly rooted and instead are easily bent or broken. While some just war ethicists might claim that just war is more "realistic" than pacifism or nonviolence, just war theory and realism should not necessarily be equated or conflated. The contributors to this volume do not use realism, as Stanley Hauerwas alleges about many just war thinkers, "to dismiss pacifism and to underwrite some version of just war."[14]

We acknowledge that nonviolence, more often than assumed, can be as realistic, or effective, as just war in resisting injustice. Just peacemaking practices and Catholic peacebuilding efforts—on which both pacifists and just war theorists have collaborated—are empirical evidence of that; and we support such nonviolent theory and practice, since they help prevent war in the first place or at least make war truly a last resort.[15] Still, we recognize that, in

---

12. Walzer, *Just and Unjust Wars*, 33.

13. Mark J. Allman, *Who Would Jesus Kill? War, Peace, and the Christian Tradition* (Winona, MN: Anselm Academic, 2008), 103-7.

14. Stanley Hauerwas, *War and the American Difference: Theological Reflections on Violence and National Identity* (Grand Rapids, MI: Baker Academic, 2011), 34.

15. See Glen Stassen, ed., *Just Peacemaking: The New Paradigm for the Ethics of Peace and War*, rev. ed. (Cleveland, OH: Pilgrim Press, 2008); and R. Scott Appleby, Robert J. Schreiter, and Gerard Powers, *Peacebuilding: Catholic Theology, Ethics, and Praxis* (Maryknoll, NY: Orbis Books, 2010).

the eyes of real realists, not only nonviolence but also just war ("with teeth") can seem unrealistic. "At least it is not clear that just war considerations can be constitutive of the decision-making processes of governments that must assume that might makes right," Hauerwas writes. "Attempts to justify wars begun and fought on realist grounds in the name of just war only serve to hide the reality of war."[16] As Christian theologians, the contributors to this volume try not to underestimate how nations, governments, and militaries really operate, but we also believe that they can do the right thing, too. We are not realists whose cynicism runs all the way down to the core; we strive to write with both eyes wide open. We strive to avoid either excessive realism or excessive idealism. Moreover, the reality of war, even if not all of us have experienced it firsthand, deeply disturbs us and discomforts our deliberations here. Even though we disagree with Sherman's dictum, we realize that war indeed is hell for all those who are scathed by it.

As for the aforementioned "blank check" attitude, my coeditor Laurie Johnston refers to how "American Catholics overall tend to be very willing—even too willing—to trust their government authorities absolutely," and she adds that some of her own students have said, "Yes, I'm a Catholic—but I'm an American first."[17] Patriotism here morphs into nationalism, making Catholics and their fellow citizens less likely to question their country's armed response to terrorism. Similar misgivings were expressed soon after 9/11 by Michael Baxter, a Catholic pacifist, and Lisa Sowle Cahill, a Catholic just war scholar, when their students at, respectively, the University of Notre Dame and Boston College slipped into excessive patriotism and its accompanying disinclination to raise moral questions when war is being contemplated.[18] It is noteworthy that pacifists and just war ethicists can agree that nationalism and militarism—and the blank-check attitude associated with them—are morally inappropriate as a default position.

To be sure, many Christian ethicists and theologians, including some who, like Cahill, contributed to this volume, brought just war principles to bear on the lead up to the war in Afghanistan—with a number thinking that some form of forceful action was justified to apprehend and stop those

16. Hauerwas, *War and the American Difference*, 34.

17. Laurie Johnston, "The Catholic Conversation since 9/11: A Moral Challenge," in *The Impact of 9/11 on Religion and Philosophy: The Day That Changed Everything?*, ed. Matthew J. Morgan (New York: Palgrave Macmillan, 2009), 114.

18. Lisa Sowle Cahill and Michael Baxter, "Is This Just War?" in *Moral Issues and Christian Responses*, 7th ed., ed. Patricia Beattie Jung and Shannon Jung (Belmont, CA: Thomson Wadsworth, 2003), 355-61, originally published in *U.S. Catholic* (December 2001), http://www.uscatholic.org.

responsible for the terrorist attacks—and in the months before the invasion of Iraq, most Christian ethicists and theologians scrupulously criticized, on just war grounds, the United States' plans for preemptive war.[19] Similar critical analysis continued during the actual fighting of these wars, as well as after the shooting supposedly stopped.[20] Likewise, the US Catholic bishops issued public statements and letters to government officials, including President Bush, that drew on criteria of the JWT in order to raise "moral concerns and questions" about the war in Iraq.[21] At the time, Pope John Paul II and other Vatican officials, including Italian Cardinal Pio Laghi, who was sent by the pope to meet with President Bush on March 5, 2003, also expressed serious reservations about whether US military action against Iraq would be a just war.[22] Moreover, when the US ambassador to the Vatican, at the time, invited American Catholic Michael Novak to give a lecture on why the Iraq war would be just, most attendees were not so persuaded on just war grounds.[23]

Thus, while it is generally true that just war theorists over the centuries have rarely issued a "no" to particular wars or to some sorts of conduct during

19. Religion News Service, "Just War: Christian Ethicists: Afghan War Is Just," *Christianity Today* (March 11, 2002), http://www.christianitytoday.com; Drew Christiansen, S.J., "After Sept. 11: Catholic Teaching on Peace and War," *Origins* 32, no. 3 (May 30, 2002): 33, 35-40; Brian V. Johnstone, C.SS.R., "The War on Terrorism: A Just War?" *Studia Moralia* 40, no. 1 (June 2002): 39-61; Scott McLemee, "100 Christian Ethicists Challenge Claim That Preemptive War on Iraq Would Be Morally Justified," *The Chronicle of Higher Education*, September 23, 2002, http://m.chronicle.com; Peter Steinfels, "Churches and Ethicists Loudly Oppose the Proposed War on Iraq, but Deaf Ears Are Many," *The New York Times*, September 28, 2002, http://query.nytimes.com.

20. Tobias Winright, "Just Cause and Preemptive Strikes in the War on Terrorism: Insights from a Just-Policing Perspective," *Journal of the Society of Christian Ethics* 26, no. 2 (Fall/Winter 2006): 157-81; Mark J. Allman and Tobias L. Winright, *After the Smoke Clears: The Just War Tradition and Post War Justice* (Maryknoll, NY: Orbis Books, 2010); David E. DeCosse, "Authority, Democracy, and the Iraq War," *Heythrop Journal* 45 (2004): 227-46; Brian V. Johnstone, C.SS.R, "Pope John Paul II and the War in Iraq," *Studia Moralia* 41, no. 2 (December 2003): 309-30.

21. United States Conference of Catholic Bishops, "Statement on Iraq," November 13, 2002, http://www.usccb.org. Subsequent statements reiterated the same questions and concerns. See "Statement on Iraq" by Bishop Wilton D. Gregory, president of the USCCB, February 26, 2003, http://www.usccb.org; "Toward a Responsible Transition in Iraq" by Bishop Thomas G. Wenski, chair of the USCCB Committee on International Policy, January 12, 2006, http://www.usccb.org.

22. Frank Bruni, "Pope Voices Opposition, His Strongest, to Iraq War," *New York Times*, January 14, 2003, http://www.nytimes.com; Gerard O'Connell, "When Bush Put John Paul II's Letter on the Side Table without Opening It," *Vatican Insider*, September 17, 2011, http://vaticaninsider.lastampa.it/.

23. David Willey, "Catholic Theologian Says Iraq 'Just War,'" *BBC News*, February 10, 2003, http://news.bbc.co.uk.

war, there have indeed been Catholic theologians, ethicists, clergy, and even popes who employ just war reasoning seriously to arrive at the "no" that Baxter expects from practitioners of the JWT.[24] Baxter himself highlights Franz Jägerstätter, Elizabeth Anscombe, and others who used just war reasoning and principles to critique unjust wars fought by their countries.[25] Jägerstätter was an Austrian peasant who refused on just war grounds to serve as a soldier for the Nazi German regime, so he was beheaded as a "traitor" to his country on August 9, 1943. A proclamation from Pope Benedict XVI, which was read at Jägerstätter's beatification on October 26, 2007, said, "We comply with the request [of the bishop of Linz, brother bishops and the Congregation for the Causes of Saints] that Franz Jägerstätter, martyr and family father, from now on can be invoked as Blessed Franz Jägerstätter."[26] Baxter points to Jägerstätter and a few others as examples of a "strict understanding of just war theory" being "faithfully theorized and practiced," and while he observes that these persons are rare exceptions, he suggests that this "should not obscure the demands of this tradition, but should make us press it upon the church all the more urgently, precisely because as the experience in Austria showed, it has had little impact on the moral discernment of Catholics."[27]

The aim of this volume is to do precisely that: to contribute to the informing of Catholics' consciences concerning just war, to equip them to discern just from unjust war, and to enable them to adhere to their convictions firmly. As theological ethicists, the contributors to this volume seriously seek to address moral questions we face in the kinds of wars prevalent, and with the sorts of weapons available, at this time. While we might not agree exactly on every detail of the JWT, we all identify with it and think it remains relevant. "Announcements of the irrelevancy, demise or uselessness of the just war tradition are commonly made," writes contributor Kenneth R. Himes, O.F.M., who contends that "the number of books published in recent years that take just war thinking seriously and offer thoughtful exposition, commentary and revision of the tradition suggests there remains a large audience of readers who find the wisdom of that politico-moral tradition still worth

---

24. For more recent applications of just war analysis in connection with Syria and Iran, see Tobias Winright, "A Just War 'No' on Attacking Syria," *The Tablet* 267, no. 9013 (August 31, 2013): 4-5; and Tobias Winright and Patrick J. Lynch, S.J., "Iran: The Challenge to Peace" *The Tablet* 266, no. 8971 (November 3, 2012): 4-5.

25. Michael Baxter, "Just War and Pacifism: A 'Pacifist' Perspective in Seven Points," *The Houston Catholic Worker*, June 1, 2004, http://cjd.org.

26. Michael Hovey, "The Beatification of Franz Jägerstätter," Catholic Peace Fellowship, http://www.catholicpeacefellowship.org.

27. Baxter, "Just War and Pacifism."

considering."[28] Whereas it is often referred to as just war *theory*, we engage it is a living, developing *tradition*. With antecedents in ancient Greek and Roman natural law philosophy, just war reasoning and principles were grafted into Christian theology beginning with Saint Ambrose and Saint Augustine in the fourth century CE, and developed through the centuries via an ongoing interplay between secular and religious sources, becoming the gold standard in the Catholic as well as other religious and ethical traditions for morally evaluating warfare.[29] The first essay in this volume, by Lisa Sowle Cahill, who is one of our more senior contributors, explores further the JWT vis-à-vis the gospel, while surveying the developments from Saint Augustine to Saint Thomas Aquinas in the thirteenth century to today.

We subscribe to a "strict constructionist" approach to just war that has "teeth"—in other words, the possibility of answering "no" when determining whether each of its criteria are met when contemplating and fighting a given war. We take seriously all of the obligations of the just war criteria, not in some minimal or negative checklist sense, but rather along the lines of a discipline that involves commitments, duties, and virtues as well as categories, criteria, and principles.[30] Elsewhere, I anchor this approach to just war, along with pacifism, for Christians, in the liturgy—especially in our eucharistic worship of the Prince of Peace and in the peace that we taste and share while doing so—and its forming and shaping us to be peacemakers.[31] Indeed,

---

28. Kenneth R. Himes, "Traditional Wisdom," review of *War's Ends: Human Rights, International Order, and the Ethics of Peace*, by James G. Murphy, S.J., *America* 212, no. 4 (February 9, 2015): 34.

29. Charles Reed, *Just War?* (New York: Church Publishing, 2004), 32.

30. For a recent book that offers a constructive account of just war as requiring communal disciplines, practices, and virtues, see Bell, *Just War as Christian Discipleship*.

31. Tobias Winright, "The Liturgy as a Basis for Catholic Identity, Just War Theory, and the Presumption against War," in *Catholic Identity and the Laity*, College Theology Society Annual, vol. 54, ed. Tim Muldoon (Maryknoll, NY: Orbis Books, 2009), 134-51, and Tobias Winright, "Gather Us In and Make Us Channels of Your Peace: Undertaking an Evaluation of War with an Entirely New Attitude," in *Gathered for the Journey: Moral Theology in Catholic Perspective*, ed. M. Therese Lysaught and David Matzko McCarthy (Grand Rapids, MI: William B. Eerdmans Publishing/SCM Press, 2007), 281-306. This connection between the liturgy and peacemaking is mentioned in National Conference of Catholic Bishops, *The Challenge of Peace* (Washington, DC: United States Conference of Catholic Bishops, 1983), par. 295. Similarly, at the end of its chapter on war and peace, the *Compendium of the Social Doctrine of the Church* says, "In particular, the Eucharistic celebration, 'the source and summit of the Christian life,' is a limitless wellspring for all authentic Christian commitment to peace" (Pontifical Council for Justice and Peace, *Compendium of the Social Doctrine of the Church* [Washington, DC: United States Conference of Catholic Bishops, 2004], par. 519). Also, the next-to-last footnote (#1102), which is by far the longest of the footnotes in that chapter, highlights the emphasis on peace that runs throughout the Mass.

according to the US Catholic bishops, "Peacemaking is not an optional commitment. It is a requirement of our faith. We are called to be peacemakers, not by some movement of the moment, but by our Lord Jesus."[32] For Catholics, this means that we may be called to resist nonviolently injustices and oppression, but it means that if others of us believe sometimes force, including lethal force, is the only way to defend the innocent, we adhere to an approach to just war reasoning that is serious and strict. This approach to just war is not, as some accuse, a "functional pacifism" or "quasi-pacifism."[33] Nor should it be confused with "holy war" or "crusades," which most Christian churches now condemn as morally unjustified. We identify with what Bell calls "a more robust vision of just war"[34] rather than the more permissive, more hawkish version that some of our fellow Catholics, such as Novak, George Weigel, and others espouse.[35] We believe that armed force can be morally justified, but as Kenneth Himes, O.F.M., puts it, "the case for war should be difficult to make. Not impossible, but difficult."[36] A burden of proof rests upon those attempting to justify war and the taking of human lives.

Still, some pacifists, similar to the realists, deny that just war is at all possible. Some, like the editorial in *La Civiltà Cattolica*, call for the jettisoning of the JWT altogether. Colman McCarthy, for instance, asks for examples of just war, and he suggests "it might be time to replace the phrase 'Just War' with 'Just Slaughter.'"[37] But other pacifists are not so dismissive. Baxter, for example, does not argue for "scrapping" just war thinking altogether.[38]

32. National Conference of Catholic Bishops, *The Challenge of Peace*, par. 333. This moral obligation for Christians, as well as for people of good will, to seek peace and an end to war is highlighted in Second Vatican Council, "Pastoral Constitution on the Church in the Modern World" (*Gaudium et spes*), in *The Documents of Vatican II*, ed. Walter M. Abbot, S.J. (Piscataway, NJ: New Century Publishers, 1966), par. 82; and *Catechism of the Catholic Church* (New York: Image/Doubleday, 1995), par. 2308.

33. James Turner Johnson, "Just War, as It Was and Is," *First Things* (January 2005): 21; Eric Patterson, *Just War Thinking: Morality and Pragmatism in the Struggle against Contemporary Threats* (Lanham, MD: Lexington Books, 2007), 25; George Weigel, *Against the Grain: Christianity and Democracy, War and Peace* (New York: Crossroad, 2008), 5.

34. Daniel M. Bell, Jr., "Discriminating Force: Just War and Counterinsurgency," *Christian Century* 130, no. 16 (August 7, 2013): 25.

35. For more on why I think the "permissive" version of just war theory is problematic, see Winright, "Liturgy as a Basis," 134–51; and Tobias Winright, "Hawks and Doves: Rival Versions of Just War Theory," *Christian Century* 123, no. 25 (December 12, 2006): 32–35.

36. Kenneth R. Himes, O.F.M., "Intervention, Just War, and U.S. National Security," *Theological Studies* 65, no. 1 (March 2004): 152.

37. Colman McCarthy, "Just War or Just More Slaughter?" *Waging Nonviolence*, August 2, 2011, http://wagingnonviolence.org/feature/just-war-or-just-more-slaughter.

38. Baxter, "Is This Just War?" 358.

Likewise, "christological pacifist" D. Stephen Long retorts, "Whether or not these strict guidelines have ever been adhered to is beside the question," because serious just war theorists and practitioners are committed to "a rigorous ethic that requires incredible self-restraint in the employment of violence."[39] Again, we confess that staunch adherence to this ethic may seem to be the exception, but we hope this volume provides a helpful resource for Catholics and others who believe that, sadly, under certain conditions when just peacemaking practices have failed (or there is not time to attempt them), the use of force, including lethal force, is justified—namely, when there is no other way to defend innocent lives from unjust aggressors. In Long's view, which I share, "Just war only makes sense if it is an alien work of love to protect the neighbor from unjust aggression."[40] As far as I can tell with regard to my fellow contributors, we do not advocate the use of lethal force for lesser loyalties, such as the flag or our "way of life" or ideas, important as they may be, such as freedom and democracy. Indeed, recent magisterial documents, such as the *Catechism of the Catholic Church*, the *Compendium of Catholic Social Doctrine*, and statements by Popes John Paul II, Benedict XVI, and Francis tend not to use the phrase "just war" but instead seem to prefer the expression "just defense" or "legitimate defense" of the innocent.[41] To be sure, beginning with Pope Paul VI, every pope has declared "never again war, never again war!"[42] And we Catholics pray for an end to war. However, David Carroll Cochran, in his recent *Catholic Realism and*

---

39. D. Stephen Long, "What about the Protection of Third-Party Innocents? On Letting Your Neighbors Die," in *A Faith Not Worth Fighting For: Addressing Commonly Asked Questions about Christian Nonviolence*, ed. Tripp York and Justin Bronson Barringer (Eugene, OR: Cascade Books, 2012), 22.

40. Ibid., 24; Allman and Winright, *After the Smoke Clears*, 30; Bell, *Just War as Christian Discipleship*, 31; and see Nigel Biggar, *In Defence of War* (Oxford: Oxford University Press, 2013), 61-91.

41. Kenneth R. Himes, O.F.M., "Hard Questions about Just War," *America* 195, no. 13 (October 30, 2006): 13; William L. Portier, "Are We Really Serious When We Ask God to Deliver Us from War? The Catechism and the Challenge of Pope John Paul II," *Communio* 23 (Spring 1996): 48, 49, 55; Drew Christiansen, S.J., "Whither the 'Just War'?" *America* 188, no. 10 (March 24, 2003): 7-11; Drew Christiansen, S.J., "After Sept. 11," 33, 35-40; Gianni Cardinale, "The Catechism in a Post-Christian World: Interview with Cardinal Joseph Ratzinger, 2003, http://www.30giorni.it/articoli_id_775_13.htm?id=775.

42. See, for example, Paul VI, "Address of Pope Paul VI to the UN General Assembly," *The Pope Speaks* 11, no. 1 (1966): 54; John Paul II, "War, a Decline for Humanity," *Origins* 20, no. 33 (1991): 531; and Rick Lyman, "Pope Francis Urges a Divided Bosnia to Heal, Declaring 'War Never Again!'" *New York Times*, June 6, 2015, http://www.nytimes.com/.

the Abolition of War, which calls for the outlawing of war, gets it right when he writes, "A narrow space for justified war still exists in Catholic doctrine."[43]

For example, in his 2007 World Day of Peace message, Benedict XVI simultaneously called for the establishment of "clearer rules" and "norms of conduct" for defending the innocent, reducing "the damage as far as possible," while repeating the papal refrain that "war always represents a failure for the international community and a grave loss for humanity."[44] What might these "clearer rules" or "norms of conduct" look like? Here Benedict footnoted the section of the *Catechism of the Catholic Church* (par. 2307-2317) that lists "the traditional elements enumerated in what is called the 'just war' doctrine" (par. 2309). Whether we call these rules "just war" criteria, criteria for "legitimate defense," "violence-reduction criteria,"[45] "just policing" criteria,[46] or the "responsibility to protect" (R2P),[47] Benedict XVI did not abandon altogether the mode of moral reasoning that involves these several criteria to be employed for considering when and how force may be used to defend innocent persons. Likewise, the editorial in *La Civiltà Cattolica*, although calling for the abandoning of just war, actually employed just war criteria to critique modern warfare, and then went on to say that the only justifiable war would be "a war of pure defense against an aggression actually taking place."[48] Kenneth Himes's contribution to this volume examines this trajectory in connection with humanitarian intervention today, including in connection with Pope Francis and the atrocities happening in Iraq and Syria committed by ISIS. So, even though the rules of the JWT have been bent and broken far too often over the centuries and in recent times, *abusus non tollit usum* ("the abuse does not negate their proper use"). In his slim book, *The Horrors We Bless: Rethinking the Just-War Legacy*, which is highly critical

---

43. David Carroll Cochran, *Catholic Realism and the Abolition of War* (Maryknoll, NY: Orbis Books, 2014), 2. In 2002, Protestant pacifist Stanley Hauerwas and Irish Catholic theological ethicist Enda McDonagh, who tended to associate with the JWT, issued "An Appeal to Abolish War," which both pacifist and just war Christians were invited to support; it can be found in Hauerwas, *War and the American Difference*, 40-42.

44. Pope Benedict XVI, "The Human Person, the Heart of Peace," World Day of Peace Message 2007, http://www.vatican.va.

45. Walter Wink, *Engaging the Powers: Discernment and Resistance in a World of Domination* (Minneapolis, MN: Fortress Press, 1992), 220-27.

46. Gerald W. Schlabach, ed., *Just Policing, Not War: An Alternative Response to World Violence* (Collegeville, MN: Liturgical Press, 2007).

47. Semegnish Asfaw, Guillermo Kerber, and Peter Weiderud, eds., *The Responsibility to Protect: Ethical and Theological Reflections* (Geneva: World Council of Churches, 2005); Tobias Winright, "Just Policing and the Responsibility to Protect," *Ecumenical Review* 63, no. 1 (March 2011): 84-95.

48. "Modern War and Christian Conscience," 453-54.

of the JWT, Daniel C. Maguire nevertheless insists that "the need is not to jettison these rules but to update them and insist on their morally binding necessity."[49] We couldn't agree more.

Traditionally, there have been two major categories of criteria: *jus ad bellum* and *jus in bello*.[50] The first, *jus ad bellum*, includes criteria that ought to be satisfied *prior* to embarking upon war. That is, these principles have to do with *why* and *when* going to war is justified. Seven criteria or principles fall under its umbrella: just cause, legitimate authority, right intent, probability of success, last resort, proportionality (on a macro scale), and comparative justice. The second, *jus in bello*, which has to do with just conduct *during* war, traditionally includes discrimination (noncombatant immunity) and proportionality (on a micro scale). In recent years, theological ethicists and others have begun to develop just war reasoning to include *jus ante bellum*, which includes just peacemaking practices that hopefully diminish the likelihood of war, and *jus post bellum*, which includes criteria and practices aimed at establishing a just and lasting peace in the wake of a war, thereby hopefully reducing the likelihood of war reigniting there.[51]

It is not the purpose of this volume to argue that just war is more faithful, better, or more realistic than pacifism. Our argument is not with pacifists. We welcome their use of what we write here to hold those of us who continue to employ just war reasoning and criteria accountable to it. The main sticking point, in my view, is this, which Long puts nicely with regard to his own Christian pacifism: "So the question put to pacifists at its boldest is, Are you willing to let your neighbors or other innocents die for the sake of your dogmatic theological convictions? And the first answer that must be given, before it then gets qualified, is yes."[52] However, when mass murder is under way or when innocent persons are threatened with genocide, for instance, and especially if they request forceful intervention from others, we believe

---

49. Daniel C. Maguire, *The Horrors We Bless: Rethinking the Just War Legacy* (Minneapolis, MN: Fortress Press, 2007).

50. For readers unfamiliar with the JWT and in need of further explanation of these criteria, see Allman and Winright, *After the Smoke Clears*, 16-17, 38-49. We rely primarily on National Conference of Catholic Bishops, *The Challenge of Peace*, pars. 84-110.

51. Allman and Winright, *After the Smoke Clears*; Mark J. Allman and Tobias L. Winright, "Growing Edges of Just War Theory: *Jus ante bellum, jus post bellum*, and Imperfect Justice," *Journal of the Society of Christian Ethics* 32, no. 2 (Fall/Winter 2012): 173-91; Maureen O'Connell, "Just *ante* bellum: Faith-Based Diplomacy and Catholic Traditions on War and Peace," *Journal for Peace and Justice Studies* 21, no. 1 (2011): 3-30; George R. Lucas, "*Jus ante* and *post bellum*: Completing the Circle, Breaking the Cycle," in *Ethics beyond War's End*, ed. Eric Patterson (Washington, DC: Georgetown University Press, 2012), 47-64.

52. Long, "What about the Protection of Third-Party Innocents?" 28.

that such lethal force may be morally justified. We do not believe we can impose pacifism and even martyrdom upon others who are undergoing such violence. But Long correctly adds that serious just war adherents must also be willing to say "yes" to the question put to pacifists, because innocents die in just wars, too, even if unintentionally as "collateral damage." And I would add that just war "with teeth" would also say "no" to some wars or actions in wars for the sake of just war convictions, and this too may lead to civilian casualties, as has happened recently in Syria. There, although just cause existed for intervention, the consequences of intervening, most just war ethicists believed, would probably outweigh any good to be sought. Civilians continue to suffer and die due to that moral reasoning, and I confess that I lose sleep knowing that. Serious just war people admit, though, that they cannot force history to come out right.

As a student of Hauerwas, I know that one of his criticisms of Christian justification of just war is that, as he puts it, "it stills the imaginative search for nonviolent ways of resistance to injustice" so that violence, rather deterministically, "becomes the only alternative."[53] Irish Catholic theologian Linda Hogan made the same assertion in a recent plenary address to the Catholic Theological Society of America. She argued that the arts and imagination can "challenge the dominance of the just war paradigm in Christian theology, to push back against its weight, and make the case for Christianity as a tradition of non-violence and pacifism."[54] However, I do not think that just war necessarily lacks imagination, and I am not persuaded that more imagination necessarily entails only pacifism. As noted earlier, just war ethicists, along with pacifists, in recent years have been using their imaginations quite a bit, generating interesting and, hopefully, helpful ideas that hone, extend, and better apply the mode of moral reasoning and the principles, practices, and commitments of the JWT towards a just and lasting peace. Just policing, just peacemaking, and R2P are but a few examples of this. I believe that the essays in this volume also reflect the creative, constructive imaginations of their contributors.

---

53. Stanley Hauerwas, *The Peaceable Kingdom: A Primer in Christian Ethics* (Notre Dame, IN: University of Notre Dame Press, 1983), 114, 123.

54. Linda Hogan, "The Ethical Imagination and the Anatomy of Change: A Perspective from Social Ethics," *Proceedings of the Catholic Theological Society* 68 (2013): 18-30. For my response, see Tobias Winright, "Response to Linda Hogan's 'Conversion and the Work of Ethical Imagination: A Perspective from Social Ethics,'" *Proceedings of the Catholic Theological Society* 68 (2013): 31-35. Both are available at http://ejournals.bc.edu/ojs/index.php/ctsa/issue/view/575/showToc.

Six men and six women authored these twelve chapters, and not all of us are from the United States. In addition to the aforementioned chapters by Lisa Sowle Cahill and Kenneth R. Himes, there are chapters on a number of urgent matters, as well as chapters that offer oft-neglected perspectives in Catholic just war ethics. As for the former, there are essays on drones and robots (Brian Stiltner), cluster munitions (Tobias Winright), self-determination and the use of force by the parties involved with efforts to secede from an existing state (Gerard F. Powers), torture and terror (Anna Floerke Scheid), environmental destruction (Laurie Johnston), and the testing of nuclear weapons (Rachel Hart Winters). Neglected perspectives are provided in the essays on women in combat and civilian immunity (Cristina Richie), intrastate conflicts in Africa (Elias O. Opongo), civilian immunity in the conflict in the Democratic Republic of the Congo (John Kiess), and, finally, returning warriors' experience of "moral injury" (Tobias Winright and E. Ann Jeschke). Of course, not every possible topic is addressed in this volume. Additional perspectives were sought, but the invited authors for those chapters, for a number of valid reasons, were unable to complete and submit their hoped-for contributions. Recently, some interesting, important viewpoints have appeared elsewhere, including an adaptation by María Teresa Dávila of Augustinian just war theory through the lens of Latino/a theology and an exploration by Ryan P. Cumming of just war theory through African American thought on war.[55] I highly recommend looking at these two works, and I look forward to similar efforts from others. I hope, moreover, that this present volume stimulates more imaginative attempts dealing with Ratzinger's question about whether war can be just in the twenty-first century.

For me, just war, or justified force, including lethal force, has not only been an academic question. I myself struggled with it when I worked for several years in law enforcement in corrections while I was a young person in college and in policing some years later. I also participated in Army R.O.T.C., including a memorable training exercise at Fort Benning in Georgia, during my undergraduate days when I considered a possible career in the military. I know that my own experience in law enforcement has impacted my vision and how I teach and write in theological ethics. Believe me, I have seen what violence can do to others; I have endured violence; and I have used force. I am not pro-war. I am not pro-violence. But I am not yet a pacifist. I also

---

55. María Teresa Dávila, "Breaking from the Dominance of Power and Order in Augustine's Ethic of War," in *Augustine and Social Justice*, ed. Teresa Delgado, John Doody, and Kim Paffenroth (Lanham, MD: Lexington Books, 2015), 145-62; Ryan P. Cumming, *The African American Challenge to Just War Theory: A Christian Approach* (New York: Palgrave Macmillan, 2013).

want to make sure that, in this twenty-first century, we who continue to use just war reasoning and principles do not fail in the way that John Courtney Murray, S.J., observed of theologians last century, when he wrote, "But there is place for an indictment of all of us who failed to make the tradition relevant."[56]

I am grateful for the many theological ethicists who are helping in this endeavor, too, including many who over the years have become my friends, a word that is ubiquitous today, but which really means something to me. I don't know what I would do without them. This includes Stanley Hauerwas, who so generously wrote the Foreword to this volume even though he is a Christian pacifist. A quarter century ago I studied under him at Duke Divinity School, and I continue to be challenged by, and to learn from, him. I am thankful for his patience, another word that means a lot more to me, and I dedicate this volume to him. It is good that we are friends. I would like to express my gratitude to all of the contributors, including especially my coeditor, Laurie Johnston. In addition to her kindness and intelligence, she, too, is patient, and she helped tremendously with soliciting and editing these essays. I really owe a lot to Jim Keane of Orbis Books for suggesting such a volume in the first place and inviting us to work on it. Besides having an excellent sense of humor, he too is pretty patient. Thanks, also, to Nathaniel Hibner, my graduate research assistant at Saint Louis University, for his help along the way. Finally, I am grateful to Susan Parsons, editor of *Studies in Christian Ethics*, as well as to Sage Publishing, for allowing me to republish as a chapter in this volume a revised and updated version of my article "The Morality of Cluster Bombing" from *Studies in Christian Ethics* 22, no. 3 (August 2009): 357-81.

---

56. John Courtney Murray, S.J., "Remarks on the Moral Problem of War," *Theological Studies* 20, no. 1 (March 1959): 53-54.

CHAPTER 1

Just War and the Gospel

LISA SOWLE CAHILL

An Enduring Dilemma

Perhaps the oldest and most basic dilemma of the Christian life is how to embrace the gospel in one's own existence while remaining inevitably embedded in a world seemingly so inimical to it. Jesus calls us to love God wholeheartedly, to love our neighbors as much as ourselves, and even to love our enemies (Mark 12:30-31; Matt 22:37; Luke 10:27; Matt 5:44). Yet not only our own survival but our very ability to love and serve other people depends on our capacity to escape substantial harms. More generally, we exist within and rely upon institutions, governments, laws, and other protections without which social life would be impossible. Even those who personally reject violence benefit from the guarantees of safety that a well-ordered society provides. People living in repressive, anarchic, or war-torn societies can especially attest to the importance of the rule of law and human security. Law and order are impossible without ways to fend off dangers, and if a threat is lethal, doesn't it call for a commensurate response?

The tension between Jesus's depiction of life under the reign of God and the practical requirements of filling this worldly role is reflected in the New Testament itself, for instance in the words of John the Baptist, Jesus's forerunner and mentor. John tells soldiers not to do violence to anyone; then, in the same breath and without demanding they leave the army, instructs soldiers to be content with their wages—perhaps a warning against currying favor with military superiors (Luke 3:14). Many of Jesus's commands seem idealistic or hyperbolic—for example, to give all you have to the poor (Luke 18:22), to forgive offenses seventy times seven (Matt 18:22), and to be as perfect as God (Matt 5:38). Certainly his instruction not to take up the sword (Matt 26:52) should not be taken as a literal command for all time.

Would Jesus deny the innocent the right to defend themselves, or to protect their nation or their neighbor from unjust aggression?

Early Christian Pacifism

The answer of historic Christianity to these questions is less than clear. While the "just war" tradition (JWT) has been mainstream since the fifth century, there has always been an active and eloquent pacifist tradition. In the first three centuries of Christianity, theologians and teachers such as Justin Martyr, Tertullian, Origen, and Cyprian were clear that to be a disciple of Jesus means to follow his countercultural example. The Christian should repudiate violence, killing, and war; and should stay out of military service, because even short of war, the military profession brings moral dangers such as gambling and prostitution. In the Roman era, it involved mandatory ceremonies by which members of the armed forces showed allegiance to the emperor by worshiping him. Interestingly—and contributing to the long-standing ambiguity about how exactly Christianity judges war—Christian tombstone inscriptions from the first three centuries do sometimes identify the deceased as soldiers.[1] Then as now, one may speculate, vociferous preaching against a practice or behavior is more likely to mean that it is in fact common than that it is actually rare.

Yet, if taken seriously, early Christian pacifism challenges the very assumption that Christians need to or should back the use of force to protect and serve, or even that Christians need to or should aim to save their own lives against unjust attack. Pacifism has been upheld by movements such as the Peace of God (tenth century) and Truce of God (eleventh century), and voices such as Peter Damian, Francis of Assisi, Desiderius Erasmus, and the sixteenth-century Anabaptists, whose heirs are the Mennonites and other historic peace churches.[2] Pacifists in recent theology include Dorothy Day, John Howard Yoder, Stanley Hauerwas, Walter Wink, John Dear, Gordon Zahn, Glen Stassen, Michael Baxter, Margaret Pfeil, and Marie Dennis, co-president of Pax Christi International, the global Catholic peace movement.

---

1. See the classic C. John Cadoux, *The Early Christian Attitude to War: A Contribution to the History of Christian Ethics* (London: Headley Bros., 1919); and John Helgeland, "Christians and the Roman Army, A.D. 173-337," *American Society of Church History* 43, no. 2 (1974): 149-63, 200.

2. See Michael G. Long, *Christian Peace and Nonviolence: A Documentary History* (Maryknoll, NY: Orbis Books, 2011).

The Emergence of the Just War Tradition

Yet pacifism has been a minority witness in Christian tradition and theology. The center of the tradition's response to state-sponsored violence has been occupied by just war thinking, labeled by Yoder the "Constantinian heresy"[3] because it took shape only after the Emperor Constantine, in the fourth century, granted Christianity status as a legally recognized religion. Before then, Christianity was seen by many as a dangerous new cult that threatened the cultural and political unity of the empire by undermining common worship of the Roman gods. The legalization of Christian worship meant that Christians now had a stake in the welfare of the empire. Christian participation in the military represented a public and civic commitment to help repudiate the Germanic peoples whose invasions increased during the life of Augustine (354–430), and resulted finally in the fall of Rome in 410 CE.

Augustine and Thomas Aquinas (1225–1274) are two seminal and still highly influential Christian theologians who defended just war as necessary to good order, justice, and peace, and therefore as justified by Christians. These two authors use different strategies to accommodate war to the gospel's message of love and nonviolence. Augustine positions war as an expression of "loving" punishment of the offending party, while Aquinas eschews the language of love and presents war as justified defense of the common good. Both of these strategies, to be discussed in more detail below, raise serious questions and problems. For instance, should Christian analysis of war be more focused on naming its inevitable abuses, excesses, and horrors, and on finding alternatives to war, than on finding reasons to validate its initiation and conduct?

Even when not "pacifist" in the strict sense, a gospel-based social ethics must concentrate first of all on building peace. Some contemporary thinkers stress that a theory of "just peace" should replace "just war." Cooperative, just, and peaceful social life requires conditions that go far deeper than fending off aggressors and vindicating the rights of injured parties by killing perpetrators. A new development in the JWT is a category of criteria for justly concluding wars and preparing for social recovery (*jus post bellum*). Many Christian social ethicists now put more emphasis on peacemaking or peacebuilding than on just war as ways to avoid and end conflict.

---

3. John Howard Yoder, "Peace without Eschatology?" in *The Royal Priesthood: Essays Ecclesiological and Ecumenical*, ed. Michael G. Cartwright (Scottdale, PA, and Waterloo, ON: Herald Press, 1998), 152.

Nevertheless, just war theory, traditionally divided into criteria of declaring or undertaking war (*jus ad bellum*) and criteria of conduct in war (*jus in bello*), still may be legitimate and useful in limiting the causes of war and in holding warriors accountable to standards of just and unjust means. It is important for all Christian citizens to scrutinize carefully the rationales for the use of force that are given by rulers, elected officials, and opinion makers. Christians have a responsibility to shape their societies in the most just ways possible. For this, they must be informed about the moral and practical validity of reasons offered for and against the use of force.

According to the North American Catholic theologian John Courtney Murray, traditional just war theory is also focused on peace, but more specifically on the justice of enforcing peace by the use of arms. Murray recognizes the evils entailed in any war. He knows that the very idea of Christian just war theory has an oxymoronic quality. "The effort of the moral reason to fit the use of violence into the objective order of justice is paradoxical enough; but the paradox is heightened when this effort takes place at the interior of the Christian religion of love." Yet war's evils may be necessary evils, even morally necessary evils, and they must be limited. The function of just war theory, therefore, is "to condemn war as evil, to limit the evils it entails, and to humanize its conduct as far as possible."[4]

Augustine

Augustine was born in North Africa, then a Roman province. Following his education in Italy, and his conversion to the Catholic faith of his pious mother, Monica, he returned to his homeland to become the bishop of Hippo. Roman political thinkers held that war could be legitimated for a good cause, an idea adopted and passed on to Augustine by his teacher and mentor in Milan, the bishop Ambrose. As a Christian and theologian, Augustine centered the life of faith on love of God as the *summum bonum,* or highest good; all else should be loved in relation to God. The inevitable tendency of human beings after the fall into sin of Adam and Eve, however, is to distort this God-designed order, placing love of self or of some created good at the center of one's universe. Sin, the falling away from love of God, is displayed in the "lust for rule" (*libido dominandi*) that according to Augustine drives human societies, politics, and governments.[5] Lust for power and

---

4. John Courtney Murray, S.J., "Remarks on the Moral Problem of War," *Theological Studies* 20 (1959): 57.

5. Augustine, *The City of God*, 1, Preface.

conquest is the hidden or not-so-hidden drive behind all projects in what Augustine calls the "earthly city."

In his major work, *The City of God*, written near the end of his life and as Rome was under foreign assault, Augustine sorts human historical life into two opposed yet intertwined and coexisting cities, the City of God and the City of "Man," the heavenly city and the earthly city. The City of God includes all those redeemed by God's grace and united in the love of God, and it is the only city in which genuine peace and social concord can be present. "The peace of the heavenly city is the perfectly ordered and harmonious enjoyment of God and of one another in God."[6] But this city cannot be identified with any actual society of people, and is only partially and tenuously present in the lives of those who follow Christ.

Contrasting to the heavenly city is the earthly city, governed by "love of self, strength, power, and profit."[7] The aims of the earthly city are temporal peace, just laws, and civil concord, but these aims too are barely realized because of sin. Temporal peace, when compared to the peace of the City of God, is no more than the "solace of our misery."[8] Nevertheless, as Augustine advises Boniface, the Christian governor of a Roman province, temporal peace is the best for which earthly societies can hope, and it is worth fighting for. Boniface should never lose sight of the aim of peace, but war may be necessary to secure it.[9]

Augustine is well aware that to advise a Christian to participate in violence for the sake of the temporal order seems on the face of it to contradict Jesus's explicit teaching as depicted in the scriptures. His strategy to reconcile Christian love with killing and war is threefold: (1) Augustine insists that love must always be the motive or intention behind any action performed by a Christian; (2) he defines war making as an act of loving punishment to correct wrongdoing, analogously to a father punishing his son;[10] and (3) he says that Jesus's command to "turn the other cheek" in the Sermon on the Mount (Matt 5:38-48) should not be taken literally. Instead, he

---

6. Ibid., 19.13.

7. Ibid., 14.28.

8. Ibid., 19.27.

9. Augustine, "Letter 189, to Boniface," in *Saint Augustine: Letters*, volume 3 of *The Fathers of the Church*, ed. Roy J. Deferrari (New York: Fathers of the Church, 1955), 269.

10. Augustine, "Commentary on the Lord's Sermon on the Mount," XX.63, in *Saint Augustine: Commentary on the Lord's Sermon on the Mount*, volume 11, of *The Fathers of the Church*, ed. Roy J. Deferrari (New York: Fathers of the Church, 1951), 90. See also "Letter 138, to Marcellinus," in *Saint Augustine: Letters*, 44.

explains, Jesus means to keep love as an intention within the heart, but "not with regard to the visible performance of the deed" (killing).[11]

Some contemporary theologians of the just war are persuaded by Augustine's view that war can be justified as a direct expression of Christian love, even for the one killed, not just the one protected. The British Anglican theologian Nigel Biggar sees just war as a benevolent use of violence to "'punish with a sort of kind harshness,' doing [the aggressor] the service of constraining him from further wrongdoing and encouraging him to repent and embrace peace."[12] Yet serious problems beset this argument. Can restraint of an aggressor honestly be characterized as an act of love toward that person if it results in his or her death, any more than the killing of an errant child by a parent? Moreover, there is an inconsistency between the second and third parts of Augustine's war-justifying strategy. If killing is really an act of love, then why does Augustine also say that, in war, love is an inner intention that differs from the outward action? Is Augustine himself ambivalent about how well the "loving punishment" rubric really explains why Christians may participate in war?

If we do grant, as Augustine's third step implies, that killing in war cannot reasonably be construed as an act of love for the one killed, then what happens to the character of the soldier who does such killing, attempting to separate it from his or her core identity as a Christian? Almost shockingly to the twenty-first-century reader, Augustine abandons virtually all restraints once war is undertaken for a just cause. The real evils in war, he maintains, are not death and destruction but faults of character such as "love of violence, revengeful cruelty, fierce and implacable enmity, wild resistance, lust of power and such like."[13] Augustine seems oblivious to the effects that repeated violent practices are likely to have on character, and to the consequences of unrestrained violence for the warrior's personal and moral integrity. It is today a well-attested fact that inflicting and suffering the devastations and atrocities of war can have disastrous results for the mental and moral well-being of surviving soldiers.

Beyond the aim of seeking to protect earthly peace by punishing evil and the requirement that war making be guided by a right intention, Augustine has another important criterion of just war: legitimate authority. It is up to the higher governmental authorities (king or emperor) to determine whether a war is just. The soldier must obey the command of a legitimate

---

11. "Commentary on the Lord's Sermon on the Mount," 1.19.59 (58).

12. Nigel Biggar, *In Defence of War* (Oxford: Oxford University Press, 2013), 61.

13. Augustine, "Reply to Faustus the Manichean," in *Writings in Connection with the Manichean Heresy*, trans. R. Stothert (Edinburgh: T. & T. Clark, 1953), 463.

authority, even if it is an "unrighteous command," and has neither the right nor the responsibility to make an independent evaluation.[14] This too does not bode well for the moral integrity of the soldier and the avoidance of war crimes.

Augustine is a landmark figure in the JWT because he establishes three of its most basic criteria: just cause, legitimate authority, and right intention. While his characterization of killing as a direct expression of love is problematic, it does represent, positively, Augustine's conviction that love must always be a part of Christian action. Christian ethics cannot deal with moral dilemmas, ambiguities, and compromises simply by saying that in those cases love need not apply. Where contemporary readers might and should draw the line, however, is in Augustine's view that it is not only permissible but sufficient to identify the work of love in times of war as killing.

Daniel Bell argues that conditions of ongoing conflict can be ended only by "counterinsurgency" efforts aimed at changing minds, hearts, cultures, and institutions of government and civil society.[15] If this is true, then shouldn't love find its most authentic expression in efforts to limit the damage of war and to rebuild trust through reconciliation and restorative justice? There is, in fact, some support for a more constructive view of the work of love in Augustine's letters, though he does not carry it into his just war theory. However dismal he may have found the prospects for genuine peace and justice in the earthly city, Augustine was surprisingly active, both alone and in concert with other bishops in North Africa, to change imperial policies to better reflect compassion, mercy, and justice. Augustine was an expert at political networking through these letters. Among the causes he took up were clemency on the death penalty, the avoidance of torture, preventing the kidnapping and sale of persons into slavery, and church sanctuary for people in danger of imprisonment and torture for nonpayment of burdensome taxes.[16]

Why didn't Augustine apply a similar approach to civil conflict and war, advocating for negotiation of conflicts, mercy toward prisoners, compassion for noncombatant victims, and restraint of violence? Augustine seems to realize the ambiguous nature of Christian justifications of violence. He also recognizes the centrality of the Christian virtue of love, and makes (if

---

14. Ibid., 464-65.

15. Daniel M. Bell, Jr., "Just War and Counterinsurgency: Discriminating Force," *Christian Century* 130, no. 16 (August 7, 2013): 23.

16. Robert Dodaro, *Christ and the Just Society* (London and New York: Cambridge University Press, 2004), 25, 217-18; and Robert Dodaro, "Between the Two Cities: Political Action in Augustine of Hippo," in *Augustine and Politics,* ed. John Doody, Kevin L. Hughes, and Kim Paffenroth (Lanham, MD, and Boulder, CO: Lexington Books, 2005).

inconsistently) some effort to distance a loving character from violent action. He takes advantage of promising opportunities to make positive differences in larger unjust systems, for instance, law, the judiciary, and the economy. It is lamentable, then, that Augustine fails to apply a similarly creative and activist approach to the transformation of war and the hate-filled violence it inevitably unleashes. The Augustinian JWT will develop and evolve in the hands of Aquinas and later authors; but it is continually plagued by the failure of its criteria to truly limit war's evils or enable the social trust so necessary to lasting peace.

Thomas Aquinas

Thomas Aquinas is a thirteenth-century Dominican priest, theologian, and papal advisor who makes important adjustments to Augustine's just war framework. As a professor at the University of Paris, he was at the center of some of the most exciting intellectual currents in Europe, especially the circulation of Aristotle's works on nature and philosophy. Scripture, Augustine, and the thought of Aristotle are the most important sources for Aquinas's greatest work, the *Summa Theologiae*.

What Aristotle brought to Christian thought about politics were the ideas that human beings are political animals, that there is a natural order to human life and society, that this order can be known by reason and chosen, and that it is enabled by natural virtues such as prudence and justice. Aquinas recognizes, with Augustine, that human nature is sinful. However, he believes that, even given original sin, human reason and free will are capable of ordering societies around the common good. While coercion is necessary to achieve valid political ends, it should not be taken for granted that wars are ordinary instruments of governance. Aquinas titles his discussion of the matter in a negative way—"Whether It Is Always Sinful to Wage War?"[17]— thus implying that it usually or often is.

Like Augustine, Aquinas stipulates that a war may be fought justly under three conditions: the authority of the sovereign, a just cause, and a rightful intention. Aquinas cites Augustine's view that war punishes evildoers but always connects punishment to broader social responsibilities: "defending the commonweal against internal disturbances" or against "external enemies." Similarly, right intention must aim at "the advancement of the good or the avoidance of evil," not at simple retribution. War is just only when

---

17. Thomas Aquinas, *Summa Theologiae* (ST), II-II.Q40.a1. The discussion in this paragraph is based on and cites this article.

necessary to protect the common good. Aquinas never describes killing in war as a form of Christian love, whether for one's fellow citizens, innocent people under attack, or the enemy. War falls under the natural virtue of justice, not the Christian virtue of love. Its purpose is "the care of the common weal."

Aquinas confronts the objection that war contradicts the Sermon on the Mount, "resist not evil" (Matt 5:39). While conceding that such precepts "should always be borne in readiness of mind," Aquinas still sees it as necessary sometimes for even a Christian warrior to "act otherwise for the common good, or the good of those with whom he is fighting" (fellow soldiers on the same side). Killing in war is not depicted as a direct act of love, nor is it paired with a separate and different inner intention of love. Rather, he seems to see Christian love as inoperative or as bracketed in the justification and conduct of war.

Means in war are also evaluated in terms of justice. For example, ambushes are not wrong, since they are a customary and expected means of war; but breaking treaties violates the "covenants of war," which are binding even among enemies.[18] In contrast to Augustine, though, Aquinas does not insist that the ruler's command is absolute. Certainly, Aquinas has a strong presumption in favor of the obedience of soldiers. But he also suggests that an unjust law is not a valid law, since the very definition of law is to serve reason and the common good.[19] Thus, a clearly unjust military initiative or command would not deserve blind obedience.

Having refused to define violence as an expression of Christian love, Aquinas now has the opposite problem to Augustine: he seems to have eliminated this essential Christian virtue from the process of war making altogether. Aquinas's corrective strategy is to assign the virtue of love to different people with nonmilitary roles. Many roles, with distinctive virtues, contribute to the good of an entire society. War is the role of rulers and soldiers, but not the role of priests and bishops; the latter are uniquely called to embody the Christian virtues of love and forbearance. They represent the sacrificial ministry of Christ, "wherefore it is unbecoming for them to slay or shed blood."[20] Aquinas's strategy for reconciling the gospel with war, then, is to connect the gospel virtue of love and the natural virtue of justice to different roles in church and society.

---

18. Ibid., a.3.
19. ST, I-II.90.a1-2.
20. Ibid., a.2.

This strategy has the merit of keeping Christian love away from direct involvement in intending and causing violence. It also protects the integral, holistic character of the warrior, who now intends and does one and the same thing. On the debit side, however, Christian love has now been defined as outside the responsibilities of some community members. Are only some Christians called and enabled to live by the radical demands of the gospel? That seems flatly to contradict the New Testament. Or do rulers and soldiers set aside these demands when fulfilling one role but conform to them when filling others, in family or local community? If so, does this too result in an unacceptable level of religious and moral schizophrenia?

Two further points in the thought of Aquinas may help us think through the dilemma of justifying war without rejecting the gospel. First is his insight that even a unitary intention can have within it degrees of commitment to the different results of an action, and even different aims. In his discussion of individual killing in self-defense, Aquinas formulates an early version of what later was to be called (in a somewhat different formulation) the principle of double effect.[21] The gist of the argument is that one act can have two effects, killing someone and protecting one's own life or the common good. Aquinas stipulates that such killing is justified when and because one's primary intention is the good and just result to be achieved, not the killing itself, which otherwise would be "unlawful."

The important point here is that Aquinas is distinguishing between two different levels or strands of intention that coexist interdependently in one choice. Violence and killing cannot be the dominant motive and purpose of the just agent, but they can be incorporated as regrettable but necessary aspects of accomplishing a good end, and even as means to that end. This analysis allows for a complex and even ambivalent intention that neither splits agency from intention nor subsumes violence under an intention that is patently incompatible with it.

It might be possible to analyze some uses of violence similarly, considering not only the ambivalence of *just* killing, as does Aquinas, but the even bigger problem of *loving* killing, as posed by Augustine. If we approach the use of mortal force to protect innocent victims within the framework of double effect, love and justice can both be seen as operative, but at different levels of intention.[22] Love in particular—and in Aquinas's account also justice

---

21. ST, II-II.Q64.a7.

22. For a similar use of double effect in the analysis of war, see Rosemary Blackburn-Smith Kellison, "Impure Agency and the Just War: A Feminist Reading of Right Intention," *Journal of Religious Ethics* (forthcoming).

(as self-defense)—is operative in the intention of the good to be achieved, saving innocent lives. The intent to kill is part of the overall intention, but in a subsidiary way. Killing is not intended in and for itself, but only as a regrettably necessary means to the ends of love and justice. This analysis does not totally resolve the problematic nature of killing from a gospel perspective. Yet it may better account for the real experiences of government representatives, military leaders, soldiers, and voters who see wars of immediate self-defense or of humanitarian intervention as necessary, as justified, and as even as embodying compassionate love. Yes, victims of genocide, torture, and repression should be protected; but sorrow, guilt, and remorse are still appropriate responses to even "justified" acts that destroy the enemy we are called to love as neighbor.

Aquinas's use of double effect helps explain how Christians can validate "just war" while affirming the indispensable nature of love in all acts and relations. But what about constructive building of peace? Aquinas has left no letters detailing his personal social efforts. But at a more theoretical level, his theology of grace and the virtues may lend aid. As usually understood, Aquinas sees the natural virtues (prudence, justice, fortitude, and temperance) as forming persons for temporal society, while the theological virtues (faith, hope, and charity) form Christians for union with God in eternal life and for life in the church on earth. But does grace have any impact on life in historical societies? Aquinas indicates that grace as a renewed relationship to God affects the *entire* life of the Christian through three concepts: the infused moral virtues (graced versions of prudence, justice, fortitude, and temperance), the gifts of the Spirit (wisdom, understanding, counsel, courage, knowledge, piety, and fear of the Lord), and the fruits of the Spirit (charity, joy, peace, patience, long-suffering, goodness, benignity, meekness, faith or fidelity, modesty, continence, and chastity).

God gives the natural virtues special support by subsuming them within one's friendship with God, so that one is better able to do "each different kind of good work."[23] The gifts are "inner promptings" that make us ready at all times to follow the Spirit's lead,[24] even in matters of reason and justice.[25] The fruits are Spirit-inspired actions that carry the dispositions of grace into the real world of personal and social relationships.[26] Through the infused moral virtues, gifts, and fruits, God is actively present in the entire Christian

---

23. ST, I-II.Q65.a3.
24. Ibid., II-II.Q68.a3.
25. Ibid., II-II.Qs45, 52, 57.
26. Ibid., Q70.a3.

life. One would assume and hope that this presence would produce a consistent awareness of the importance of peace, as well as constant efforts to build it even in times of war.

Just War and the Gospel Today

Going beyond their just war theories, there are hints in the thought of these two major thinkers that suggest creative ways to reconcile the clashing demands of discipleship and citizenship. With Augustine, love must be operative in every Christian action (but not quarantined in the "internal" forum). With Aquinas we can say that love does not operate in the same way in every Christian action, though love is always active in moral discernment to bring every situation closer to the gospel. Just as "war involves justice with regret,"[27] it involves love with regret. It also must involve love's healing and reconciling power. While just war theory is certainly meant to repel injustice, restrain war, and promote justice, it can never be separated in either intention or action from a simultaneous "Christlike commitment to nonviolence."[28]

Christian love works to counter all circumstances when war is a danger or a reality. Christian theorists of war and peace are shifting the balance and focus toward peacebuilding, even within or alongside theories of just war. The Catholic scholar of international relations, Maryann Cusimano Love, stresses "just peace" not "just war."[29] Just peace criteria should be operative in every phase of conflict and conflict resolution and entail the participation of all stakeholders, especially women, not just victors or elites, as well as active conflict prevention, education, economic development, and the building of participatory and transparent government. Mark Allman and Tobias Winright give biblical and theological reasons to conclude every conflict on terms that lead to long-term peace.[30] The evangelical theologian

---

27. Richard B. Miller, "Aquinas and the Presumption against Killing and War," *Journal of Religion* 82, no. 2 (2002): 190, 203.

28. See Laurie Johnston, "The Catholic Conversation since 9/11: A Moral Challenge," in *The Impact of 9/11 on Religion and Philosophy: The Day That Changed Everything?*, ed. Matthew J. Morgan (New York: Palgrave Macmillan, 2009), 113-24, cited phrase at 115.

29. "Peace by Piece: On Peacebuilding with Maryann Cusimano Love," *U.S. Catholic* 76, no. 9 (September 2011): 12-16, http://www.uscatholic.org/; and "What Kind of Peace Do We Seek?" in R. Scott Appleby, Robert J. Schreiter, and Gerard Powers, eds., *Peacebuilding: Catholic Theology, Ethics, and Praxis* (Maryknoll, NY: Orbis Books, 2010).

30. Mark J. Allman and Tobias L. Winright, *After the Smoke Clears: The Just War Tradition and Post War Justice* (Maryknoll, NY: Orbis, 2010).

Glen Stassen collaborated with religious and political thinkers and activists to identify national and international practices that prevent war.[31] Some "transforming initiatives" are nonviolent direct action, cooperative conflict resolution, sustainable economic development, strengthening of the UN, and reduction of the arms trade.

Theologian Eli McCarthy has identified seven core practices that can ready Christians to engage in nonviolent peacemaking when violence threatens. These include training in nonviolent resistance and unarmed civilian peacekeeping and defense.[32] The Catholic Peacebuilding Network brings together theorists and activists interreligiously and internationally to help local communities build conditions of peace in war-torn zones, such as Mindanao, the Philippines, the Great Lakes region of Africa, and Colombia.[33]

The declaration and means of regrettable wars must be limited by the evolved criteria of just war, including just cause, right intention, last resort, legitimate authority, proportion, reasonable hope of success, and noncombatant immunity, as well as by the newer criteria of *jus post bellum*. But these criteria should never be separated from, and will never be effective without, a critical, constructive, and creative determination to make peacebuilding more powerful than war.

---

31. Glen Stassen, *Just Peacemaking: The New Paradigm for the Ethics of Peace and War* (Cleveland, OH: Pilgrim Press, 2008).

32. Eli Sasaran McCarthy, *Becoming Nonviolent Peacemakers: A Virtue Ethic for Catholic Social Teaching and U.S. Policy* (Eugene OR: Wipf & Stock, 2012).

33. See the website at the Kroc Institute, University of Notre Dame, http://cpn.nd.edu/; and Schreiter, Appleby, and Powers, *Peacebuilding*.

CHAPTER 2

A Taste of Armageddon: When Warring Is Done by Drones and Robots

BRIAN STILTNER

War by Remote Control

The late 1960s television show *Star Trek* excelled in one of the purposes of science fiction: helping us think about a contemporary controversial practice by imagining its use in a future world. In the episode "A Taste of Armageddon," the starship *Enterprise* visits a solar system in which two planets, Eminiar and Vendikar, are locked in a centuries-old war. Long ago, these two planets decided to reduce the physical destructiveness of their war by conducting it solely with computers. Each side would launch virtual attacks and the computers would calculate the death toll. The attacked side would then have 24 hours to send that many of its own citizens—people specifically identified by the computers—to disintegration booths. If either side refused to abide by this practice, the terms of their treaty would be discarded and physical bombings would resume. The leaders of the planet Eminiar, visited by Captain Kirk and some of his crew, are so fearful of the older style of warfare that they maintain the simulated war with its real, deadly consequences.

Before the crew of the *Enterprise* realize what is going on, their starship is virtually attacked by Vendikar. The leaders of Eminiar tell Captain Kirk that all of his crew have been killed in the simulation, so they must report for disintegration within a day. Kirk finds the scenario perverse. When his attempts to reason with Eminiar's leaders get nowhere, he disrupts the war by destroying their main computer. He believes that the Eminians have been lulled into complacency because they no longer see all the horrific consequences of war. Nonetheless, their terror at resuming conventional warfare is shared by the Vendikans, who contact them to open up negotiations for peace. Leaving the solar system, Kirk believes that his gamble was worth it. After all, he says, the Eminians, who seem motivated to keep an orderly society, recognize that "actual war is a very messy business. A very, very messy business."

This episode sheds light on the swift rise in the use of drones for counter-terrorist warfare. Like the computers used by the two planets, unmanned weaponized drones have been touted as tools that enable necessary fighting to continue, but more bearably. These weapons have played an increasing role in the United States' pursuit of Taliban and al-Qaeda fighters and leaders. Supporters of drone attacks enthuse that the United States is "taking out" many al-Qaeda leaders and combatants, with no loss of American soldiers' lives and with very few civilian deaths. Yet critics caution that war by remote control lulls the United States into a false sense of security and makes it difficult for Americans to see the all-too-messy consequences of war for civilians. War with drones looks effective and safe—for us. But is it?

Weaponized drones are just one of several unmanned systems already being used in the theaters of Iraq and Afghanistan. Rather than focus on the ethical and legal use of drones in asymmetrical warfare, which has been the subject of several other important books and articles,[1] this chapter will address the ethical issues attending *unmanned* weapons, both drones and robots. Humans' experience with technology is typically that once a genie is out of the bottle, there is no putting it back in. So there is every reason to believe that unmanned and robotic systems will figure increasingly in the warfare of the future. It is important to keep in mind that such systems need not only be used for fighting. There are relatively uncontroversial, even virtuous, applications for military robots and drones. But since these technologies have already been used for fighting, with great controversy, the key question here is whether the just war tradition (JWT) has the resources to keep their use directed to ethical ends. In principle, the answer is "yes," but as with any other application of just war principles, we have to follow the discipline of the theory to gain any benefits from it.

Science Fiction Has Become Military Reality

It will be helpful to sketch a picture of the unmanned technologies already in use and what might be coming down the pike. The four main uses for unmanned systems are reconnaissance and surveillance, disarming bombs,

---

1. See John Kaag and Sarah Kreps, *Drone Warfare* (Malden, MA: Polity Press, 2014); Bradley Jay Strawser, ed., *Killing by Remote Control* (New York: Oxford University Press, 2012); and Claire Finkelstein, Jens David Ohlin, and Andrew Altman, eds., *Targeted Killings: Law and Morality in an Asymmetrical World* (New York: Oxford University Press, 2012).

attacking, and rescue. Both drones and robots have been used for all four purposes.[2]

Drones, also known as unmanned aerial vehicles (UAVs), are flying machines operated by a remote human operator but featuring varying amounts of self-control. Many of them can stay up in the air for 24 hours or more over Iraq, Afghanistan, Pakistan, or Yemen and be controlled by someone operating a joystick at an operations center in the United States. The Predator, a 27-foot-long plane, which was first used for reconnaissance and surveillance in the Balkan wars of the 1990s, saw heavy use in the Afghanistan war. General Tommy Franks said in the early years of the war, "The Predator is my most capable sensor in hunting down and killing Al-Qaeda and Taliban leadership and is proving critical to our fight." P. W. Singer reports, "The ugly little drone has quickly become perhaps the busiest US asset in the air. From June 2005 to June 2006, Predators carried out 2,073 missions, flew 33,833 hours, surveyed 18,490 targets, and participated in 242 separate raids. Even with this massive effort, there is demand for more."[3]

There are drones of all sizes and for all purposes, from the 40-foot-long Global Hawk to the 38-inch, 4-pound Raven. The Global Hawk is used in Iraq in much the same way as the Predator, while the Raven is used by soldiers for surveillance.

> In a sort of irony, soldiers launch the tiny plane using the same over-the-shoulder motion that the Roman legionnaires used in war two thousand years ago, just tossing a robot instead of a javelin. The Raven then buzzes off, able to fly for ninety minutes at about four hundred feet. Raven carries three cameras in its nose, including an infrared one. Soldiers love it because they can now peer over the next hill or city block, as well as get their own spy planes to control, instead of having to beg for support from higher-ups.[4]

This vignette illustrates that drones are used not only for shooting. Nor are they used only abroad. After Hurricane Katrina, drones searched for survivors.[5] More controversially, the Department of Homeland Security uses at

---

2. There are several books that report on the technical, military, and political aspects of drones; few books also consider military robots. The best book-length examination to date of both systems, and a primary resource for this chapter, is P. W. Singer, *Wired for War: The Robotics Revolution and Conflict in the Twenty-First Century* (New York: Penguin, 2009).

3. Ibid., 35.

4. Ibid., 37.

5. Ibid., 41.

least ten drones to patrol the United States–Mexico border and wants to purchase more.[6]

While drones have been used for reconnaissance and rescue, their most controversial purpose is to kill. To get a handle on the deadliness of drone attacks is difficult, in large part because the administrations of presidents George W. Bush and Barack Obama have been very secretive about the deaths caused by drones, about when and where drones have been used, and about their legal rationales for using drones. A well-respected bipartisan report provides a helpful summary of American use over the past decade:

> Unmanned aerial vehicles have been used extensively in Afghanistan and Iraq, for intelligence, surveillance and reconnaissance (ISR) purposes, to carry out strikes and to provide close air support to ground troops. They have also become a weapon of choice for counterterrorism strikes in regions where US troops are not engaged in ground combat. Between 2004 and 2014, US UAV strikes in Pakistan are estimated to have killed approximately 2,000 to 4,000 people, while US strikes in Yemen are estimated to have killed several hundred people. A small number of UAV strikes are believed to have occurred in Somalia, and there are also unconfirmed reports of US UAV strikes in a handful of other countries, including Mali and the Philippines.[7]

The second major unmanned technology is robots, which are more common than people might realize. "All told as of 2008, some twenty-two different robot systems were operating on the ground in Iraq."[8] PakBot is a lawnmower-sized robot, and Talon is a tank-sized machine. Both robots were used to search the wreckage at Ground Zero and then employed in Afghanistan and Iraq to detonate improvised explosive devices (IEDs). Another robot, called SWORDS, "is basically Talon's pissed-off big brother, with its gripping arm replaced with a gun mount."[9] In other words, robotic systems, although so far mostly used for reconnaissance and disarming IEDs, can be weaponized like drones. Both drones and robots are controlled by humans in their main operations, yet they rely upon sophisticated computer chips and the power of wired networks and big data to work autonomously

---

6. Trahern Jones, "U.S. Set to Deploy More Drones along U.S. Borders, Despite Concerns about Effectiveness and Cost," Walter Cronkite School of Journalism and Mass Communication, September 24, 2013, http://cronkite.asu.edu.

7. Gen. John P. Abizaid (ret.) and Rosa Brooks, co-chairs, *Recommendations and Report of the Task Force on US Drone Policy*, Stimson Center, June 2014, http://www.stimson.org.

8. Singer, *Wired for War*, 32.

9. Ibid., 30.

much of the time. There is no reason, in principle, why they cannot be programmed to make decisions to kill on their own.

This point raises the issue of how drones and robots will be used as part of a systematic strategy of computerized warfare in the future. Singer describes two different strategies that are already being put into use. The first is the "mothership" strategy, which is modeled on how the US Navy is already using its unmanned systems. Since it is difficult for submarines to move into shallow waters and since traditional sonar gives away one's location, unmanned submarines are being used to expand the reach of traditional subs and ships. Naval officers see robotic minisubs as the figurative eyes, ears, and teeth that extend the reach of the mothership, which could even be a permanent sailing base at sea.[10] The other strategic concept is the "swarm." Weapons scientists have studied natural predators for inspiration. The most efficient predators hunt in packs; swarms are made up of independent parts without a single leader necessary to coordinate them. These concepts are being used to plan coordinated attack by swarms of drones and robots. "Much like being surrounded by bees, the experience of fighting against swarms may also prove incredibly frustrating and even psychologically debilitating. . . . With the simple rules guiding them and the simpler, cheaper robots that they require, there is no limit on the size of swarms. iRobot has already run programs with swarms sized up to ten thousand, while one DARPA researcher describes swarms that could reach the size of 'zillions and zillions of robots.'"[11]

Singer concludes, "Whatever doctrine prevails, it is clear that the American military is getting ready for a battlefield where it sends out fewer humans and more robots."[12] As on the planets of Eminiar and Vendikar, the attacks may involve no humans, but the deaths certainly will. What does the JWT have to say about this brave new world?

A Brave New—or the Same Old—World?

To answer the question about the current relevance of an ethical tradition born some 1,600 years ago (dating its Christian formulation to Augustine), it would be helpful to reflect on whether the current situation is really as new as it seems. Advances in weapons technology in every age tend to throw the ethics of war into confusion for a time. There is often a feeling that a

---

10. Ibid., 227.

11. Ibid., 234. iRobot is the company that created the PakBot. DARPA is the Defense Advanced Research Projects Agency, a company that creates robots for the US military.

12. Singer, *Wired for War*, 236.

new weapon is too destructive, too efficient, too far reaching, or too secret
to be controlled by just war principles. For some ethical theorists, the newness entails that the weapon must be flatly rejected. For others, the newness
entails that the just war criteria are no longer relevant.

An interesting example is the medieval attempt to prohibit crossbows.
The medieval crossbow was a considerable technical advance on earlier bows,
because its arrows could be propelled over three hundred yards and pierce
chainmail armor. "This weapon was frightening because its lethal force
could be projected over unprecedented distances, wholly disrupting the
contemporary chivalric conventions of armed conflict."[13] In 1139, the Catholic Church's Second Lateran Council forbade the use of crossbows. But the
prohibition effort was so unsuccessful that Gratian, compiling canon law
just a decade after this council, made no reference to the ban. As I concluded
with my coauthor David Clough in *Faith and Force,* "Here is an example of
important social conventions supported by powerful vested interests being
overturned by the raw military effectiveness of a new weapons technology.
Not even Christian combatants could resist using crossbows, which meant
that everyone ended up adopting them."[14] In light of this and other failed
attempts to forbid the use of certain weapons, those of a realist bent often
claim that such attempts are naïve.

Yet just war thinkers believe that we must keep trying to control the
means of war, difficult though the task is. A measure of control is better
than no control at all. What's more, just war principles can shape public discussions about weapons, sometimes creating enough of a public consensus
that prohibitions work. For example, there is broad—and, in my opinion,
largely effective—international consensus that no nation should possess
biological and chemical weapons. There is also an international consensus
that no nation should use nuclear weapons; but because the international
discussion took place in earnest only after several nations possessed nuclear
weapons, it was politically feasible to draw the line only at the initial nuclear
club of five countries.[15] The limitations on all three types of weapons are
enforced in treaties, using standards drawn from the JWT, as mediated

---

13. David L. Clough and Brian Stiltner, *Faith and Force: A Christian Debate about War*
(Washington, DC: Georgetown University Press, 2007), 111.

14. Ibid., 112.

15. This line did not hold, but only four other countries have become nuclear states since,
three of them being the only countries not to ratify the 1968 Treaty on the Non-Proliferation of
Nuclear Weapons (North Korea's status as withdrawn from the treaty is complex and contested).
The Non-Proliferation Treaty has been ratified by more countries than any other arms-control
treaty. See the UN Office on Disarmament Affairs, http://www.un.org.

through international law. These limitations are among the successes of just war theory: not ending all wars, unfortunately, but preventing some wars and bringing judgment and constraint to other wars.[16]

Whether the tradition can also underwrite a consensus on the use of drones and robots remains to be seen. It will be helpful to take stock of how unmanned military systems are like and unlike past weapons. Weaponized drones and robots appear to be *similar* to many weapons of the past in several ways:

- They kill.
- They are used because they advance war aims. Nations, armies, and combatants adopt them either to gain a competitive advantage or to try to even up the playing field.
- Too much faith can be placed in them. Hyperbolic rhetoric surrounds new weapons. Political and military leaders often excitedly claimed that a new weapon is going to make a decisive difference or end a war. Almost always, they overpromise.[17]
- The user—whether a nation or a soldier—can give over too much power to the weapon. This happens when the use of the weapon influences strategy and policy rather than the reverse. In other words, the weapon is used because it can be, without sufficient consideration given to long-term consequences. This dynamic happens to some degree with just about every breakthrough in weapons technology.
- Many new weapons encourage a myth of precision. The weapons get more deadly and precise, but never precise enough to remove all moral concerns. The crossbow was more precise and allowed the shooter to fight from a safe distance, but no safer once the other side got crossbows, too. Precision-guided munitions (PGMs), which broke into the public's attention during the 1991 Persian Gulf War, still killed civilians. Drones and PGMs are limited by what a camera can see and by what a human operator thinks the camera is showing.
- Unmanned systems, like any weapon developed for traditional warfare against other countries, can be used domestically. This is true of guns,

---

16. See Clough and Stiltner, *Faith and Force*, 222.

17. Certainly there are times that a new weapon made a decisive change in a war, but the change is never as wonderful as the rhetoric states. The extreme example is the United States dropping two atomic bombs on Japan to precipitate the end of World War II. Their use caused enduring moral controversy, while historians continue to debate whether World War II would have ended soon enough without the bombings. See the discussion in Clough and Stiltner, *Faith and Force*, 122-24 and 132-35, and the resources listed in 262 n. 40.

body armor, helicopters, and so on—and, as noted above, it is already true of drones.[18]

- These weapons can spread to other nations and even nonstate actors. The black-market trade in small arms has been a huge problem for the international community. Not infrequently, arms that the United States gives to its allies end up in the hands of its enemies and are directed back against US soldiers.[19] There is no reason the same thing won't happen with drones and robots. In fact, it happens already, as when Iraqi militants repurposed an IED-detonation robot and outfitted it with an IED to send back at American soldiers.[20]

- Weapons of any sort very often breed resentment among the civilian populations on which they are used. In guerilla wars throughout history, large nations have been drawn into fights in which they appear as behemoths strewing indiscriminate destruction. Fairly or not, the large nation with the superior technology is placed in the role of Goliath against David, giving local civilians more reason to sympathize with insurgents. Theologian Paul F. M. Zahl says that the same happens with drones: "This method of fighting reduces people on the ground to a condition of absolute helplessness, because they cannot fight back against unmanned drones. . . . It creates resentment in the people we are fighting. . . . People cannot be expected to take this one-sided warfare 'lying down.'"[21] Placing too much faith in a weapon can blind leaders to such consequences.

Alongside these similarities, there are three ways that the unmanned systems are markedly *different* from all previous weapons. The first is that the operator can be extremely distant from the fighting. The only previous weapons that have something of this feature are long-range missiles such as cruise missiles launched from land, ship, airplane, or submarine, and intercontinental ballistic missiles (ICBMs) armed with nuclear warheads. But these are blunt weapons that do major damage. The drone is new in being a

---

18. In protest of the lack of laws and policies controlling the use of drones within the United States, Kentucky Senator Rand Paul famously conducted a traditional filibuster for 13 hours on March 6-7, 2013. The *New York Times* editorialized on the types of domestic policies that Congress should enact in "Putting Drones to the Test" (January 5, 2014). So far there has been little action from Congress.

19. For one recent example, see Rowan Scarborough, "Fast & Furious, Part II: No Way to Keep U.S. Weapons out of Enemy Hands in Syria," *Washington Times*, September 23, 2013, http://www.washingtontimes.com.

20. Singer, *Wired for War*, 219.

21. Paul F. M. Zahl, "It's an Unfair Fight," *Christianity Today*, August 1, 2011, 64.

rather precise weapon that enables an operator to take a great deal of time to think about whether, when, how, and whom he will shoot, and then to do so—from thousands of miles away. Many American drone operators go to an office of sorts, figuratively working "from 9 to 5" while they fight in a war. Then they return to their families and personal life. While some are not troubled by the incongruity, others have found the situation psychologically stressful, even to the point of suffering post-traumatic stress disorder.[22]

The second difference is that the drone is a weapon that fits perfectly with a new style of open-ended, nontraditional war. The "war on terror" is the term that American leaders, especially during the administration of President George W. Bush, have used to describe the pursuit and elimination of terrorist groups anywhere in the world. There are many novel features of this military campaign, including that the groups do not fit the traditional status of combatants, which has served as a justification by the Bush and Obama administrations to conduct military actions outside the rules of international treaties and just war standards.[23] In the case of drones, the questionable actions have included: (a) the military use of drones by agencies other than the military, namely, by the Central Intelligence Agency (CIA); (b) sending drones into the airspace of other countries with whom we are not at war, particularly Pakistan and Yemen, in the pursuit of terrorists; and (c) killing persons when they are not carrying weapons and not currently engaging in any act of aggression.

The third difference has been alluded to in the above discussion of the mothership and swarm doctrines: unmanned systems are designed to think for themselves, at least to a degree. This is one of the three components of anything that counts as a robot. A robot has *sensors* that read the environment; *processors,* or artificial intelligence, that decide how to respond; and *effectors* "that act upon the environment in a manner that reflects the decisions, creating some sort of change in the world around a robot."[24] While current robotic weapons systems depend on a human operator to do anything deadly, there is no reason the machines will not become increasingly smart and autonomous. The swarm doctrine is premised on the idea that

---

22. Elisabeth Bumiller, "Air Force Drone Operators Report High Levels of Stress," *New York Times,* December 19, 2011, A8. This report is cited by Abizaid and Brooks, *Recommendations,* 25.

23. Kaag and Kreps suggest that both the Bush and the Obama administrations have failed to support the legality of most of their drone strikes. "The more restrictive interpretations of *jus ad bellum* conclude that the only place where drone attacks are plausibly legal is in Afghanistan, where the United States initiated a war of self-defense after the 9/11 attacks. Consequently, drone attacks are not legal in countries with which the United States is not in a declared conflict, such as Pakistan, Yemen, and Somalia" (*Drone Warfare,* 86).

24. Singer, *Wired for War,* 67.

thousands of "dumb" drones or robots will work together in a sophisticated network that will continually adapt to the fighting environment in real time. The swarm will think for itself and decide how to respond.

Can War with Drones and Robots Be Justly Conducted?

Should one be more impressed with the similarities or the differences between old and new weapons? A reasonable approach is to take account of both. The political, economic, cultural, and military conditions that prompt the creation of new weapons are as old as humanity: people are motivated by power and fear, and they are prone to engage in wishful thinking. Just war principles can address drones and robots along the same lines as crossbows, chemical weapons, and nuclear weapons, because behind the use of all of them are very similar motivations. But each weapon type requires its own particularized response, based on the nature of the weapon and the context of its use. So how do the long-standing just war criteria apply to drones and robots? This section will briefly summarize the application of the just-conduct *(jus in bello)* and just-decision *(jus ad bellum)* criteria and then raise questions of accountability.

The two *jus in bello* criteria govern how weapons are used. The apparent innovation with drones and other PGMs are that they make it much easier to respect the criterion of *discrimination,* which requires that weapons and acts of fighting must distinguish between combatants and noncombatants, never intentionally targeting the latter. Drones respect this criterion in their design. Their precision can potentially make a campaign waged with them morally better than the same campaign waged with larger, "dumber" bombs. But their technical precision does not automatically make them free of moral problems. First, the technical precision of drones can mislead their operators. Christian just war theorist Daniel M. Bell, Jr., notes, "The 'soda straw' optics of drones may inhibit the ability to discriminate appropriately because they exclude the surrounding context. For example, I was once told of a drone being used to take out a bridge. The narrow field of view of its optics did not include a passenger train that was approaching the bridge and did not have time to stop."[25] Second, the distance at which drones are used might make it psychologically easier to fire them, increasing the chances of abuse. Finally, it is not easy to decide who is a proper target in asymmetrical

---

25. Daniel M. Bell, Jr., "The Drone Wars and Just War," *Journal of Lutheran Ethics* 14, no. 6 (June 2014), http://www.elca.org/JLE/Articles/71, paragraph 6.

counterterrorist warfare. The legal and ethical issues are very murky.[26] A drone can set its sights on a house where cameras saw a man enter—an American citizen who is active in al-Qaeda. This situation is nothing like a solider on a battlefield with a gun in his hand, so is this man a legitimate target? Many ethicists and international lawyers say "no," but American drone policy has permitted such people to be killed.

The second *in bello* criterion, *proportionality,* holds that the use of a particular weapon must reasonably promise to produce more overall good than harm. The reason for this stipulation is that the ongoing use of weapons even in a discriminating manner can add up to a morally problematic result. The classic principle of double effect, which guides the application of discrimination, allows some low level of collateral damage—of civilians who are accidentally or unintentionally killed in the prosecution of a justified war. The principle even allows some such civilian deaths to be "foreseen" as long as they were not the intended result. But what is a low level and how scrupulous does an army have to be? Double effect can operate as a fig leaf if it is reduced to the claim that one did not intend to kill civilians. In addition, the concept of proportionality can also be abused, because the standards of what is too much violence in light of the hoped-for result is difficult to establish. Because of these problems, the just war theorist Michael Walzer has famously articulated the tradition's concept of "due care," which is a positive commitment to save civilian lives even when that means soldiers put themselves at risk.[27]

It is not clear whether the United States has been scrupulous enough. At least early on in the drone wars, it very arguably was not. The New America Foundation conducts an ongoing analysis of deaths in the US drone campaign in Pakistan. It estimates that in 48 strikes conducted by the Bush administration, up to 557 people were killed, with the civilian death rate falling between 20 and 37 percent of the total. While the Obama administration has conducted many more strikes (328) that have caused many more deaths (up to 2,932), the Foundation estimates the civilian death toll in these strikes as 5 to 10 percent of the total.[28] Perhaps even 5 to 10 percent reflects a lack of due care, but the significant decline also suggests that the United States *can* better control drones *if it wants to.*

---

26. Kaag and Kreps, *Drone Warfare,* 82-86.

27. Michael Walzer, *Just and Unjust Wars,* 3rd ed. (New York, Basic Books, 2000), 152-57.

28. New America Foundation, "Drone Wars Pakistan: Analysis," http://securitydata. newamerica.net. I calculated the casualty rate based on the data this site reported as of August 20, 2014.

With such trends in view, a June 2014 report of a bipartisan commit-tee with several former senior military and intelligence officials argued that drones do not cause disproportionately high civilian causalities. This report, issued by the Stimson Center, states, "The frequency and number of civil-ian casualties resulting from US drone strikes also appear to have dropped sharply in recent years, as UAV technologies have improved and targeting rules have been tightened."[29] The data has been hotly contested by support-ers and critics of drones, but all acknowledge that it is difficult to get a pre-cise picture because of the secrecy with which American administrations conduct drone attacks. The Stimson panel is by no means a champion of drones, but it believes that the greatest ethical and legal concerns are found under the other part of just war theory.

America's use of drones in counterterrorist warfare raises a number of questions under the *jus ad bellum* criteria. Is the possibility of future terror-ism from a certain group a *just cause* for sending military strikes against that group? Does the United States have the *legitimate authority* under inter-national law to conduct drone attacks in countries with whom it is not at war? Have other strategies been exhausted, making bombings a *last resort*? Is the strategy of drone strikes *proportionate*, in that it is likely to do more good than harm in the long run, bringing a *reasonable hope of peace*? And have the strikes been carried out with *morally right intentions*? Bell raises important challenges to current drone practice on the last two points. An assessment of proportionality has to consider how the whole policy affects America's standing in the eyes of other countries. Bell comments,

> The best insights of counter-insurgency theory argue for a shift from an "enemy-centric" approach that focuses primarily on destroying an elusive enemy to a "population-centric" approach that focuses on pro-tecting civilians and communities from harm. The drone wars of recent years are oddly out of step with this insight and to the extent that they make a just conclusion of the war more difficult, they run afoul of the just war tradition.[30]

As for right intention, Bell states, "No matter how precise the weaponry or how close the trigger to its effects, if the one pulling the trigger is not a person formed in the virtues that characterize a just war people, then that technology will only amplify vice."[31] Similarly, the Stimson report "is espe-cially critical of the secrecy that continues to envelop drone operations and

---

29. Abizaid and Brooks, *Recommendations*, 25.
30. Bell, "Drone Wars," paragraph 15.
31. Daniel M. Bell, Jr., "Let Character Prevail," *Christianity Today,* August 1, 2011, 65.

questions whether they might be creating terrorists even as they are killing them."[32]

Considered from both directions—*in bello* and *ad bellum*—just war theory clearly mandates rigorous reflection, control, and accountability. Such qualities have been lacking in American drone policy, yet they are urgently needed as unmanned war threatens to expand. Several ethical recommendations emerge from the just war theorists and nonprofit organizations that have studied unmanned systems:

- The Stimson panel leads its list of eight recommendations with the need for the United States to "conduct a rigorous strategic review and cost-benefit analysis of the role of lethal UAVs in targeted counter-terrorism strikes." It also urges increased transparency in US policy and more robust oversight and accountability mechanisms.[33]
- Weaponized drones and robots should be acknowledged as the tools of war that they are and used solely by military agencies, not in clandestine departments of the government. They ought to be used only in military campaigns under the standards of military ethics and international law. The White House indicated its interest in moving in this direction in May 2013, but has not yet done so.[34]
- Human beings should always retain responsibility for decisions to kill. In its report *Losing Humanity: The Case against Killer Robots,* Human Rights Watch argues that "robots with complete autonomy would be incapable of meeting international humanitarian law standards. The rules of distinction, proportionality, and military necessity are especially important tools for protecting civilians from the effects of war, and fully autonomous weapons would not be able to abide by those rules." This report calls for international laws and national policies to prevent the development, production, and use of fully autonomous weapons, and for roboticists to develop a professional code prohibiting the same.[35]
- The international community needs to develop mechanisms of accountability. The temptation is especially keen for small nations

---

32. Mark Mazzetti, "Use of Drones for Killings Risk a War without End, Panel Concludes in Report," *New York Times*, June 26, 2014, A11.

33. Abizaid and Brooks, *Recommendations,* 14-15 and 41-49.

34. I made this recommendation in my op-ed, "Follow Just War Rules," *Christianity Today*, August 1, 2011, 65, and the Stimson panel recommends it as well (Abizaid and Brooks, *Recommendations,* 14-15 and 43).

35. Human Rights Watch, *Losing Humanity: The Case against Killer Robots,* November 2012, http://www.hrw.org, 3-5 and 46-48.

wishing to exert their influence (hence the smaller nations joining and trying to join the nuclear club) and for superpowers who have resources and technology that no one else has. Currently, the United States is in this position with drones and robots. It won't be for long, though. It should learn a lesson from the late 1940s when it was the only nation with atomic weapons. By holding itself to a different standard than other nations and by actually using these weapons, even if for ostensibly good purposes, the United States harmed its moral standing in the eyes of the world. Its bombings of Hiroshima and Nagasaki are still mentioned by rogue leaders as evidence of America's hypocrisy. The Stimson report foresees a similar problem emerging with drones: other nations will appeal to America's use to justify their own.[36] The United States has a chance to lead on establishing standards for drones, robots, and similar technologies, but the window is closing.

Back to the Future

Based on just war criteria, we must raise serious questions about the wisdom of warring with drones and robots. While drone systems are not inherently indiscriminate or disproportionate, they have been too heavily relied on by American leaders in an age where the public is understandably reluctant to see American soldiers deployed in hot combat but eager to be assured that terrorist leaders are being killed. Unmanned systems create moral hazards when we conduct war from a far remove, and they will create more hazards if we start turning over decisions about targeting and killing to machines.[37]

How much control are we willing to cede? One science fiction dystopia is that the robots take over, as in the *Terminator* movies. We would seem to be far away from that future, but not so far that we should not be planning for it. The principle should be that *a human being* always decides on a deadly action. Sure, persons are flawed in many ways, but they are morally and legally accountable, and they understand the human stakes of war, even when they try to ignore them.

Another science fiction dystopia is the one that began this chapter: that technological war becomes so seemingly pristine that we slide into endless war. The *Star Trek* episode sheds light not just on computerized war in general but on the US "war on terror" in particular. America's pursuit of

---

36. Abizaid and Brooks, *Recommendations*, 37.
37. Kaag and Kreps use the concept of moral hazard extensively in chap. 5 of *Drone Warfare*.

terrorists through drones is like the simulated war in the episode, but in only one direction: computer-aided attacks are ordered up, with one side experiencing the deaths and the other side hardly ever seeing the results.

While Christianity has only been mentioned briefly in this chapter, here is certainly a place where the churches and faithful citizens can bring a distinctive perspective to the just-war discussion. As Bell rhetorically asks, "What kinds of moral communities are necessary to resist the politics of expediency that renders drones so tempting to our political leaders? Perhaps churches that embrace just war need to speak up and remind those leaders that, as Walzer said, we are willing to bear the risk, the cost, the sacrifice necessary to avoid killing civilians and shattering communities . . . in short we are willing to bear the costs of waging war justly."[38] Drones and robot armies will test us, the people, as to whether we are up the challenge. Are we willing to say "no" to something that is being done just because it *can* be done? The JWT gives us the resources; we must be willing to use them. The first step is moral perception: having the courage to look into what acts are being done in our name and remembering that actual war is a very, very messy business.

---

38. Bell, "Drone Wars," paragraph 29.

CHAPTER 3

The (Im)Morality of Cluster Munitions

TOBIAS WINRIGHT

In May 2008, representatives of 107 governments gathered in Dublin, Ireland, to draft an international treaty categorically banning the production, use, and export of cluster munitions, as well as committing nations to destroy their stockpiles within eight years.[1] Over 90 nations signed it in Oslo, Norway, seven months later. Norway, the Republic of Ireland, Sierra Leone, and the Holy See were the first four states to ratify the Convention on Cluster Munitions. On August 1, 2010, after thirty states had ratified it, the convention became binding international law to which ratifying states are expected to adhere. At present, 112 states have signed it, with 83 of them also ratifying it. As with the 1997 Ottawa Treaty banning landmines, the convention reflects a consensus among nations, human rights groups, and religious organizations about cluster bombs and the pernicious threat they pose in particular to innocent civilians. Benedict XVI, who was pope at the time the convention took effect, felt "great contentment" that "the international community has demonstrated wisdom" in banning "these insidious explosives."[2]

Indeed, during and after recent armed conflicts—such as the US-led wars in Afghanistan and Iraq, the hostilities between Israel and Hezbollah in southern Lebanon in 2006, the fighting between Russia and Georgia in the southern Georgian province of Ossetia in 2008, and the Syrian civil war in 2012—graphic news accounts about innocent civilians injured or killed by cluster munitions have stirred world public opinion. In an article appearing in *Time* in May 2003, Michael Weisskopf shares the story of an Iraqi family in Karbala. After hiding from two days of US bombing, Jabar and her

---

1. An English text of the Convention on Cluster Munitions is available on the Internet at http://www.clusterconvention.org.

2. "Pope Welcomes Cluster Munitions Ban, Urges More Countries to Sign," Catholic News Agency, August 1, 2010, http://www.catholicnewsagency.com.

six-year-old daughter Duaa Raheem emerged from their house in order to get some water. A black plastic object shaped like a C-cell battery attached to a white ribbon attracted Duaa's curiosity, so she grabbed it and took her discovery home to share with her two sisters, three-year-old Duha and eight-year-old Saja. On their kitchen floor, as she situated the device on her lap and twisted a screw, it exploded, sundering Duaa in half while also killing Duha and severely injuring Saja. The grief-stricken mother's bitter words are conveyed by Weisskopf: "We thought we were safe because the bombs had stopped," says Jabar. "My daughters were stolen from me."[3] Such incidents are not rare. According to a preliminary report released in November 2006 and followed up by another in May 2007 from Handicap International, an organization that campaigns against cluster bombs, 98 percent of the casualties caused by these munitions are civilians, with 27 percent of these being children.[4]

Opponents of cluster munitions claim that these weapons are inherently indiscriminate, which is why there are so many civilian casualties from them; thus, these weapons themselves are immoral and never justified for use. International law scholar Virgil Wiebe, who has served as a consultant to the Mennonite Central Committee and who cofounded the Cluster Munitions Coalition, a network of NGOs, faith-based groups, and professional organizations campaigning against cluster munitions, alleges that these weapons are per se indiscriminate, "given the inherent nature of cluster bombs as wide-area munitions."[5] In his view, civilian deaths from cluster bombs are practically unavoidable and, thus, to be expected. Similarly, the then-president of the US Conference of Catholic Bishops, Wilton D. Gregory, in a statement issued on the eve of the US-led war against Iraq in 2003, warned, "Any decision to defend against Iraq's weapons of mass destruction by using our own weapons of mass destruction would be clearly unjustified." Gregory continued, the "use of anti-personnel landmines, cluster bombs and other weapons that cannot distinguish between soldiers and civilians, or between times of war and times of peace, ought to be avoided."[6] The weapons themselves, in this statement, rather than how they are used, are regarded as mor-

---

3. Michael Weisskopf, "The Bombs That Keep on Killing," *Time,* May 12, 2003, 43.

4. Lucy Fielder, "Injuries in Lebanon Revive Bid to Ban Cluster Bombs," *Christian Science Monitor,* November 7, 2006, 11. See *Fatal Footprint: The Global Impact of Cluster Munitions* (November 2006), and *Circle of Impact: The Fatal Footprint of Cluster Munitions on People and Communities* (May 2007), http://www.handicap-international.org.uk.

5. Virgil Wiebe, "Footprints of Death: Cluster Bombs as Indiscriminate Weapons under International Humanitarian Law," *Michigan Journal of International Law* 22, no. 1 (2000): 87.

6. Bishop Wilton D. Gregory, "Statement on Iraq" (Washington, DC: United States Conference of Catholic Bishops, March 19, 2003), http://www.usccb.org. For a similar perspective from

ally unjustified. Likewise, the World Council of Churches regards these weapons as "an indiscriminate instrument that confounds the intentions of its users and brings terrible consequences to its victims."[7] Again, the weapons themselves are indiscriminate, and their use is going to result in civilian casualties regardless of the intent of those in the military who employ them.

However, several nations still have not signed or ratified the convention, including the United States, Russia, and China. Why hasn't the United States supported the treaty? According to Stephen Mull, who is a former acting assistant secretary for political-military affairs, cluster munitions have "a certain military utility" and are necessary to protect American troops and interests.[8] US Air Force Major Thomas J. Herthel also emphasizes the military efficacy of cluster munitions, but he moreover argues that these weapons "are not indiscriminate by their very nature."[9] He is confident that cluster bombs can be improved technologically and used lawfully by the military so as to minimize collateral damage that is proportionate to intended military gains. As of 2003, the United States suspended its use of cluster munitions in combat and has been conducting the sort of research, testing, and development that Herthel prioritizes.

Therefore, although the opponents of cluster munitions, with the convention, have won this argument, at least for those states that have ratified it, there remain nations, such as the United States, that are unconvinced about these weapons being inherently indiscriminate. Which point of view is right? In what follows, I consider cluster munitions and their use vis-à-vis the just war tradition (JWT). Rather than resting content with asserting that cluster munitions are inherently indiscriminate, this essay instead submits these weapons and their use to more careful moral analysis. For as Paul Ramsey wrote four decades ago in connection with incapacitating gases, "Too many have too quickly slapped the notation 'immoral' upon any such weapons. No such notation belongs on any weapon, but only on a weapon's use or the action for which the weapon is intended. . . ."[10] More recently, in his *The Just War Revisited*, which contains a chapter on the topic of "immoral weapons,"

the Vatican, see Archbishop Sylvano Tomasi, "'Culture of Prevention,' Not Cluster Bombs, Will Ensure a Just Security," *L'Osservatore Romano,* June 2, 2004, 10.

7. World Council of Churches, "Statement on Cluster Munitions" (Geneva: Central Committee of the WCC, February 13-20, 2008), http://www.oikoumene.org.

8. Quoted in Daniel Allen, "A Cluster of Fallacies," *Foreign Policy in Focus* (June 3, 2008), http://fpif.org.

9. Thomas J. Herthel, "On the Chopping Block: Cluster Munitions and the Law of War," *Air Force Law Review* 51, no. 1 (2001): 264, 267.

10. Paul Ramsey, *The Just War: Force and Political Responsibility* (New York: Charles Scribner's Sons, 1968), 466.

Oliver O'Donovan similarly questions whether weapons themselves can be considered intrinsically indiscriminate, since discrimination "has to do with the intention of attack, not with the technical limitations or grossness of the means."[11]

Accordingly, even if it is indeed possible to say that these weapons are per se indiscriminate, I seek in this essay to provide the missing moral legwork that Ramsey and O'Donovan would call for in order to arrive at this conclusion. Moreover, I will address the points Herthel has raised and, contrary to his conclusions, argue in favor of the ban as a result of a moral assessment of cluster munitions and their use through attention to the *jus in bello* principles of discrimination, proportionality, and the framework of double-effect reasoning.

Clarifying Clusters: What, Where, When, Why, and by Whom?

Early versions of cluster bombs were used by the Soviets and Germans during World War II, and the US military has employed them in almost every conflict from the Vietnam War on.[12] According to a special report in *USA Today*, the United States used in its 2003 war against Iraq nearly 10,800 cluster munitions.[13] Technically known as Cluster Bomb Units or CBUs, these weapons are actually canisters dropped by aircraft or launched from land and sea by artillery, missiles, or rockets.[14] Inexpensive to manufacture, each canister contains up to 650 bomblets, or submunitions, which are dispersed across a wide area over a target. The bomblets sometimes come with a small parachute, so that they float toward their target. Often brightly colored,

---

11. Oliver O'Donovan, *The Just War Revisited* (Cambridge: Cambridge University Press, 2003), 79.

12. Wiebe, "Footprints of Death," 91. Rob Nixon asserts that the United States has used cluster bombs in more conflicts than any other nation; see Rob Nixon, "Of Land Mines and Cluster Bombs," *Cultural Critique* 67, no. 3 (Fall 2007): 164.

13. Paul Wiseman, "Special Report: Cluster Bombs Kill in Iraq, Even after Shelling Ends," *USA Today*, December 11, 2003, 1a; Nixon, "Of Land Mines and Cluster Bombs," 166.

14. For the details on cluster munitions I am drawing from Barbara Hilkert Andolsen, "'The Vision Still Has Its Time': A Social-Ethical Cryptanalysis of the Signs of the Times," *Proceedings of the Annual Convention of the Catholic Theological Society of America* 57 (2002), 45-46; Herthel, "On the Chopping Block," 234-35; Nixon, "Of Land Mines and Cluster Bombs," 168; Claire Schaeffer-Duffy, "War's Lethal Leftovers," *National Catholic Reporter* 38, no. 5 (August 2, 2002): 7-9; Wiebe, "Footprints of Death," 89-90, 111; Virgil Wiebe and Titus Peachey, "War's Insidious Litter: Cluster Bombs," *Christian Science Monitor*, June 9, 1999, 11; and Wiseman, "Cluster Bombs Kill in Iraq," 1a, 6a-7a.

small, and coming in various shapes resembling batteries, tennis balls, soda cans, or hockey pucks, each submunition, in turn, contains shrapnel, steel pellets, or ball bearings that are released when detonated in mid-air or on impact. Like a hand grenade, these metal fragments can kill or injure many enemy soldiers, especially when they are in mass formation. Not only are cluster munitions an antipersonnel weapon, as "dual use" devices they are also designed to be antimateriel in that the shrapnel can penetrate and render inoperable enemy tanks, armored personnel carriers, and grounded aircraft. Some cluster munitions, moreover, contain an incendiary feature that causes fires if the submunition lands on flammable materials or fuel.

Cluster munitions thus are different from unitary or single warhead munitions designed to strike a single point. They could be likened to a shotgun blast as opposed to a bullet fired from a rifle. Years ago, when I worked as a law enforcement officer, I might have had to use my shotgun, with shells containing numerous small pellets that disperse and target a wider area, in order to increase the likelihood of stopping a life-threatening individual. Cluster munitions are like the shotgun shell, and cluster submunitions are comparable to the shotgun pellets released from the shell.

Because cluster submunitions blanket a wide area, referred to as their "footprint," which can be as large as two football fields, or approximately one square kilometer, opponents of these weapons warn that the likelihood of hitting civilians, along with legitimate military targets, is increased. As Rob Nixon critically observes, to refer to these weapons as "cluster" bombs is actually a misnomer, given that what "distinguishes cluster bombs is less their clustering than the dispersal of their malign effects."[15]

Concern has also been expressed about the lingering effects of cluster munitions even after hostilities have officially concluded. Many bomblets fail to explode on impact for two basic reasons. First, submunitions may not detonate if they land on a soft surface, such as sand, mud, weeds, water, or snow. These remain "live" and thus are a continuing threat. Second, there is the possibility of mechanical failure. Some bomblets simply fail to explode. The latter, like those that land on soft surfaces, still pose an ongoing threat to unsuspecting civilians who later come into contact with them. Cluster submunitions had "dud" rates ranging from 5 percent to 30 percent in Kosovo and Afghanistan, depending on the particular type of cluster bomb and the conditions where used. In Kosovo, this meant that between 15,000 and 90,000 unexploded bomblets remained on the ground.[16] Here the

---

15. Nixon, "Of Land Mines and Cluster Bombs," 165.
16. Schaeffer-Duffy, "War's Lethal Leftovers," 8; Wiebe, "Footprints of Death," 95-96.

comparison with shotgun pellets breaks down, for these individual pellets themselves do not detonate, either on impact or later on. There are no "dud" shotgun pellets. Rather, as Wiebe puts it, many unexploded cluster bomblets are "de facto landmines" that continue to be "indiscriminate killers for decades to come."[17] In addition, remaining unexploded ordnance impacts the environment, interferes with the efforts of displaced civilians to return to their homes, and impedes farming, fishing, and other important social-economic matters.

During its conflict with Hezbollah in the summer of 2006, Israel launched some 2.6 million to 4 million submunitions into southern Lebanon. The UN estimates that one million did not explode and that two-thirds were scattered in populated areas. A very high percentage—as many as 40 percent—of the bomblets used in Lebanon did not explode immediately and remained active on the ground, harming civilians and even experienced demolition experts after the conflict had ended.[18] Many landed on balconies, outside front doors, in trees and gardens, and some inside homes. These seriously hampered southern Lebanon's economic recovery for years, especially with regard to their agriculture, which specializes in olives, bananas, tobacco, and wheat. Similar protracted consequences may be found in the wake of other conflicts.

In Laos, where bombing by the United States ended in 1973, two or three Laotian civilians continue to be killed, with another six or seven injured, per month due to unexploded submunitions ordnance left over from the Vietnam War.[19] The United States dropped 80 million cluster bomblets on Laos, with 10 percent failing to explode on impact, leaving 8 million to 24 million unexploded submunitions scattered across the country.[20] Farmers continue to be impeded from cultivating land to grow rice due to the unexploded ordnance. Laotian farmer Phousavien Phetdonxay owns about 12 acres of land, but he cultivates only one because of safety concerns about unexploded ordnance. Thus rural areas as well as urban population centers can be drasti-

---

17. Wiebe, "Footprints of Death," 87; Nixon, "Of Land Mines and Cluster Bombs," 172.

18. Donald Steinberg, "US Should Ban Bomblets and Get on the Right Side of History," *Christian Science Monitor*, July 20, 2007, 9; Curt Goering, "A Call to Abolish Cluster Bombs," *Christian Science Monitor,* October 23, 2006, 9; Fielder, "Injuries in Lebanon," 11. Michael L. Gross gives attention to the use of cluster munitions by Israel against Hezbollah in southern Lebanon, focusing in particular on discrimination, proportionality, and double effect, in "The Second Lebanon War: The Question of Proportionality and the Prospect of Non-Lethal Warfare," *Journal of Military Ethics* 7, no. 1 (January 2008): 10-12.

19. Wiseman, "Cluster Bombs Kill in Iraq," 10a.

20. Ibid.; Wiebe, "Footprints of Death," 92, gives slightly higher estimates of between 9 and 27 million unexploded submunitions.

cally affected by cluster submunitions during hostilities and long after they have ended. Not only does this ordnance destroy civilian lives; it also can be inimical to their way of life. In sum, cluster munitions wreak mass destruction when deployed as well as decades after the shooting putatively stops.

Criticizing Clusters: An Early Effort

Appearing in the journal *Foreign Affairs* in the immediate wake of the Vietnam War in 1974, "Weapons Potentially Inhumane: The Case of Cluster Bombs," authored by Michael Krepon, was perhaps the first scholarly essay to examine critically cluster munitions and their use. In its war in Vietnam, the United States developed cluster bombs to target a larger area more effectively and to help American aircraft avoid enemy anti-aircraft fire. With dense and extensive tree-canopied jungles in which to hide, North Vietnamese forces, anti-aircraft artillery units, and surface-to-air missile batteries were difficult to strike. US aircrews struggled to engage and neutralize these defenses in one pass, with single bombs, and from high altitudes.[21] Cluster munitions, and in particular, the CBU-24, which was first tested in 1966, offered a solution. As a flak-suppression weapon, it dispersed hundreds of submunitions—safely for US aircrews who could deploy them in a single pass and from a high altitude—that pockmarked a wide area so as to destroy these targets. Nicknamed "guavas" by the North Vietnamese, these cluster munitions soon became "the darling of the aviators" in the US Air Force.[22]

Given their usefulness and effectiveness, little debate accompanied the introduction of the CBU-24s into the US arsenal. There was neither political nor public discussion of these weapons. Krepon reported that the Joint Chiefs wished to avoid a prolonged public debate that might interfere with the CBU-24s' deployment, as had happened with napalm.[23] Focus was kept on the military utility of these cluster munitions, and they were portrayed as conventional weapons that can lawfully be used. Thus, as Vice Admiral Lloyd M. Mustin, who was director of operations for the Joint Chiefs of Staff, commented in an interview, "Once we tested them, the immediate question became 'How many can we make?'"[24]

---

21. Herthel, "On the Chopping Block," 237.
22. Michael Krepon, "Weapons Potentially Inhumane: The Case of Cluster Bombs," *Foreign Affairs* 52, no. 3 (April 1974): 595, 598, 603.
23. Ibid., 600.
24. Quoted in ibid., 598.

Extensively used in North Vietnam and in eastern Laos, cluster bombs were deployed less frequently in South Vietnam, perhaps because of American concerns about collateral damage to friendly civilians, which would be an implicit acknowledgment of the threat these weapons pose to civilians generally. They were dropped not only on anti-aircraft batteries in the jungle, but also on urban population centers. Six North Vietnamese cities—Hanoi, Haiphong, Nam Dinh, Thai Binh, Vinh, and Viet Tri—were especially targeted; and their wide footprint, according to Krepon, "must have caused extensive civilian casualties, and in a high ratio to the military damage it unquestionably inflicted on its intended targets."[25]

As a scholar specializing in arms and security issues, Krepon asked some critical questions three decades ago about the use of cluster munitions during the Vietnam War. He worried about the momentum of "the bureaucratic war machine" toward "maximizing the possibilities of wide-scale damage to save American lives."[26] In Krepon's view, the CBU-24 was "the most indiscriminate antipersonnel weapon," both in its design and its practical deployment, used in Vietnam, and he expressed a deep concern that the rules of international law were "too fragile and hazy to protect civilians from the devastation" resulting from these munitions and their use.[27] Nevertheless, he offered, as the title of his article suggested, only a tentative judgment of the weapons as "potentially inhumane." It is still unclear whether the problem is more with their use rather than with the cluster munitions themselves.

John C. Ford, S.J., and
"The Morality of Obliteration Bombing"

For guidance in examining whether weapons per se can be regarded as indiscriminate, and therefore immoral, or whether it is how they are used that is the moral problem, I turn here to a famous article, "The Morality of Obliteration Bombing," published in 1944 in the Jesuit journal *Theological Studies* by the American Catholic moral theologian John C. Ford, S.J., who offered a serious just war analysis of the strategy of area, or obliteration, bombing by military forces on both the Allied and Axis sides during World War II. In a recent book about Ford, Eric Marcelo O. Genilo notes that this article is

---

25. Ibid., 604.
26. Ibid., 605.
27. Ibid., 595, 605.

considered "the most influential article in the journal's history."[28] It inspired similar treatments of weapons and their use in subsequent decades and other conflicts. In an article appearing in 1964, James W. Douglass extended Ford's incisive analysis to address the morality of nuclear bombing and deterrence.[29] Similarly, in 1995 when the United States, the United Kingdom, and France were threatening air strikes against Serbs in Bosnia, J. Bryan Hehir drew on Ford's work to emphasize the importance and nonnegotiability of the principle of noncombatant immunity.[30]

Ford began by affirming the abiding relevance of the principles of the JWT. Although Ford acknowledged that much of the warfare of the early twentieth century involved devastation heretofore unimaginable, he nevertheless adamantly maintained that limited, and thus just, war is possible.[31] Not only did he condemn Germany's policy of *Blitzkrieg*, but Ford turned critical attention to the Allies' carpet bombing of cities in Germany and Japan. In doing so, he did not mean to morally equate Germany and the Allies. Rather, Ford accepted the view that the United States was in a just war against the Axis powers, at least with regard to the *jus ad bellum* criteria. At issue for him, however, was a particular means used in the conduct of the war, which falls under the purview of the *jus in bello* criteria, namely, obliteration bombing.

Ford did not attempt to evaluate morally obliteration bombs themselves; instead, he focused on the strategy of *using* bombs in a certain way. He distinguished between precision bombing, which involves definite, limited targets, and obliteration bombing, which aims at larger, unlimited targets that are "not a well-defined military objective, as that term has been understood in the past."[32] Indeed, Ford culled many quotes from British and American sources at the time indicating that the United Kingdom and the United States employed a "strategic plan of wiping out German cities."[33] The

---

28. Eric Marcelo O. Genilo, *John Cuthbert Ford, SJ: Moral Theologian at the End of the Manualist Era* (Washington, DC: Georgetown University Press, 2007), 1-2; John Howard Yoder, *When War Is Unjust: Being Honest in Just-War Thinking*, 2nd ed. (Maryknoll, NY: Orbis Books, 1996), 41. Ford's article is mentioned, quoted, or anthologized in several articles and books, more so in recent decades than when it was published.

29. James W. Douglass, "The Morality of Thermonuclear Deterrence: Can We Resolve the Conflict between Absolute Principle and Strategic Necessity?" *Worldview* 7, no. 9 (October 1964): 4-5.

30. J. Bryan Hehir, "Kosovo: A War of Values and the Values of War," *America* 180, no. 17 (May 15, 1999): 10.

31. John C. Ford, "The Morality of Obliteration Bombing," *Theological Studies* 5, no. 3 (September 1944): 267.

32. Ibid., 261.

33. Ibid., 263.

air forces of these nations aimed "on purpose" to destroy industrial centers, railroads and communications, and residential districts where workers lived, "so that absenteeism will interfere with industrial production."[34] Of course, when employees were injured and killed in their residences, so too were their families. "The principal moral problem raised by obliteration bombing," Ford wrote, "is that of the rights of non-combatants to their lives in war time."[35]

Here he brought to bear the *jus in bello* criterion of discrimination, also known as noncombatant immunity. This principle requires militaries, when targeting, to distinguish between combatants and noncombatants, and to aim at combatants, not noncombatants, directly and intentionally. To intentionally and directly take the life of an innocent person is always wrong and considered murder, including during war. Soldiers are legitimately targeted, even if they are only materially guilty, because of "their immediate cooperation in violent unjust acts that made them legitimate objects of direct killing."[36] By inserting "even if . . . only materially guilty," Ford is alluding to a distinction having to do with one's culpability when cooperating in an evil action that is intended and done by others, such as one's nation or one's leaders—in this case, an unjust war.[37] One who *formally* cooperates in the evil act shares in the culpability of the leader, so this would include any soldiers who really intended what Hitler sought to achieve through warfare. Ford regarded any soldier "under arms" as guilty at least in this sense. In contrast, a soldier or citizen who *materially* cooperates in the evil act does not share the leader's or the nation's evil intent and does not approve of the evil act. But if it is *immediate* material cooperation, in which the soldier's or citizen's action is essential to the evil being done, so that the leader's or nation's evil action could not be accomplished without it, then this immediate moral cooperation is not morally licit. Those persons are also guilty and therefore legitimately targeted as "combatants." *Mediate* material cooperation is permissible, though, because the act done by the person is basically good and his or her performance of it is not needed by the leader or the nation to carry out the evil action.

---

34. Ibid., 264-65.

35. Ibid., 269.

36. Ibid., 272.

37. On the principle of cooperation with evil, I am relying on Benedict M. Ashley, O.P., Jean Deblois, C.S.J., and Kevin D. O'Rourke, O.P., *Health Care Ethics: A Catholic Theological Analysis*, 5th ed. (Washington, DC: Georgetown University Press, 2006), 55-56; and Nicanor Pier Giorgio Austriaco, O.P., *Biomedicine and Beatitude: An Introduction to Catholic Bioethics* (Washington, DC: Catholic University of America Press, 2011), 264-65.

Contrary to those who held that all citizens of an enemy nation are to be presumed guilty, Ford argued that most citizens were at most to be considered as mediate material cooperators. To the claim that the line demarcating combatants from noncombatants is too blurred or impossible to identify or respect, Ford countered with a 25-line list—including bakers, dressmakers, piano tuners, nurses, dentists, school teachers, professors, nuns, stenographers, and children—and asked whether "these persons are so guilty that they deserve death, or almost any violence to person and property short of death. . . ."[38] In his view, the distinction between combatant and noncombatant remains perennially valid, even in modern warfare.

More recently, in his *The Just War Revisited*, Oliver O'Donovan also highlights the distinction between the guilty and the innocent, along with the distinction between formal and material cooperation in the doing of wrong by one's nation. The distinction is not always clear or black-and-white, and O'Donovan acknowledges that drawing the line is difficult to do. That is, material cooperation (i.e., immediate) in wrongdoing can include politicians, mechanics, truck drivers, and others who are not in uniform, but, on the other hand, doctors, chefs, and lawyers wearing a uniform are not necessarily combatants.[39] Nevertheless, the distinction is not impossible to observe. Echoing Paul Ramsey, who drew upon Samuel Johnson, O'Donovan writes, "Yet while we puzzle over the twilight cases, we cannot overlook the difference between day and night: a soldier in his tank is a combatant, his wife and children in an air-raid shelter are non-combatants."[40]

Of course, Ford recognized—as does O'Donovan—that the other side of the coin with regard to the principle of discrimination is that unintentional, indirect killing of civilians is permissible.[41] Euphemistically referred to as "collateral damage," discrimination does not require that noncombatant casualties be avoided altogether. Still, on the Allies' strategy of area bombing of cities such as Dresden, Ford asked, "Looking at obliteration bombing as it actually takes place, can we say that the maiming and death of hundreds of thousands of innocent persons, which are its immediate result, are not directly intended, but merely permitted?"[42] Here he had in mind those who tried to invoke the principle of double effect to defend obliteration bombing.

---

38. Ford, "The Morality of Obliteration Bombing," 283-84, 286.

39. O'Donovan, *The Just War Revisited*, 36, 38-39.

40. Ibid., 38. See Ramsey, *The Just War*, 145-46.

41. Ford, "The Morality of Obliteration Bombing," 281-82; O'Donovan, *The Just War Revisited*, 43.

42. Ford, "The Morality of Obliteration Bombing," 291.

Ford outlined double effect as follows: "The foreseen evil effect of a man's action is not morally imputable to him, provided that (1) the action in itself is directed immediately to some other result, (2) the evil effect is not willed either in itself or as a means to the other result, (3) the permitting of the evil effect is justified by reasons of proportionate weight."[43] Accordingly, those attempting to justify obliteration bombing might argue that, while civilian injuries and deaths accompany such bombing, these casualties are not the aim, or intent, of those who are conducting obliteration bombing. Noncombatant injuries and deaths are not intended, although they are foreseen. Nor are these harms the means to an end. Rather, civilian casualties, which are admittedly an evil effect, are a secondary one, accompanying the good effect, namely, the destruction of the military target. In addition, these civilian casualties are an evil that is outweighed proportionately by the good of defeating the enemy, shortening the war, and saving our own soldiers' lives. Ford, however, thought that all of this constituted a seriously flawed application of double-effect reasoning.

With regard to intent, Ford noted that the destruction of property, including that belonging to civilians, is obviously directly intended; indeed, Allied leaders acknowledged as much.[44] In addition, Ford quoted British and American sources who openly stated that their intent through obliteration bombing was to accomplish "the progressive destruction and dislocation of the German military, industrial and economic system and the undermining of the morale of the German people to the point where their capacity for armed resistance is fatally weakened."[45] Furthermore, drawing on the work of John K. Ryan, Ford argued that any good gained by such bombing was actually incidental to the evil.[46] In other words, the evil effect was, first, immediate and direct; any military advantage, on the other hand, was secondary and derivative. Injuring and killing civilians, as well as obliterating their property, was actually a means to an end. In Ford's view, the area bombing by the Allies of civilian population centers was a form of "civilian terrorization." As for proportionality, Ford noted that obliteration bombing resulted in an evil that is "certain and extensive and immediate," namely, the

---

43. Ibid., 289. A helpful treatment of double effect in connection with noncombatant immunity and bombing, including the United States' dropping of the atomic bomb on Hiroshima, is provided in William C. Mattison III, *Introducing Moral Theology: True Happiness and the Virtues* (Grand Rapids, MI: Brazos Press, 2008), 171-77.

44. Ford, "The Morality of Obliteration Bombing," 291.

45. Ibid., 294; quoting from *Target: Germany: The Army Air Force's Official Story of the VIII Bomber Command's First Year over Europe* (New York: Simon & Schuster, 1943), 117.

46. Ford, "The Morality of Obliteration Bombing," 292; see John K. Ryan, *Modern War and Basic Ethics* (Milwaukee, WI: Bruce, 1940), 105ff.

"infliction of enormous agonies on hundreds of thousands and even millions of innocent persons"; whereas, the ultimate good sought, namely, the shortening of the war and the saving of American soldiers' lives, was a future, more remote good that was more speculative.[47] Other outcomes were possible, including the opposite effect from what the Americans envisioned. As Ford points out, the obliteration bombing by the Germans of English cities instead stiffened the resolve and resistance of the British rather than undermined their morale.[48] Because "in the practical estimation of proportionate cause it is fundamental to recognize that an evil which is certain and extensive and immediate will rarely be compensated for by a problematical, speculative, future good," Ford doubted that the proportionality prong of double-effect reasoning was satisfied. He added that even if obliteration bombing were to shorten the war and save American soldiers' lives, another long-term effect should give pause—that is, "we still must consider *what the result for the future will be if this means of warfare is made generally legitimate.*"[49]

Ford thus offered a carefully reasoned moral analysis of obliteration bombing by Allied forces during World War II. Employing double-effect reasoning, with attention to the *jus in bello* principles of discrimination and proportionality, he mustered a potent ethical critique of this means of warfare. Yet, he did not condemn the bombs as inherently indiscriminate. Rather, Ford argued that it is possible to fight in accordance with just war principles and reasoning "even when war is waged against an enemy who has no scruples in the matter."[50] But what would he have said about weapons, such as cluster munitions, that seem inherently less amenable to discriminate or proportionate use?

The Problem: Cluster Bombs or Cluster Bombing?

Most of Wiebe's essay focuses on how cluster munitions have actually been used, with problems arising because of their wide footprint, especially when deployed near civilian areas, which is why, at the time, short of a ban, he recommended at least making the use of cluster munitions illegal in civilian areas.[51] There is still the problem of unexploded cluster ordnance, however, which Wiebe views as de facto land mines and therefore inherently

---

47. Ford, "The Morality of Obliteration Bombing," 298-99.
48. Ibid., 301.
49. Ibid., 302.
50. Ibid., 267.
51. Wiebe, "Footprints of Death," 87.

indiscriminate.[52] Most of the supporters of the Convention on Cluster Munitions emphasized how these bombs themselves are inherently indiscriminate and, therefore, unjust.

Yet, on the surface, as Ramsey and O'Donovan noted earlier, to describe any given weapon itself as immoral because it is inherently indiscriminate seems mistaken. The principle of discrimination is a moral guideline for the conduct of war and how battles are fought. It has to do with moral agents who intend something when acting, rather than with an instrument, tool, or weapon. After all, as O'Donovan observes, "instruments are apparently adaptable to different ways of acting."[53] The examples he gives are a surgeon's scalpel and a pirate's cutlass. It is possible that the surgeon's scalpel could be used to commit murder, and a pirate's cutlass conceivably could be used to perform a surgical operation to save someone's life. Years ago, when I worked in law enforcement, police officers sometimes used their flashlight as a baton, and I suppose that a baton could be used in ways other than as a weapon—perhaps as a stick that could be extended to someone who was out of reach and who is stuck in quicksand. But that same baton might be used as a weapon in ways that are either lawful or unlawful (i.e., when it is excessive force or brutality). Again, it is how something is used, rather than the instrument itself, that usually matters with regard to discrimination and intent. As Herthel notes, it is possible to use any lawful weapon unlawfully.[54]

Herthel argues that cluster munitions are a lawful weapon that may be deployed lawfully. He believes that cluster munitions have military utility as an effective weapon and that they can indeed be intentionally used as such. Military units can discriminate between combatants and noncombatants, deploying cluster weapons—even with their wide footprint—specifically against troop and convoy columns, anti-aircraft units, tank formations in an open field, or aircraft on a runway preparing to take off.[55] Special care is taken, in his view, to minimize noncombatant casualties; if these occur, they are unintentional.

So, for example, Catholic ethicist Barbara Hilkert Andolsen credits the US military with carefully selecting bombing targets in Afghanistan, ensuring that they were truly legitimate military objectives, and thereby minimizing collateral civilian casualties.[56] She does not believe that the US military deliberately targeted cluster bombs at or near civilian areas. To be sure, it

---

52. Ibid., 103.
53. O'Donovan, *The Just War Revisited*, 78.
54. Herthel, "On the Chopping Block," 266.
55. Ibid., 258-59, 264.
56. Andolsen, "'The Vision Still Has Its Time,'" 47.

does not appear, in my view, that cluster munitions have been intentionally used by the United States to kill or hurt civilians in the same way that obliteration bombing was conducted during World War II. No quotes similar to those that Ford highlighted from British and American politicians and commanders are to be found today. There do not seem to be any comparable official calls for indiscriminate cluster bombing of civilian residential or industrial areas—except for an alarming statement by then Secretary of Defense Donald Rumsfeld, who said that women and children who were killed in eastern Afghanistan were there "of their own free will, knowing who they're with and who they're supporting and who they're encouraging and who they're assisting."[57] While not exactly saying that these civilian deaths were intended, Rumsfeld verges on asserting that the women and children were considered combatants because of their alleged immediate material support of the enemy.

O'Donovan offers the following hypothetical question as a test of intention concerning means: "if it were to chance that by some unexpected intervention of Providence the predicted harm to non-combatants did not ensue, would the point of the attack have been frustrated?"[58] If the answer is yes, then the noncombatant deaths were not accidental, but instead were intended as either part of the means or even the goal of the attack. In O'Donovan's view, the dropping of the atom bombs on Hiroshima and Nagasaki fail this test. And Rumsfeld's remark comes about as close as possible to failing as one can get, but I'm not convinced it is representative. I hope not.

Even if cluster bombs can be used discriminately, what about the high percentage of submunitions that fail to detonate immediately upon impact? Is it possible to say that this *unexploded* ordnance itself—rather than how cluster munitions are used—is indiscriminate? Wiebe thinks so when he asserts that such unexploded cluster submunitions are de facto land mines. Regardless of the intent of those who deploy cluster bombs, such dud ordnance poses an ongoing threat to combatants and noncombatants alike. For his part, O'Donovan acknowledges that a land mine (he does not deal with cluster munitions) is a weapon that, "while not incapable of discriminate use, is somewhat resistant to it."[59] Still, this comment falls short of calling land mines inherently indiscriminate—and I suspect O'Donovan would have a similar view of unexploded cluster munitions. As for Herthel, he believes Wiebe's analogy between cluster munitions and land mines is erroneous.

---

57. Eric Schmitt, "A Nation Challenged: The Bombing; Pentagon Says U.S. Airstrike Killed Women and Children," *New York Times*, March 13, 2002, A14.

58. O'Donovan, *The Just War Revisited*, 45.

59. Ibid., 81.

Cluster munitions are not designed to function like land mines, the latter of which are actually made to lie dormant and detonate later.[60] Rather, cluster munitions are designed to be antipersonnel and antimateriel weapons, to explode on initial impact and destroy military targets. That cluster munitions may be inaccurate and have dud rates is indeed a problem, in Herthel's view, but not one that is unique to these particular weapons. He points out that all munitions, from a rifle round to a 2,000-pound bomb, are incapable of being 100 percent accurate, and that Europe was littered with unexploded ordnance following World War II.

True enough, but considering the fact that cluster munitions have high dud rates—recall that estimates were 40 percent of the cluster munitions used by Israel against Hezbollah in southern Lebanon in 2006—and the fact that 98 percent of the casualties from cluster munitions are civilians, cluster bombs are a weapon that, while perhaps not incapable of discriminate use—to modify O'Donovan above—is *highly* resistant to it. As Nixon observes, these are "predictable" disasters that are "reenacted every time" cluster munitions are used.[61] In other words, we have here not only foreseeable collateral damage but a foreseeable *pattern* of noncombatant casualties. The US military is currently testing new cluster munitions with the goal of lowering the dud rate to 1 percent. Yet, as the statement from the World Council of Churches warns, "Lowering the rate of duds to even one percent still creates unacceptable levels of lethal and dangerous contamination in the targeted area. One percent of a million bomblets is 10,000 bomblets."[62] Thus, the risks associated with the inaccuracy of cluster munitions are greater than with some of the other weapons to which Herthel refers.

Before moving on from this consideration of discrimination and intention to consider this high number of noncombatant casualties in relation to proportionality, something else that O'Donovan touches on leads me to contemplate expanding how intent ought to be understood with regard to cluster munitions. In his discussion of the surgeon's scalpel and the pirate's cutlass, where our focus was on how these instruments are used rather than on the instruments themselves, O'Donovan points out that each device is designed with a purpose in mind. Either instrument can conceivably be used in ways that were not originally envisioned when they were invented, but they were designed nevertheless with some specific purpose in mind. Thus, intent can be found not only in connection with a weapon's use but also in its very design. The process of making, designing, and even decorating weap-

---

60. Herthel, "On the Chopping Block," 233, 265.
61. Nixon, "Of Land Mines and Cluster Bombs," 168-69.
62. World Council of Churches, "Statement on Cluster Munitions," endnote 8.

ons is an intentional act. Accordingly, it may be possible to deem a weapon as inherently indiscriminate if it is intentionally designed to kill civilians. An example that O'Donovan considers is a biological weapon designed to spread a deadly virus through a city's water supply.[63]

This point leads me to ask why cluster munitions are designed and decorated in ways that lend themselves to be mistaken by civilians, especially children, for soda cans, tennis balls, batteries, and the like. While an individual soldier or military unit might not be guilty of acting indiscriminately in deploying these cluster munitions, there is still room here to suggest, I think, that the collective agent (i.e., the nation, the government, the military) that builds and uses them—and does nothing to modify the bombs so that they no longer resemble toys or soft drinks—is morally blameworthy. In Afghanistan, for instance, where the United States dropped cluster bombs and humanitarian food parcels that were both yellow in color, leading some Afghan civilians to mistake the bombs for food, the Americans were forced to broadcast warnings to the population and later to change the color of the parcels.[64] This shows that there is a choice, and therefore intentionality, in the matter.

What I have said here about intent in design should also apply to likely flaws. Given the dud rates of cluster munitions, why haven't technological fixes been pursued sooner and more ardently? To minimize noncombatant casualties because of their wide footprint, perhaps cluster munitions could be produced that are precision guided. To get the dud rate as close as possible to 0 percent, perhaps cluster munitions could be manufactured with self-destruct timing devices. That these kinds of alternatives are now being researched and developed demonstrates again that there is a choice in the matter. Indeed, in O'Donovan's judgment, "the foresight that *disproportionate* noncombatant damage will be done combined with a *failure to intend to avoid* that disproportionate damage, presumes an intention to do that damage."[65] Those who choose, from start to finish, to make and deploy cluster bombs ought therefore to do everything feasible to circumvent and minimize foreseeable noncombatant injuries and deaths.

So, intention indeed may be still involved vis-à-vis cluster munitions, even if it is not as explicit as we usually assume. And even if intent is not clearly involved, only foreseeing something does not necessarily excuse someone entirely. After all, under several circumstances one can be blamed

63. O'Donovan, *The Just War Revisited*, 80; Herthel, "On the Chopping Block," 265.

64. See "Radio Warns Afghans over Food Parcels," BBC News, October 28, 2001, http://news.bbc.co.uk/2/hi/world/monitoring/media_reports/1624787.stm.

65. O'Donovan, *The Just War Revisited*, 44.

for unintended side effects.[66] For instance, if someone drives under the influence of alcohol and kills someone with a car, such an effect from driving while intoxicated should have been foreseen as a possibility. The driver is thus morally blameworthy. He or she has not committed murder, but manslaughter. The death was neither intended nor totally accidental. The agent may not have foreseen the bad side effect of his action, though he should have foreseen it as a distinct possibility, which then could have been prevented or avoided. The alarmingly high number of noncombatant casualties due to cluster munitions, however, does not seem to me to be merely a possibility but, instead, a probability. Another example of when an agent is morally responsible for unacceptable side effects that are unintended but foreseen is sometimes referred to as "depraved-heart murder." If a person who owns an airplane blows it up for the insurance money, foreseeing but not intending the passengers' deaths that result from the explosion, this is a type of murder—usually second-degree murder—though it is not an intentional killing. The agent in this action has exhibited a "callous disregard for human life" that results in death, or as one writer put it, the agent's action is "predicated by recklessness—and not caring about recklessness—rather than intent."[67] Given the pattern of noncombatant casualties resulting from cluster munitions, we may be dealing therefore with something akin to depraved-heart murder.

Thirteenth-century theologian Thomas Aquinas, whose discussion of whether an innocent person may kill an unjust attacker in self-defense is widely regarded as a precedent for double-effect reasoning,[68] also addressed when a person might be morally responsible for foreseen, though unintended, effects that are certain to result from that person's action. For example, in his several references to the parable of the wheat and the tares (Matt 13:24-40), Aquinas interpreted Jesus's story as a warning against harming innocent persons, even unintentionally, when one is dealing with evil.[69] Furthermore, in his treatise "On Evil," Aquinas referred to a scenario in which a

---

66. Mattison, *Introducing Moral Theology*, 172.

67. "Freddie Gray Charges: What Is 'Depraved Heart Murder'?" *The Guardian,* May 1, 2015, http://www.theguardian.com.

68. Thomas Aquinas, *Summa Theologica,* trans. Fathers of the English Dominican Province (Westminster, MD: Christian Classics, 1981), II-II.64.7.

69. Ibid., II-II.64.2, and at least five other places, according to LeRoy B. Walters, "Five Classic Just-War Theories: A Study in the Thought of Thomas Aquinas, Vitoria, Suarez, Gentili, and Grotius" (Ph.D. diss., Yale University, 1971), 160ff. See also G. E. M. Anscombe, "Medalist's Address: Action, Intention and 'Double Effect,'" *Proceedings of the American Catholic Philosophical Association,* vol. 56, ed. Daniel O. Dahlstrom et al. (Washington, DC: American Catholic Philosophical Association, 1982), 12-25.

branch falls as a result of a woodcutter's chopping a tree in a forest. If the forest is not regularly traveled by persons, no moral blame is attributed to the lumberjack if the branch kills someone. The victim's death is unintended, even if it is a foreseen as a somewhat remote possibility. However, if the forest is indeed regularly traveled by people, the woodcutter is morally culpable if the falling branch kills someone. According to Aquinas, "But if evil is always or in most cases associated with the good intrinsically intended, the will is not excused from sin, although the will does not intrinsically intend the evil."[70] In a way resembling the aforementioned case of depraved-heart murder, Aquinas believed agents are morally responsible for unintentional effects if they are foreseen as probable or certain. It is difficult to imagine how the foreseen probability that 98 percent of the casualties from cluster munitions are noncombatants passes this moral test.

Usually noncombatant injuries and deaths that are foreseen as possible and truly not intended are morally evaluated under proportionality. Nearly all references to this criterion in the literature explain it as requiring that the good gained must outweigh the evil accompanying it. The focus is on how to distinguish acceptable from unacceptable consequences. O'Donovan thus views proportion as "elastic, a matter of more or less."[71] Applying proportionality, understood in this way, to cluster bombing in Afghanistan, Andolsen holds that their use is "morally acceptable if . . . any harm unintentionally inflicted upon innocent civilians during bombing is proportional to the importance of the military objective."[72] She factors into the "harm unintentionally inflicted upon innocent civilians" side of the balance sheet cluster munitions' dud rates and the duration of time over which they may cause harm to noncombatants and interfere with a society's capacity to return to a state of ordered justice. Given that 98 percent of the casualties from cluster munitions are noncombatants, and given the way that unexploded ordnance impedes farming, resettling of displaced people into their homes, and the like, it is hard to see how the use of cluster munitions passes the proportionality test.

Moreover, there appears to be an interesting twist here in connection with what Ford said about proportionality and obliteration bombing. Again, he criticized obliteration bombing for resulting in an evil that is "certain and extensive and immediate," namely, the "infliction of enormous agonies on

---

70. Thomas Aquinas, *On Evil*, ed. Brian Davies, trans. R. Regan (New York: Oxford University Press, 2003), 1.3.15.

71. O'Donovan, *The Just War Revisited*, 43.

72. Andolsen, "'The Vision Still Has Its Time,'" 47; see Herthel, "On the Chopping Block," 248, 267–68; and O'Donovan, *The Just War Revisited*, 62.

hundreds of thousands and even millions of innocent persons," while the ultimate good sought, namely, the shortening of the war and the saving of American soldiers' lives, is a future, more remote good that is more speculative.[73] Cluster munitions, however, are effective—assuming that Herthel is right—in a way that is certain and immediate in achieving the good sought, namely, the destruction of a legitimate military target and the saving of American soldiers' lives. But the evil that results from cluster bombing is also certain, given the high dud rates and percentage of noncombatant casualties. This evil may not be so immediate—and thus is a more future evil—but neither is it speculative.

But there is another way to understand proportionality in connection with the use of force. For instance, not only are police officers expected to use discriminate force, intending only to subdue or stop a dangerous suspect, they are also supposed to employ *proportionate* force. Often referred to as a use of force continuum, police officers possess a range of use of force options that may be utilized depending on a subject's level of resistance or noncompliance.[74] If a suspect resists arrest with punches, an officer is not justified in resorting to his firearm. She has at her disposal, instead, several intermediary options, such as a baton or pepper spray. Police must use only the amount of force necessary to subdue the suspect. Proportionality refers not simply to the consequences—good and bad—that are weighed; rather, proportionality also has to do with weighing the alternatives and using the appropriate, fitting *means*.

This approach to understanding proportionality may be congruent with how Aquinas understood it. As moral philosopher G. E. M. Anscombe has noted, Aquinas may have had in mind proportionate means rather than ends or effects.[75] Accordingly, one ought not to use a sledgehammer to swat a mosquito on her neighbor's forehead; it would be disproportionate and morally wrong, notwithstanding her good intention. Viewed in this way, the military's decision to use a cluster bomb should have to do with how it is the most fitting means to accomplish a legitimate military objective. If other effective means are available, especially if it is foreseen that they involve the likelihood of fewer noncombatant casualties, then these should instead be utilized.

---

73. Ford, "The Morality of Obliteration Bombing," 298-99.

74. See John Kleinig, *The Ethics of Policing* (Cambridge: Cambridge University Press, 1996), 107; and Tobias L. Winright, "The Challenge of Policing: An Analysis in Christian Social Ethics" (Ph.D. diss., University of Notre Dame, 2002), 320-27.

75. Anscombe, "Medalist's Address," 24-25.

A final note about proportionality should be mentioned. Ford's warning about the possible precedent that obliteration bombing set for the future of warfare, combined with his suggestion that such a strategy actually stiffened rather than diminished the resolve of the enemy population to resist, should give nations today pause before they use cluster bombs. If there is a just war criterion that worldwide public opinion takes seriously today, it is noncombatant immunity (i.e., discrimination). Weapons such as cluster munitions, which result in high numbers of civilian casualties, undermine the moral credibility of nations that use them. Moreover, a dangerous precedent is set that might lead to other nations using them, including against the nation that has used them. In addition, judgments about proportionality should take into consideration the long-term effects of cluster munitions on civilians and on the environment. Like other weapons of mass destruction (WMD), cluster munitions can be regarded as weapons of long-term destruction (WLTD), and *jus post bellum* requires cleanup efforts by the nation that uses them.[76]

Conclusion

In this essay I have attempted to examine more closely the claim that cluster munitions are inherently indiscriminate because of the extremely high percentage of civilian casualties that result from their use. I have argued that the principles of discrimination and proportionality offer real traction for a substantive and critical moral evaluation of cluster munitions and their use. The cumulative weight of these considerations leads me to conclude that the use of cluster munitions is not morally justified at this time. I hope this essay has shown that we can justify the ban enacted by the Convention on Cluster Munitions based on reasoning and principles from the JWT rather than simple or premature assertions about these weapons' inherent immorality.

---

76. Mark J. Allman and Tobias L. Winright, *After the Smoke Clears: The Just War Tradition and Post War Justice* (Maryknoll, NY: Orbis Books, 2010), 165-72.

CHAPTER 4

Humanitarian Intervention and the Just War Tradition

KENNETH R. HIMES, O.F.M.

The purpose of this essay is to address the question of whether armed force can be used for humanitarian purposes. The most commonly cited articulation of a favorable view of humanitarian military intervention is found in an international commission's report, *The Responsibility to Protect*.[1] My examination of armed humanitarian intervention will show how it accords with the just war tradition (JWT). Prior to addressing that matter, however, it is important to understand the broader context of the JWT—namely, its relation to politics and the ideal of peace—as well as the changed international order that situates the discussion of humanitarian military intervention.

The Purpose of Politics

An oft-quoted statement about war is that of the nineteenth-century German military thinker Carl von Clausewitz, who wrote that "war is the continuation of politics by other means."[2] For many, the comment suggests Clausewitz was cynical about war or simply resigned to it as a regular occurrence throughout human history. Instead the Prussian author was suggesting that although events in war are unpredictable and not easily controlled, there is a dimension of war that is rational and goal oriented, just like politics. There can be reasonable and purposeful choices behind the decision to go to war. Indeed, war is "the continuation of politics."

---

1. International Commission on Intervention and State Sovereignty, *The Responsibility to Protect* (Ottawa: International Development Research Centre, 2001), http://www.idrc.ca.

2. Carl von Clausewitz, *On War*, trans. and ed. Michael Howard and Peter Paret (Princeton, NJ: Princeton University Press, 1984), 87.

Good politics aims at good governance, the oversight of a community of people such that the well-being of the group is sought, promoted, and maintained. The state is the institution through which governance of a society occurs.

Within Catholic social teaching the theory of the state is an outgrowth of a communal vision of the human person. While upholding the dignity and uniqueness of each person, the Catholic social tradition also maintains that the full development of any person is realized only in community. Human beings achieve their true self through involvement in a dense web of overlapping relationships creating a variety of communal experiences. The state establishes public order for the multiplicity of social groupings—familial, professional, religious, economic, political, educational, cultural, and recreational—that make up society.

Few things are so clearly expressed in Catholic social teaching as the idea that the state exists to protect and promote the common good.[3] Because God has created human persons as social there is an obligation incumbent upon us all to contribute to the common good that benefits each and every person. This common good requires a political institution to protect and promote it. So in that sense the state is a necessary institution for ordering society toward the common good.

In Catholic teaching the common good has been described as "the sum of those conditions of social life whereby persons, families and associations more adequately and readily may attain their own perfection."[4] Most often the common good is used in reference to a nation, but the term also may refer to smaller as well as larger groups. The Catholic tradition sees the common good of the society as including the relationships of individual members. To contribute to the common good enriches both the self and others at the same time. "Belonging to everyone and to each person," the good "remains 'common', because it is indivisible and because only together is it possible to attain it."[5]

A fundamental task of a good political community is to secure a person's rights and to locate a person's duties. Besides personal rights and duties, Catholic social teaching cites a variety of elements encompassed by the

---

3. "The responsibility for attaining the common good, besides falling to individual persons, belongs also to the State, since the common good is the reason that political authority exists"; see Pontifical Council for Justice and Peace, *Compendium of the Social Doctrine of the Church* (Vatican City: Libreria Editrice Vaticana, 2004), n. 168.

4. Vatican II, "Pastoral Constitution on the Church in the Modern World" (*Gaudium et spes*), n. 74.

5. Pontifical Council for Justice and Peace, *Compendium of the Social Doctrine*, n. 164.

common good: establishment of a sound legal system with just laws, coordination of social institutions that enable participation and sharing in human association, care for the poor and infirm, support for education, promotion of economic development and prosperity, the securing of peace, and encouragement of international structures of cooperation and security. If war is to be continuous with politics, therefore, the aim of any just war must be to help establish or maintain a political order that serves the common good.

Understanding Peace

Besides its connection to the common good it is also important to see how a just war must serve peace. A clear lesson from the Jewish and Christian traditions is that peace is not merely the absence of war. Yet this way of thinking about peace is common. Whenever a war ends—the shooting stops between warring parties—we say that peace has been restored. The end of hostilities is thought of as the onset of peace. Such an approach equates peace with nonwar.

Alternatively, peace can be understood as a positive concept. Throughout the Catholic tradition there is a way of speaking about peace as a rightly ordered political community. This is the peace that St. Augustine described by the expression *tranquillitas ordinis*.[6] A state of tranquility is the result of a political community that is rightly ordered, which means that people live in truth, charity, freedom, and justice directed toward the common good. It is a peace sought through the construction of institutions and practices that permit men and women to live together as a political community.

Peace, however, has its counterfeit expression. Recall the ancient historian Tacitus's description of how the Britons bitterly described their Roman conquerors, *solitudinem faciunt, pacem appellant* ("they make a desert and call it peace").[7] There is, in short, a false "peace" that is little more than silent acquiescence due to oppression and fear.

Because there can be no true peace without a political order that is just, measures to correct injustice are a way to build peace. Thus, we have systems of public safety and law that protect each person's basic rights, punish those who violate the rights of others, and develop measures to compensate

---

6. Augustine, *The City of God*, ed. David Knowles; trans. Henry Bettenson (New York: Penguin Books, 1972), Bk 19, §13.

7. Tacitus, *Agricola*, trans. M. Hutton; rev. R. M. Ogilvie (Loeb Classical Library; Cambridge, MA: Harvard University Press, 1980), §30.

victims. In the United States we expect rival parties to resolve their differences without using violence but through the processes of our legal system.

Internationally, however, the situation is different. While Catholic social teaching has promoted and praised the work of those who strive to create a true international order, there is a structural flaw in the system. No institution of international order plays the role that the state performs in domestic society to resolve disputes and secure justice for all parties. True, there are at present some building blocks for an international order, but the analogy between the domestic and the international order still limps.

In large part, this is due to the inability of any agent of international order to guarantee the rights of a nation-state. The structural flaw of international politics is that no actor is acknowledged as the effective overseer of global order. Consequently, Catholic social teaching does not deny a state's right or duty to employ armed force in limited circumstances. Because peace without justice is no true peace, and no international authority is adequate to the task of securing international justice, there is a recognition that an individual nation may have recourse to armed force under certain conditions.

For those who define peace as simply the absence of war, the claim that a war may be fought for the sake of peace is self-contradictory. However, precisely because peace is not merely the absence of war but the establishment of a just political order, it is possible for a war to be fought for the sake of securing genuine peace. This is not to claim that a war can create peace; it is only to acknowledge that armed force can remove obstacles to peace, for example, depose tyrants, stop genocide, or deter aggression. Thus there is a true sense that one can win a war (remove an obstacle to true peace) yet fail to win the peace (not proceed to build a just political order that promotes the common good).

Of course we must place limits on the violence done in the name of justice and peace. To allow for some war does not mean all war is legitimate, nor are all actions in war permissible. This is the backdrop to the many debates and developments within the JWT. Because in modern times even a justifiable war causes great harm, we must never presume war is always the best, or even a useful, way to help bring about peace.

Just Cause and War

We have seen that good governance requires that the leaders of a state protect and promote the common good, and that includes a number of elements such as human rights, care for the vulnerable, and establishing structures of international cooperation and security. Throughout history, therefore, just causes for war have included punishment of wrongdoers, vindication of rights, self-defense, and the maintenance of international order by resisting aggression.

Return to that dictum of Clausewitz about how "war is the continuation of politics by other means." Just as politics is meant to be a purposeful enterprise whereby a nation advances its interests, so also with war. There must be a larger aim to which it is directed, and the violent means of warfare must be able to achieve the aim. In the eyes of many observers, because of the incredible suffering caused by World Wars I and II, as well as the onset of the nuclear age with its potential for catastrophic devastation, modern warfare largely lost its purposeful quality. War no longer seemed to be a sensible way for a nation to advance legitimate interests.

The modern papacy adopted such an outlook. In 1963, John XXIII challenged the reasonableness of war in the encyclical letter *Pacem in terris*.[8] Paul VI, John Paul II, Benedict XVI, and the present pope, Francis, have all added their voices to oppose war. The lone exception permitted was the case of national defense when the very existence of a nation was threatened by an aggressor's attack.

A Transformed Context

The decades after World War II were dominated by the Cold War competition of the dominant superpowers and their respective allies. That is no longer the case, and we are witnessing an evolution in international order. There are three elements to the new global context that are particularly significant for discussing armed humanitarian intervention. First, the narrowing of what might count as a just cause for war had much plausibility when contemplating the prospect of nuclear war between the superpowers. However, with the collapse of the Soviet Union the concern over nuclear war lessened markedly. A consequence of the changed relationship between Moscow and Washington was the space created for other actors on the world scene.

By the 1990s the altered situation between the superpowers allowed smaller states to pursue their own interests without the limitations that the superpowers had imposed. Consequently, a measure of international instability was introduced as old rivalries and tensions emerged within regions

---

8. "Thus, in this age which boasts of its atomic power, it no longer makes sense to maintain that war is a fit instrument with which to repair the violation of justice"; see John XXIII, *Pacem in terris*, n. 127.

that had been controlled for generations by the Soviet Union. Ethnic, cultural, and religious identities that had been repressed or strictly contained now resurfaced. Not only were there conflicts between states, but also within them as the façade of national unity collapsed in different places. The tribal tensions in Rwanda, the ethnic and religious differences in regions of the former Yugoslavia, the weak state and missing sense of nationalism in Somalia, and the religious and ethnic conflicts that bedeviled Sudan are examples of where outside observers saw the need for interventions to end violence.

A second element in the changed international order is the rise of the human rights movement. During the Cold War there were various interventions carried out under a variety of pretexts, but the underlying motive was usually one side's effort to maintain or gain some advantage in the contest between the great powers. Humanitarian intervention, however, is aimed at halting mass and flagrant violations of the fundamental human rights of people by their own government.[9] Opposing the atrocities of repressive governments and alleviating the harsh suffering of ordinary people have strong appeal in an age that endorses human rights as fundamental to the dignity of the person.

Whereas individual states are still seen as the ordinary mechanism for protecting rights there is growing appreciation for the role of a broader audience in the defense and protection of basic human rights. This is what is meant by the "internationalization" of human rights claims. Confronted by a pattern of extraordinary human rights abuses within a state, the consciences of men and women everywhere are shocked. These are crimes against humanity, not only against the laws of a state.

Of course, grave and persistent violations of human rights by a state are a threat not only to the domestic population but also to international order and peace. The creation of refugees fleeing across borders, the disruption of economic life through limitations on trade or access to resources, the cross-border loyalties of race, religion, or ethnicity that will arouse concern in other states—these are likely results stemming from widespread repression within a nation. Other states, especially neighboring ones, cannot afford to be indifferent to a government's gross abuses of its people.

A third element of the transformed international context is the rethinking of the meaning of state sovereignty. Properly speaking, intervention is

---

9. While I refer to the direct actions of a government as the cause of the crimes against its own population, it is possible that a humanitarian intervention will be considered when the government is not the direct actor. It could be the case that the targeted government is complicit in the evil of other agents, or is simply ineffectual in protecting the population from the wrongdoing of a domestic actor other than the state.

a form of interference. Intervention may be defined as "dictatorial interference in the internal affairs of another state involving the use or threat of force, or substantially debilitating economic coercion."[10] A humanitarian military intervention is the use of armed force by one state (or an association of states) against a targeted state that is not done in response to that state's external aggression but in reaction to the targeted state's domestic situation.

State sovereignty is a norm of international law. Intervention violates the targeted state's claim of sovereignty over its territory. Those advocating the legitimacy of humanitarian military intervention have argued that the idea of sovereignty must not be understood in a manner that allows a state, in effect, to wage war unhampered upon its own people. The interventionist claim is that ever since the modern system of international order was forged in the middle of the seventeenth century the state received undue emphasis to the neglect of other actors. Due to the rise of human rights movements, the United Nations, and other transnational agents (e.g., European Union, International Criminal Court, Red Cross, Catholic Church, Internet), the idea that only states ought to have standing in international law is undergoing erosion.

In the face of these new factors it simply is not realistic for a state to maintain the same old claims to absolute sovereignty over its population when so much of what used to fall under the domestic jurisdiction of a state is now subject to international forces. Our understanding of sovereignty must evolve to fit the times. The dramatic revolutions in information, communication, travel, business, and environmental awareness, as well as other areas, have led to a new understanding of interdependence. What happens in one state's domestic affairs cannot be contained within its borders but has a spillover effect into other populations.

A standard account of Catholic political theory regarding the state supports those arguing for a revised theory of state sovereignty.[11] Within the Catholic perspective, sovereignty never became separated from the broader notion of an order of political goods. Political sovereignty is a part of that order, not its entirety. The good of the individual, of the family, and of religious, cultural, and economic organizations, all represent genuine limits to sovereignty. And since the unity of the human family is a genuine political good, too, the international order also places a restriction on sovereignty.[12]

---

10. Jack Donnelly, "Human Rights, Humanitarian Intervention and American Foreign Policy: Law, Morality and Politics," *Journal of International Affairs* 37 (1984): 311-28, at 311.

11. Heinrich Rommen, *The State in Catholic Thought* (St. Louis: B. Herder Book Company, 1945).

12. Ibid., 400.

When a state abuses its sovereignty by refusing to recognize the goods it is called to serve, it undercuts the very moral foundation for its own existence. Sovereignty cannot be used as immunity for a state to violate its own reason to exist. As the US bishops have noted, there is a "real but relative moral value to sovereign states. The value is real because of the functions states fulfill as sources of order and authority in the political community; it is relative because boundaries of the sovereign state do not dissolve the deeper relationships of responsibility existing in the human community."[13] A state's sovereignty is to be respected, but its claim is limited and relative.

The Responsibility to Protect

Having discussed the background to the issue, it is possible to turn now to the question of humanitarian military intervention. In 1999 Kofi Annan, then secretary general of the United Nations, asked government leaders to establish a working policy that might guide future crises when vulnerable populations were victimized by their own governments. In response to that call the Canadian government sponsored the International Commission on Intervention and State Sovereignty (ICISS), which proposed the doctrine of the Responsibility to Protect or R2P.[14] The idea of R2P emerged from what the commission saw as a gap between the reality of massive human suffering and the existing rules and mechanisms for managing international order. To plug the gap the commission identified an international obligation—the responsibility to protect—that may require others to intervene in the internal affairs of a state undergoing extreme humanitarian crisis.

The R2P proposal was discussed at the 2005 UN World Summit where the participants declared, "Each individual State has the responsibility to protect its populations from genocide, war crimes, ethnic cleansing and crimes against humanity." The summit concluded that the wider international community shares in this responsibility and through the UN may use "appropriate diplomatic, humanitarian and other peaceful means . . . to help protect populations" from these crimes. It further concluded that military means might be used to exercise this responsibility if peaceful means prove inadequate.[15]

---

13. National Conference of Catholic Bishops, *The Challenge of Peace* (Washington, DC: US Catholic Conference, 1983), n. 237.

14. See note 1.

15. United Nations General Assembly, 2005 World Summit Outcome Document (September 16, 2005), nn. 138-39, http://daccessdds.un.org.

It must be remembered that the use of armed force is the last, not the first, resort in ending genocide, ethnic cleansing, and other violations of basic human rights. In the UN World Summit's declaration there was caution about the role of armed intervention and concern about bodies other than the UN Security Council being used to authorize armed intervention.[16] The nations of the world, acting through the UN and in other forums, have an obligation to use all the means available in international relations and not only armed force when confronting a humanitarian crisis. That should not be forgotten, even if this chapter is focused on the last resort of armed violence.

Both the ICISS and the UN World Summit documents speak of responsibility and duty. Each state has a duty to protect its own people from genocide and mass atrocities; other states have a responsibility to assist the targeted state in fulfilling its obligation to its citizens; and the entire international community has the duty "to take timely and decisive action, using Chapters VI, VII, and VIII of the UN Charter, in situations where a state is manifestly failing to protect its population."[17]

The Catholic Church and Humanitarian Intervention

The church's position on humanitarian intervention was first articulated by John Paul II in response to the practice of ethnic cleansing in Bosnia-Herzegovina during the early 1990s. In a speech to foreign diplomats assigned to the Vatican, John Paul acknowledged the validity of the "principles of state sovereignty and non-interference" in international order, but he insisted that these norms "cannot constitute a screen behind which torture and murder may be carried out."[18] For John Paul, neglect of the obligation to assist those suffering from a humanitarian crisis is a "culpable omission." And to make clear the context of his assertion of a duty to act, he stated, "Once the possibilities afforded by diplomatic negotiations and the procedures provided by international agreements and organizations have been put into effect, and nevertheless, populations are succumbing to the attacks of an unjust aggressor, states no longer have a 'right to indifference.'

---

16. Alex Bellamy, "The Responsibility to Protect—Five Years On," *Ethics and International Affairs* 24, no. 2 (2010): 143.

17. Alex Bellamy and John Tessitore, "EIA Interview: Alex Bellamy on the Responsibility to Protect" (February 16, 2009), http://www.cceia.org.

18. John Paul II, "Address to the Diplomatic Corps Accredited to the Holy See," *L'Osservatore Romano* (Weekly Edition in English) 26 (January 20, 1993), 3.

It seems clear that their duty is to disarm this aggressor, if all other means have proved ineffective."[19]

John Paul returned to the topic a few years later with a comment in his 2000 World Day of Peace message. After discussing the right of people to humanitarian assistance, the pope turned to the topic of humanitarian intervention. "Clearly, when a civilian population risks being overcome by the attacks of an unjust aggressor and political efforts and non-violent defence prove to be of no avail, it is legitimate and even obligatory to take concrete measures to disarm the aggressor."[20] Four years later, the papal viewpoint found expression in the *Compendium of the Social Doctrine of the Church*.[21]

The church's teaching on armed intervention for humanitarian purposes became a topic for discussion in the summer of 2014 with the crisis in northern Iraq. Assessing the actions of the terrorist group known as the Islamic State, Archbishop Silvano Tomasi, Vatican representative to UN agencies in Geneva, concluded that "when all other means have been exhausted, to save human beings the international community must act. This can include disarming the aggressor." Concurring with that judgment, the Vatican nuncio to Iraq, Archbishop Giorgio Lingua, stated on Vatican Radio that the US airstrikes in northern Iraq were "something that had to be done, otherwise [the Islamic State] could not be stopped."[22]

Tomasi claimed that John Paul II's teaching provided "a clear orientation and precise guidelines" for humanitarian intervention. Those guidelines are that such action "must not be unilateral, but internationally recognized"; that "all other means—dialogue, negotiations—for protecting the innocent must be exhausted"; and that "real assistance for those whose rights are being trampled must be provided."[23]

A few days earlier Pope Francis had written to UN Secretary General Ban Ki-moon, urging the international community "to take action to end the humanitarian tragedy now under way" in northern Iraq. The pope went on

---

19. Ibid., 2-3.

20. John Paul II, "Peace on Earth to Those Whom God Loves!" (World Day of Peace Message, January 1, 2000), n. 11, http://www.vatican.va.

21. The text reads, "The international community as a whole has the moral obligation to intervene on behalf of those groups whose very survival is threatened or whose basic human rights are seriously violated. As members of an international community, States cannot remain indifferent; on the contrary, if all other available means should prove ineffective, it is 'legitimate and even obligatory to take concrete measures to disarm the aggressor'"; see Pontifical Council, *Compendium*, n. 506, quoting the 2000 World Day of Peace Message.

22. Both comments are found in Cindy Wooden, "Time to Act: Church Teaches Duty to Intervene to Prevent Genocide," Catholic News Service, August 12, 2014.

23. Ibid.

to write that the effort should aim "to stop and prevent further systematic violence against ethnic and religious minorities."[24] After that letter was made public, the pope was asked a question during a press conference about the US airstrikes against the Islamic State forces. Francis replied,

> In these cases where there is unjust aggression, I can only say that it is licit to stop the unjust aggressor. I underscore the verb "stop"; I don't say bomb, make war—stop him. The means by which he may be stopped should be evaluated. To stop the unjust aggressor is licit, but we nevertheless need to remember how many times, using this excuse of stopping an unjust aggressor, the powerful nations have dominated other people, made a real war of conquest. A single nation cannot judge how to stop this, how to stop an unjust aggressor. After the Second World War, there arose the idea of the United Nations. That is where we should discuss: "Is there an unjust aggressor? It seems there is. How do we stop him?" But only that, nothing more.[25]

There are four things worth noting about the papal answer. First, as Francis himself emphasized, he used the word "stop" not "make war." There is a humanitarian crisis, and the cause of that crisis, the aggression of the Islamic State, ought to be stopped. Second, the means to be used must be "evaluated." Third, in the past there have been alleged humanitarian interventions that served as cover for wars of conquest. Finally, the determination to intervene should not be done unilaterally but through the UN.

Francis affirmed the fundamental idea of a duty to assist innocent victims of a humanitarian crisis, but he was hesitant to conclude armed intervention as the most appropriate response. Instead he called for an evaluation of the proposed means of intervention. One reason for the papal hesitancy is the risk that under the guise of humanitarian motives more self-interested ambitions may be at work. In part, that is why unilateral action ought to be avoided, because it can too easily slide into national interest and away from authentic humanitarian intervention.

Pope Francis does not deny or undercut the idea of a moral duty to protect innocents victimized by aggressive actors. Yet he wisely cautions that

---

24. "Pope to UN SecGen: Int'l Action to Stop Iraq Violence," August 8, 2014, http://www.news.va.

25. Francis Rocca, "Pope Talks Airstrikes in Iraq, His Health, Possible US Visit," Catholic News Service, August 18, 2014, http://ncronline.org. Also, on March 13, 2015, Tomasi said that the crisis in Syria and Iraq requires "more coordinated protection, including the use of force to stop the hands of an aggressor"; see John L. Allen, Jr., "Vatican Backs Military Force to Stop ISIS 'Genocide,'" *Crux*, March 13, 2015, http://www.cruxnow.com.

the decision for armed intervention is fraught with difficult judgments. The claim that there is a duty to intervene for humanitarian purposes highlights the obligation that falls upon competent actors when confronting the evils of genocide, war crimes, ethnic cleansing, and crimes against humanity.

However, it must be asked if such a duty is to be understood in an actual or *prima facie* way. *Prima facie* is a Latin expression meaning "at first sight" or "at first glance." So a *prima facie* duty is one that appears to be real upon first consideration or at first sight. The theory of humanitarian intervention establishes a presumptive (*prima facie*) moral duty that other nations ought to intervene on behalf of the victimized population. Translating that into the actual practice of intervention, however, requires further steps. In other words, the movement from moral principle to practical action is neither automatic nor straightforward.

Moving from Policy to Practice

Making a moral argument for the duty to intervene is just one step. Our actions must be guided by moral concerns, but that alone is insufficient for wise policy judgments. Political, economic, social, historical, military, and psychological forces all are at work in policy deliberations. Political leaders must act on their moral ideals; but they do so in the world as it is, and this places constraints on both their ability to act and the range of actions available.

The ICISS report provided guidance for a decision about humanitarian intervention. Under the heading of "principles for military intervention" the report cites just cause, right intention, last resort, proportional means, reasonable prospects, and right authority. All six of these principles will be readily found in the literature of the JWT. Drawing upon that tradition helps to clarify the moral issues as well as the policy decision.

Just Cause. Without granting absolute status to sovereignty, even human rights advocates acknowledge the potential chaos if nation-states could no longer expect their sovereignty required respect from other nations. Thus, caution is necessary when making an appeal to override a nation's sovereignty. The nature of the humanitarian crisis must be widely agreed upon. Wary voices suggest only genocide and nothing less justifies intervention. The fear is there are simply too many evils committed in the world for nations to assume they must call upon troops to right all the world's wrongs. A clear and bright line such as genocide prevents excessive claims for humanitarian intervention.

Yet others argue the genocide rule is too strict and ignores the vast majority of humanitarian crises. While the violation of human rights must be egregious and pervasive so as to grievously affect thousands of individuals, evils such as ethnic cleansing, rampant torture and rape, arbitrary arrests and detentions without trial, mass executions of political opponents, and deliberate targeting of civilian populations in military assaults meet those standards. To restrict humanitarian intervention only to genocide is too narrow and would permit far too much unnecessary suffering. One should not deny the reasonableness of intervention when there are clear trends over time toward greater suffering with evident government complicity.

Right Intention. If just cause establishes the rationale for why the intervention should occur, the criterion of right intent requires that the interveners be clear and specific about what it is that will be done with military force. Since the stated cause must be to protect the basic human rights of a victimized group, it must be made evident what armed force will do to secure that aim. Some goals are ill served by military action, while others may be beyond the capability of military intervention.

An intervention may begin with a humanitarian purpose, but there is a risk that other self-interested war aims may come to dominate, thereby affecting the manner by which the intervention is carried out. Right intent calls for vigilance to make sure that the goals and strategies of the military intervention correspond to the just cause. Once the goal(s) of armed force is clear, we must ask what is the causal chain that links military intervention to the desired end of stopping the humanitarian crisis.

Last Resort. Armed intervention is more than interference in the domestic affairs of a state; it is the most extreme form of interference among nations, and as such ought to be subject to greater restriction than less coercive forms of interference. One such restriction is that other, less radical types of interference—diplomatic pressures, economic assistance, support for the political opposition, sanctions, and blockades—ought to be tried and found wanting before recourse to armed intervention is considered.

Proportional Means. Judgments about proportionality, the good attained relative to the harm caused, are never a matter of precise calculation but can only be reflective and informed decisions by wise and prudent persons. In the case of humanitarian intervention one must consider the cost in lives lost and suffering created in order to alleviate the suffering and save the lives of others. Such a tragic choice is something no one wishes to confront, but the sad nature of international relations is that the choice is presented. Great suffering and loss of life are happening; hence the call for intervention. Will armed intervention exacerbate the evil or alleviate it? Given the uncertainties of large-scale military action, the answer is not always clear.

Two concerns loom large among advocates of intervention. First is that safeguards against escalation must be clear and enforceable. There is the risk that the intervener will find it necessary to increase the level of military action, either to achieve the original aim or simply to save face before the world. The risk is that escalation will exceed proportionality, so safeguards and checks should be in place to insure against this.

A second and related concern is that there be a strategy for withdrawal so that the intervention does not continue indefinitely. Any strategy for intervention should have an accompanying plan for how to terminate the military engagement to avoid raising the level of the intervention beyond the measure of proportionality. If the first concern is one of scale, this second concern is one of duration. The intervention should be no larger or longer than is necessary to secure the safety of the victimized population.

Reasonable Prospects. If right intent has been followed it should be clear what the aims of the intervention are. Have those aims been achieved so that the ultimate goal, the end of the evil that justified the intervention, has been brought about? Is the strategy to do that the creation of a new government? Establishment of protected enclaves? A negotiated peace among the disputants? Cessation of the worst of the atrocities?

In addition to defining the nature of success and determining the relation of armed force to that success there remains the large question of the likelihood of achieving the intervention's goal. Will it be possible to defeat the forces of oppression? What are the odds of success? The cause may be just, the goals of the armed intervention clear and appropriate, yet uncertainty about the prospect of the military effort may be significant enough to deter those seeking to aid the victims.

The issue of feasibility leaves proponents of humanitarian intervention open to the charge of inconsistency, but the charge is mistaken. Treating similar cases dissimilarly is inconsistent, but treating different cases differently is good sense. As already noted, questions of feasibility will depend on a number of factors. Differences between one crisis and another concerning the military risk, the likelihood of multilateral cooperation, the extent and severity of human rights violations, a government's complicity, competing commitments for limited resources, and the amount of domestic support will necessitate examining each case closely to determine the right course of action.

Right Authority. It must be stressed that multilateral interventions are to be preferred over unilateral ones. Concerted action by several nations is not foolproof as a safeguard against national self-interest, but it does offer a check on any one nation using humanitarian intervention as a cover for its own purposes. Insisting on multilateral intervention is a sensible threshold to cross in order to prevent a nation rushing headlong into foolish interventions or deceiving itself as to the real motives for its intervention.

The United Nations and the developing body of international law are imperfect attempts at forming a structure for addressing international conflicts. Still, despite their failings, these institutions deserve support as building blocks of international order. In a world where weaker nations are wary of the power of stronger nations to impose their will, we should only with great reluctance undercut whatever fledgling structures help to move international relations beyond the rule of might.

Nonetheless, there will be times when the UN Security Council, due to the self-interest of its permanent members, will be inadequate to the task of timely humanitarian intervention. Then other multilateral organizations must act. When the case for intervention is made in such a way that it becomes morally compelling to multiple nations, there is at least the hope that humanitarianism will be the dominant if not sole motive. And the willingness of others to join in the military action is a reasonable standard of evidence to demonstrate genuine support and not just passive acquiescence by allied or client nations to a major power's viewpoint.

Conclusion

The case for intervention must be presented in such a manner that the support of the international community will be marshaled to combat genocide, war crimes, ethnic cleansing, and crimes against humanity. The ability to explain a proposed armed humanitarian intervention according to the principled framework of the JWT is a wise approach to forge consensus on behalf of military action.

Chapter 5

Self-Determination and the Ethics of Force

GERARD F. POWERS

Catholic just war analysis suffers from a gap. Some half of the world's conflicts, including some of the most violent and intractable, are over competing claims of self-determination, often involving efforts to secede from existing states.[1] Much attention has been devoted to the identity conflicts—over religion, ethnicity, and nationality—that fuel these secessionist claims. But there is almost nothing in the Catholic social ethics literature or in official Catholic social teaching on self-determination itself, the morality of the use of force by the parties to the conflict, and the morality of outside intervention on behalf of secessionists or the existing state. This gap is especially surprising in light of the fact that, from Bosnia-Herzegovina and Northern Ireland to East Timor and South Sudan, Catholic leaders, including the Holy See, have often taken rather clear positions on these secessionist claims and on the use of force in these conflicts, especially those that have involved humanitarian interventions.

A Catholic ethic of war and peace that is capacious enough to deal with today's conflicts requires the development of an ethic of self-determination and a corresponding ethic of the use of force to deal with secessionist conflicts. This essay suggests first that a Catholic ethic of self-determination considers secession, or full independence, not a right but a remedy in cases of systematic, prolonged injustice. It then suggests that forceful secession is harder to justify than self-defense by an existing state against aggression but easier to justify than forceful revolution. Finally, it concludes that intervention on behalf of a legitimate secession should not, in most cases, be treated as an ordinary case of collective self-defense but rather should be considered

---

1. From 1989 to 2009, 64 of 130 conflicts were intrastate conflicts over territorial issues related to self-determination (e.g., efforts to gain greater autonomy or full independence). See Uppsala Conflict Database, September 16, 2010, compiled by Rachel Miller for Peter Wallensteen, *Understanding Conflict Resolution*, 3rd ed. (London: Sage, 2011).

an exceptional case that requires broad international authorization, prefer-ably by the UN Security Council.

Toward a Catholic Ethic of Self-Determination

The church has been deeply engaged in addressing conflicts over secession, taking a wide range of approaches that are sometimes difficult to reconcile.[2] Some have claimed that the church contributed to the violent breakup of Yugoslavia by supporting independence movements in Slovenia, Croatia, and Bosnia-Herzegovina, and by the Vatican's early recognition of these new nation-states. In the Philippines, by contrast, the church has opposed Muslim efforts to secede. It is tempting to dismiss these and other cases as examples of an unhealthy mix of religion and nationalism. While that is sometimes true, an examination of the cases in light of general principles of Catholic social teaching elicits a framework for a coherent ethic of self-determination, which, in exceptional cases, permits forceful secession.

Three Catholic Approaches to Secession

The church's position on self-determination has covered the spectrum of supporting alternatives to full independence, consensual divorce, and force-ful secession.

Less than Sovereign Alternatives:
Northern Ireland and the Philippines
In the case of Northern Ireland, the church supported the long-term aspi-ration of many, mostly Catholic, nationalists for a united Ireland. But the church insisted on constitutional and political efforts to resolve conflicting claims of self-determination. It vehemently denounced the IRA's permissive use of just war criteria to legitimize its terrorist violence, while criticizing abuses by British troops, the Protestant-unionist-dominated police, and Loyalist paramilitaries. The church supported self-determination measures short of a united Ireland, such as the cross-border institutions, power sharing within Northern Ireland, and protection of minority and human rights that were incorporated into the 1998 Good Friday Agreement. The church also

---

2. This section is drawn from a talk presented at a conference, "Theology, Conflict, and Peacebuilding: An Intercontinental Conversation," held at St. Vincent School of Theology and Adamson University in Manila, the Philippines, and cosponsored by DePaul University's Center for World Catholicism and Intercultural Theology, December 12-13, 2014.

insisted on the ultimate importance of overcoming sectarianism and promoting reconciliation between Catholics and Protestants, nationalists and loyalists.[3]

In Mindanao, in the southern Philippines, the church has responded in a variety of ways to the decades-long conflict involving various Muslim rebel groups seeking independence. The bishops' January 2015 statement, their most comprehensive on the peace process with the Moro Islamic Liberation Front (MILF), the largest of the armed rebel groups, reflected the challenges involved in balancing competing justice claims. They supported creating new Bangsamoro autonomous areas and recognition of ancestral domain of the indigenous peoples (Lumad) as ways to recognize their aspirations for self-determination. At the same time, they insisted on the overarching right of the Philippines to its sovereignty and territorial integrity. They also highlighted the need to address the economic, social, and political marginalization of Muslims and Lumads, while protecting the fundamental human rights of Christians and others.[4] Regarding the use of force, the church has condemned violence by Abu Sayyef, the MILF, and other armed groups, while also criticizing the government's human rights abuses. It has recognized the right and duty of the Filipino government to use limited military force against these armed groups but has condemned "total war" as a solution, insisting that dialogue is the only path to peace. The church has defined its own role primarily in terms of promoting civic and interreligious dialogue and engagement for peace as a way to overcome the deep historical divide between Christians, Muslims, and the Lumad, and has supported a range of efforts designed to cultivate a culture of peace in a region that has known little but war for generations.[5]

CONSENSUAL DIVORCE: SOUTH SUDAN

South Sudan became an independent state in 2011 after a referendum on independence that many feared would ignite a new genocidal conflict. The independence referendum was part of the 2005 Comprehensive Peace Agreement, which brought a cease fire to a conflict that had raged between the Arab- and Muslim-dominated Sudanese government and the mostly

---

3. For a fuller account, see Gerard F. Powers, "Testing the Moral Limits of Self-Determination: Northern Ireland and Croatia," *The Fletcher Forum of World Affairs* 16, no. 22 (Summer 1992): 29, 30-34.

4. Catholic Bishops' Conference of the Philippines, "Guide Our Feet into the Way of Peace (Lk 1:79): Pastoral Statement on the Draft Bangsamoro Basic Law," January 24, 2015, http://www.cbcpnews.com.

5. Reina C. Neufeldt, "Interfaith Dialogue: Assessing Theories of Change," *Peace & Change* 36 (2011): 344-72.

Christian and animist southern Sudan from 1955 to 1972 and again from 1983 to 2005. The Catholic and Anglican churches helped pave the path to a cease fire and full independence with a multipronged peacebuilding effort. Their "people-to-people" peace process in the 1990s helped reconcile warring tribes in southern Sudan; their parallel civil society peace process helped cement the 2005 peace agreement; and their civic education campaign and logistical support were instrumental in ensuring a peaceful and credible referendum on independence. The bishops' statements focused heavily on the need for a free and fair referendum. They rejected a unity based on Muslim and Arab domination of other religious, linguistic, and ethnic identities, and a Sudanese government that marginalized and repressed those on the periphery. But they were clear that popular will was determinative, and that, whatever the outcome of the referendum, the task would be "to bring about a unity embracing all, in a just, free and open society, where the human dignity of every citizen is safeguarded and respected."[6]

FORCEFUL SECESSION: YUGOSLAVIA

In Yugoslavia, the church supported secession for Slovenia, Croatia, and Bosnia-Herzegovina, including the use of force to defend the newly independent states.[7] While the church was long split between integrationists who supported the Yugoslav ideal of integrating diverse nationalities into one state and religious nationalists who equated Catholic identity with exclusivist and chauvinistic forms of Croatian nationalism, the church took a middle position in 1991. It justified secession in part as a means to protect historic national, cultural, and religious identities, but its main justification was to escape from a Serb-dominated, communist, and (by then) failed Yugoslavia and to integrate with a more democratic Western Europe.[8]

The Vatican led the way in recognizing the new states, largely as a defensive measure in the face of a failed Yugoslavia and a destructive war in Croatia. Even after Croatia and Slovenia declared independence in 1991, the Catholic bishops of Yugoslavia and the Vatican presumed that newly independent republics could, through negotiation, remain integrated into

---

6. Sudan Catholic Bishops' Conference, "A Future Full of Hope," July 22, 2010, http://cpn.nd.edu.

7. A comparable case is the church's role in East Timor's struggle for independence; see Arnold S. Kohen, "The Catholic Church and the Independence of East Timor," *Bulletin of Concerned Asian Scholars* (January-June 2000): 19; and Patrick A. Smythe, *"The Heaviest Blow": The Catholic Church and the East Timor Issue* (Munster: Lit Verlag, 2004).

8. For a fuller account, see Powers, "Testing the Moral Limits," 34-39; Pedro Ramet, "Religion and Nationalism in Yugoslavia," in *Religion and Nationalism in Soviet and East European Politics*, ed. P. Ramet (Durham, NC: Duke University Press, 1989), 319, 322.

a reconstituted confederal Yugoslavia. When negotiations over a confederal solution failed, the Vatican supported full independence, conditioned on maintaining the existing boundaries of Yugoslavia's republics and respecting minority and human rights. The church consistently opposed the Croatian extremists' efforts to create an ethnically "pure" Greater Croatia, and to partition Bosnia along ethnic-religious lines. [9]

Given the church's support for an independent Bosnia, Croatia, and Slovenia, it reiterated traditional Catholic teaching about the right and duty of these new states to defend themselves against aggression in accord with the just war tradition (JWT) and the laws of war.[10] While some Catholic leaders spoke of a sacred duty to defend the nation, church support for the use of force in self-defense was relatively restrained. Even during the worst of the ethnic cleansing in Bosnia-Herzegovina, the bishops did not embrace lifting the arms embargo imposed by the UN for fear of widening and escalating the conflict. Rather, with Pope John Paul II, they appealed for (mostly nonmilitary forms of) "humanitarian intervention" by the international community "to disarm the aggressor" and begin a process of demilitarizing the region.[11]

How might one reconcile these four very different cases? Drawing on general principles from Catholic social teaching and considering how the church has addressed specific cases of secession, a Catholic moral framework for self-determination could be summarized in the following way. The Irish and Mindanao cases and the proposals for a confederal Yugoslavia, with their emphasis on less-than-sovereign means of respecting self-determination, should represent the paradigmatic moral case. South Sudan's consensual divorce represents the morally preferable approach when less-than-sovereign alternatives are not viable alternatives. The Yugoslav case illustrates how this approach does not exclude, in extraordinary cases, unilateral, or nonconsensual, secession as a last-resort remedy.[12]

---

9. For a detailed account of the church's role in the conflict, see Gerard Powers, "Religion, Conflict, and Prospects for Reconciliation in Bosnia, Croatia, and Yugoslavia," *Journal of International Affairs* 50, no. 1 (Summer 1996): 221-52.

10. See, e.g., Croatian Catholic Bishops, "Urgent Appeal from the Bishops of Croatia," Zagreb, July 30, 1991, jloughnan.tripod.com/croatbpssay.htm.

11. John Paul II, "Address to the Diplomatic Corps," January 16, 1993, in *Origins* 22, no. 34 (February 4, 1993): 587; also Cardinal Vinko Puljic, Archbishop of Sarajevo, "Address at the Center for Strategic and International Studies," March 30, 1995, Catholic News Service, April 3, 1995, 7.

12. My initial effort to develop this moral framework is found in Powers, "Testing the Moral Limits," 29.

General Principles Relevant to Self-Determination

Before elaborating on this moral framework, it is useful to step back and consider several particularly relevant elements of the church's cosmopolitan and communitarian political ethic, defined by the twin goals of protecting human dignity and promoting the common good.

First, a Catholic international ethic is *human-centric*, not state-centric; states remain important, but the human person and the global human family are the ultimate objects of concern. While the church gives great weight to respect for sovereignty, this is not an absolute norm; it can be overridden where necessary to accommodate secessionist claims that will better protect fundamental human and minority rights.

A second element is a *positive conception of peace*. Much of Catholic teaching and practice, particularly the JWT, is about maintaining a negative peace—i.e., avoiding war and helping to prevent and manage violent conflicts around the world. But Catholic teaching also insists on the importance of a positive political peace: *tranquillitas ordinis*, the peace of a rightly ordered political community, with people living in truth, charity, freedom, and justice directed toward the common good. The claims of both existing nation-states and secessionist groups within those states should be judged not just by whether they will threaten a negative peace but also by whether they will contribute to a positive peace.

Third is *solidarity*. As a communitarian ethic, Catholic teaching places great value on protecting what is distinctive about different religious, cultural, national, and ethnic identities. But as a cosmopolitan ethic, it also emphasizes what is universal and shared among different peoples. Solidarity is about creating unity out of diversity. It challenges the zero-sum thinking of extreme nationalists who claim that their candle can burn brightly only if they extinguish their enemy's. The church, therefore, distinguishes between inclusive forms of civic nationalism and legitimate expressions of patriotism, on the one hand, and the "idolatry" of chauvinist, militant, and exclusivist forms of religious nationalism, on the other. Solidarity calls for collaboration, not competition, among individuals, groups, and nations to build the structures of cooperative security that can promote authentic human development and the common good.[13]

A fourth element—*strengthening international law and international institutions*—is a concrete manifestation of the virtue of solidarity, and a necessary

---

13. See Kenneth Himes, "Peacebuilding and Catholic Social Teaching," in *Peacebuilding: Catholic Theology, Ethics, and Praxis*, ed. R. Schreiter, S. Appleby, and G. Powers (Maryknoll, NY: Orbis Books, 2010), 273-75.

means to achieve both a negative and a positive peace. "International community" is not an oxymoron, as some political realists argue, but something all states—and others, such as civil society actors—have an obligation to help protect and strengthen. States have an obligation to help develop a cooperative security regime based in strengthened international norms and institutions that can reduce and eventually eliminate the occasions when nations feel compelled to resort to force and that can improve their capacity to address global problems that even the most powerful nations cannot expect to solve on their own.[14] Given the centrality of international law, the United Nations, and other international institutions to this vision of cooperative security, the church will give considerable deference to existing international law and institutions in addressing self-determination and the use of force.

Fifth, the *principle of subsidiarity* applies to self-determination in at least two ways. On the one hand, since authority should be exercised at the *lowest level possible*, overly centralized states or a global super state that does not adequately represent or devolve authority to lower levels would seem problematic.[15] On the other hand, subsidiarity also requires that authority should be exercised at the *highest level necessary* to deal with the range of complex economic, political, and security issues that are part and parcel of a globalized world.[16] That element of subsidiarity would argue against a proliferation of microstates that might well lack the capacity to address regional and global issues by themselves or in collaboration with other nations.

These general norms—a human-centric ethic that qualifies the right of sovereignty; a positive conception of peace defined in terms of justice and the national and global common good; a solidarity that rejects exclusivist nationalisms and finds unity in diversity; support for strengthening international law and institutions; and a subsidiarity that values both decentralization and centralization—provide a context for elaborating a Catholic theory of self-determination.

Self-Determination as a Moral Right

The term "self-determination" is rarely used in official church documents. The *Compendium of the Social Doctrine of the Church* mentions, without

---

14. The Second Vatican Council urged "the establishment of some universal public authority acknowledged as such by all, and endowed with effective power to safeguard, on behalf of all, security, regard for justice, and respect for rights"; see *Gaudium et spes*, no. 82.

15. Pontifical Council for Justice and Peace, *Compendium of the Social Doctrine of the Church* (Washington, DC: US Conference of Catholic Bishops, 2005), no. 441.

16. John XXIII, *Pacem in terris*, no. 140.

elaboration, "a right to self-determination and independence" in the context of economic globalization.[17] While he does not use the term, Paul VI, in *Populorum progressio*, calls for "an ever more effective world solidarity [that] should allow all peoples to become the artisans of their destiny."[18] The 1971 Synod of Bishops argued that global inequalities necessitated "a certain responsible nationalism [that] gives them the impetus needed to acquire an identity of their own. From this basic self-determination can come attempts at putting together new political groupings allowing full development to these peoples."[19] In one of the few efforts in a church document to define general criteria for self-determination, the US bishops' 1993 statement, *The Harvest of Justice Is Sown in Peace*, defined self-determination as a right of peoples "to participate in shaping their cultural, religious, economic, and political identities."[20] These statements parallel the definition of self-determination in international law.[21]

These passages suggest that self-determination is a norm analogous to the norm of participation. It is the freedom of a people to participate in shaping its own future, especially but not only its political future. Participation is necessary for and an expression of individual and communal identity and development. It is also a means for ensuring the protection of individual and communal rights, either within a nation or vis-à-vis other nations. Marginalization, or lack of participation, is associated with the violation of basic rights and limits the ability of individuals and peoples to contribute to the common good.

A Right to What?

If self-determination is about participating in shaping one's own future, what does that entail politically? While it has been in flux since the end of the Cold War, international law has generally taken a restrictive view that limits secessionist self-determination, or full independence, to countries escaping colonial rule or foreign military occupation. Under the principle of

---

17. *Compendium of the Social Doctrine of the Church*, no. 365.

18. Paul VI, *Populorum progressio*, par. 65.

19. Synod of Bishops, *Justice in the World* (1971), par. 17.

20. National Conference of Catholic Bishops, *The Harvest of Justice Is Sown in Peace* (Washington, DC: U.S. Catholic Conference, 1991), 28-29.

21. The "self-determination of peoples" is a "principle" in article 1(2) of the UN Charter and a "right" in common article 1 of the human rights covenants. The UN General Assembly's 1970 "Declaration on Friendly Relations" defines self-determination as a right of all peoples "freely to determine, without external interference, their political status and to pursue their economic, social and cultural development."

uti possidetis, colonies that become independent must retain their colonial borders.

This restrictive approach to secessionist self-determination prioritizes the territorial integrity and political unity of existing states over secessionist claims. It presumes that self-determination can and should be achieved by what Hurst Hannum calls "less-than-sovereign" alternatives,[22] such as power sharing, minority rights regimes, and various kinds of autonomy in federal and confederal systems. This is the default Catholic position that is reflected especially in the Irish and Mindanao cases.[23]

Several concerns would seem to justify this approach. A proliferation of new states could replicate problems secession was meant to resolve by creating unviable microstates or transforming dominant majorities into trapped minorities, such as Serbs in Croatia and Protestants in a united Ireland. Limiting self-determination to "less-than-sovereign" alternatives protects order by preventing the violent Balkanization that could occur if the numerous states with self-determination movements faced armed rebellions.

But a broad rejection of secession means tolerating violations of the right to self-determination in cases of tyranny, repression of minorities, and failed states. In some cases, the status quo is more violent than the alternative. It is inconsistent to permit secession in the colonial context but not in other cases where peoples suffer comparable kinds of subjugation. Moreover, denying the right to secede has neither prevented violent secessionist movements nor encouraged states to accommodate legitimate minority rights and aspirations.

A much more permissive approach to self-determination is what Allen Buchanan calls the *primary right* approach.[24] The primary right approach assumes all peoples should have their own state. It grounds a right to independence in a people's distinctive history, culture, language, and other objective characteristics—as well as in the subjective desire to secede, as evidenced, for example, by referenda for independence in Croatia in 1991 and South Sudan two decades later.

22. Hurst Hannum, *Autonomy, Sovereignty, and Self-Determination: The Accommodation of Conflicting Rights* (Philadelphia: University of Pennsylvania Press, 1990), 233.

23. The *Compendium* begins a brief discussion of minority rights with an acknowledgment, without elaboration, of the fact that "For every people there is in general a corresponding nation, but for various reasons national boundaries do not always coincide with ethnic boundaries" (par. 387).

24. See, e.g., Alan Buchanan, "Secession, State Breakdown, and Humanitarian Intervention," in *Ethics and Foreign Intervention,* ed. Deen Chatterjee and Donald Scheid (Cambridge: Cambridge University Press, 2003), 189-211; Tom Farer, "The Ethics of Intervention in Self-Determination Struggles," *Human Rights Quarterly* 25, no. 2 (May 2003): 382.

This approach appreciates the importance of independence for maintaining one's distinctive identity and respects democratic decision making, but it suffers from several problems. First is the problem of infinite divisibility. Given the sheer number of peoples, the world would be littered with unviable microstates. Second is insularity. The assumption that all peoples have a right to, and can only protect their identity by means of, an independent state tends to reinforce insular forms of ethno-nationalism, as opposed to more open forms of civic nationalism. Third, a people's right to a sovereign state should not be based only on distinctive identity and the desire to be independent. The essential test of a new state's legitimacy should be its commitment and capacity to fulfill the functional purposes of sovereignty: to create a just and stable political order and contribute to the global common good.[25] Specifically, the new state must be able to maintain a viable economy, establish the rule of law, protect basic human rights, especially minority rights, and play a constructive and peaceful role in international affairs.

The more restrictive *remedial right* approach resolves some of the problems with a primary right to secede. According to Buchanan, secession is not a right but is a last-resort remedy in the face of persistent, systematic, and grave injustice. Given the instabilities and imponderable consequences associated with secession, the presumption is for achieving self-determination through means that respect the territorial integrity and unity of the existing state. But that presumption many be overridden in cases of systematic injustice and where the new states retain the original state's boundaries. This approach seems consistent with evolving state practice since the end of the Cold War. In noncolonial contexts, such as the breakup of Yugoslavia, the principles of effectivity and *uti possidetis* have been interpreted to allow recognition as an independent state when a major substate entity, such as a province in a federal system, has effective control over its territory and people and maintains the internal boundaries of the original state. The new states have also been expected to meet other criteria, such as a commitment to protect minority and other human rights.

As with state practice, evolving church practice reflects this remedial-right approach. This approach has several elements. First, self-determination is a moral right analogous to the right of participation. Secession is a remedy, not a right, and is only appropriate as a last resort in cases of serious, systematic and long-standing injustice. Second, the "what" that is to be determined is not to be understood univocally as sovereign statehood but consists of a

---

25. *The Harvest of Justice Is Sown in Peace*, 29.

number of less-than-sovereign options, as well as secession as a last-resort remedy. In the Irish and Mindanao cases, the church emphasized the need and possibility of protecting the rights and identities of, and promoting reconciliation among, conflicting national, ethnic, and religious communities regardless of the ultimate political solution. In the Croatia and Sudan cases, however, the bishops concluded that secession was justified because "less-than-sovereign" alternatives were not available or would not remedy long-standing violations of basic human and minority rights by the central government. Third, popular will and objective indicators of national identity are not sufficient to establish the right of a people to independent statehood; the more important criterion is whether a people have the capacity and will to fulfill the purposes of sovereignty.

Self-Determination and the Use of Force

Two separate but related questions about the use of force are raised by remedial secession. First, if unilateral secession is permitted in exceptional cases, can the seceding entity use military force to achieve independence and can the central government use force to prevent it? Second, under what circumstances may foreign states intervene on behalf of either party?

Forceful Secession

Two approaches to war that are often found in conflicts over self-determination are not compatible with Catholic teaching: holy war and amoral realism. While they would vigorously resent the comparison, Croatian and Serbian nationalist extremists fighting over Croatian secession were engaged in a form of holy war not altogether different from that perpetrated by the Islamic State in Iraq and Syria (ISIS). Both the extreme nationalists and ISIS hold that war has no moral limits because the enemy is less than human (an infidel or an inferior culture) and because war is necessary to defend ultimate values, whether nationalist or religious. According to amoral realists, the use of force, whether on the side of the central government or the secessionists, should be judged by whether it serves national interests and not be constrained by moral and legal norms.

In Catholic teaching, the JWT and pacifism, or principled nonviolence, are the two morally legitimate approaches to the ethics of war. Nonviolence has always been a part of the tradition, but since Vatican II and especially since the end of the Cold War, it has received greater emphasis, with papal statements routinely declaiming that "war is not the answer."[26] The genocidal violence that has so often been associated with secessionist civil wars has reinforced the church's skepticism about the ability of modern war to meet just war criteria. At the same time, the success of nonviolence in the demise of Soviet communism, the overthrow of dictatorial regimes in the Philippines and Serbia, and the peaceful breakup of the Soviet Union and Czechoslovakia have demonstrated the efficacy of nonviolence and political dialogue in achieving dramatic political changes that most thought could only take place through war.[27]

Nevertheless, principled nonviolence is considered an option for individuals not governments. In a sinful world without an international authority to control and resolve conflict, military force is sometimes considered a tragic necessity to establish or maintain order.[28] But war must be governed by the moral criteria of the JWT. A minority of Catholic scholars adopts a permissive interpretation of just war that begins with a presumption that war is a tool of statecraft necessary to preserve justice; therefore, force is easier to justify, including by those seeking to overthrow repressive regimes.[29] Official church teaching adopts an increasingly strict, or restrictive, approach that begins with a strong presumption against war and considers war a failure of statecraft. The just war criteria are therefore to be strictly construed, making it very difficult to justify when, why, and how to use military force.[30] Especially in cases of forceful secession, a just war analysis must be tied to a broader peacebuilding ethic that can provide a framework for the state- and nation-building and reconciliation that are inherent in secession.

How do these general norms governing the use of force apply to the specific problem of secessionist self-determination? The *Catechism* addresses the more general issue of armed resistance to oppressive regimes by reiterat-

---

26. *Compendium of the Social Doctrine of the Church*, no. 497.

27. John Paul II, *Centesimus annus* (1991), no. 23. See also Drew Christiansen, S.J., "Catholic Peacemaking, 1991-2005: The Legacy of Pope John Paul II," *Review of Faith and International Affairs* 4, no. 2 (Fall 2006): 21-28. A growing body of literature analyzes the efficacy of nonviolent resistance. See, e.g., Erica Chenoweth and Maria J. Stephan, *Why Civil Resistance Works: The Strategic Logic of Nonviolent Conflict* (New York: Columbia University Press, 2011).

28. *Gaudium et spes*, no. 79.

29. See George Weigel, "The Development of Just War Thinking in the Post–Cold War World: An American Perspective," in *The Price of Peace: Just War in the Twenty-First Century*, ed. C. Reed and D. Ryall (Cambridge: Cambridge University Press, 2007).

30. See, e.g., J. Bryan Hehir, "From the Pastoral Constitution of Vatican II to *The Challenge of Peace*," in *Catholics and Nuclear War*, ed. Philip J. Murnion (New York: Crossroad, 1983), 71-87. For an overview of the US bishops' application of this strict approach to US military interventions since the 1980s, see Gerard Powers, "The U.S. Bishops and War since the Peace Pastoral," *U.S. Catholic Historian* 27, no. 2 (Winter 2009): 73-96.

ing just war criteria. Armed resistance to oppression by political authority is not legitimate unless all the following conditions are met: (1) there is certain, grave, and prolonged violation of fundamental rights; (2) all other means of redress have been exhausted; (3) such resistance will not provoke worse disorders; (4) there is well-founded hope of success; and (5) it is impossible reasonably to foresee any better solution.[31]

While these criteria mimic those for self-defense against aggression, in the JWT as in international law it has traditionally been much more difficult to justify revolutionary violence than self-defense in conflicts between states.[32] Revolutions have been considered to be justified, as a last resort, in cases of tyranny and systematic repression. But the self-appointed leaders of rebel groups have a difficult time establishing legitimate authority.[33] Moreover, revolutions pose a threat to order, often involving disproportionate and uncontrollable violence without serious prospects for success in creating a more just polity.[34] James Turner Johnson contends, however, that contemporary ethics has "significantly tilted toward favoring the right of rebellion."[35] That more favorable view reflects a greater concern for human rights and justice as a foundation for a stable order. The emergence of the concepts of a responsibility to protect (R2P) and a right to democracy are examples. Regime change is also increasingly promoted, and sometimes accepted, as a legitimate objective of both nonviolent and violent campaigns. The success of "people power" movements to overthrow dictatorial regimes in the Philippines, the Soviet bloc, and the Middle East is an example of the former. The use of the Reagan Doctrine to justify the Contra war in Nicaragua and the preventive war doctrine in Iraq are examples of the latter. Given these developments, it is not surprising that the international community has also taken a more permissive approach to secession since the end of the Cold War, welcoming the consensual breakup of the Soviet Union and Sudan, and acquiescing in and even supporting armed secession in Bosnia, Kosovo, and East Timor.[36]

---

31. *Catechism of the Catholic Church* (New York: Image Books, 1995), no. 2243.

32. According to Christine Gray, there is no right in international law to use force to secede except in cases of decolonization or occupation. See *International Law and the Use of Force* (Oxford: Oxford University Press, 2008), 64.

33. James Turner Johnson, "*Ad Fontes*: The Question of Rebellion and Moral Tradition on the Use of Force," *Ethics & International Affairs* 27, no. 4 (Winter 2013): 373.

34. Nigel Biggar, "Christian Just War Reasoning and Two Cases of Rebellion: Ireland 1916–1921 and Syria 2011–Present," *Ethics & International Affairs* 27, no. 4 (Winter 2013): 399.

35. Johnson, "*Ad Fontes*," 375.

36. I have developed this line of argument more fully with respect to the French intervention in Mali in Gerard Powers, "The Ethics of Intervention," *Sicherheit und Frieden/Security and Peace* 2 (2014): 119–24.

Whatever one makes of these developments, there is a lot of wisdom in retaining strict criteria, so that forceful secession is clearly the exceptional case.

First is *just cause*. The threshold for interstate conflicts is defense against aggression. The standard for forceful secession should be higher: serious, systematic, and long-standing injustice.

Second and more difficult is the question of *legitimate authority*. As noted earlier, it should not be enough to show control of people and a defined territory under the principles of effectivity and *uti posseditis*. More is required, notably a capacity and will to fulfill the purposes of sovereignty defined in terms of respect for human rights, especially minority rights, and promotion of the common good at the national and international levels. This test is very difficult to meet in cases of armed revolution, where a new government needs to be created from scratch, often by an irregular band of self-appointed armed leaders. But under the revised understanding of *uti possidetis*, a secessionist government should be able to meet this test because it would be an existing major substate governmental entity with a track record.

A third hurdle is *probability of success*. This criterion is far more difficult to meet in cases of secession than in cases of self-defense in interstate conflicts because the objective is not just a return to the pre-aggression status quo ante. Rather, success is measured in terms of the creation of a new nation-state that is more just, peaceful, and prosperous than the existing unified state. The litany of failed efforts at state building is long. The fate of the rump state left behind after secession also has to be a factor in judging success. As with legitimate authority, the one factor that makes success more likely in cases of remedial secession than revolutions to overthrow a government is the *uti possidetis* requirement that a secessionist body already have authority over a major existing administrative unit, which makes the successful transformation into an independent state more likely.

Last resort and *proportionality* are related hurdles. If less-than-sovereign alternatives are not viable, the strong preference is for a South Sudan–like consensual divorce. But consensual divorce is often not feasible in cases that justify remedial secession. Nonviolent resistance is another option, but nonviolent movements rarely succeed in seceding.[37] Forceful secession, however, increases the risk the conflict might become genocidal, as secessionists battle the central government as well as trapped minorities who oppose secession.

---

37. See, e.g., Erica Chenoweth and Maria J. Stephan, *Why Civil Resistance Works: The Strategic Logic of Nonviolent Conflict* (New York: Columbia University Press, 2011).

A final consideration is the *jus post bellum*. If forceful secession is to be morally acceptable in the exceptional circumstances that meet a strict interpretation of just war criteria, a host of postsecession issues arise. The *jus post bellum* is in a formative stage of development. A minimalist approach might be appropriate for interstate conflicts in which neither country subjugates or occupies the other. In those cases, a victor's responsibilities might be limited to ensuring a just peace settlement that restores the prewar status quo. A victorious secessionist might be tempted to adopt such a minimalist understanding of postwar responsibilities, especially given the long-term, systematic injustice that justified secession in the first place. Since secession entails state building, however, the *jus post bellum* responsibilities must be closely tied to the requirements of legitimate authority and probability of success. That is, the secessionist must take concrete steps to create a just and peaceful state, as well as to be a good neighbor and a good global citizen. That broad agenda would include, among many other things, instituting minority-rights protections and perhaps affirmative measures to help trapped minorities rebuild and become integral members of the new state; ensuring a just distribution of vital assets between the new state and the rump state and equitable terms for benefiting from natural resources; and promoting reconciliation among different ethnic, religious, and national groups within the new state and between that state and the rump state.[38]

There are many self-determination cases that could meet the threshold for just cause, fewer that could establish their legitimate authority, and fewer still that could also meet concerns about probability of success and proportionality, as well as their *jus post bellum* obligations. As a result, forceful secession is harder to justify than self-defense by an existing state against aggression but easier to justify than forceful revolution.

Intervention on Behalf of Secession

The legitimacy of intervention depends on the moral and legal legitimacy of the secession. If the secession is not legitimate, intervention at the invitation of the secessionist group violates the sovereignty of the existing state and, if militarily significant, can constitute aggression against that state. If the existing government is not legitimate, intervention at the invitation of that state to prevent secession is not legitimate. If the secession is legitimate, intervention on behalf of the illegitimate existing government violates the

---

38. For an overview of different approaches to *jus post bellum* and reconciliation, see Kenneth Himes, "Peacebuilding and Catholic Social Teaching," 282-92; Daniel Philpott, "Reconciliation: A Catholic Ethic for Peacebuilding in the Political Order," in *Peacebuilding*, 92-124.

sovereignty of and, if militarily significant, can constitute aggression against the new state. Is the converse also true? Is it legitimate to intervene militarily at the invitation of a new state that has established its legitimacy under the criteria for remedial secession? (Different criteria than I suggest below might apply to various kinds of nonmilitary aid to a new state, but here I will address only militarily significant forms of intervention.)

If upholding sovereignty is the principal goal, a symmetrical and permissive approach to the use of force would justify military intervention to defend the new state as a classic form of collective self-defense. In international law, collective self-defense is permitted under Article 51 of the UN Charter at the invitation of a state that is the victim of an armed attack. This approach makes good sense insofar as it would be counterproductive and even hypocritical to establish a remedy of secession but then deny the new state the international support necessary for it to defend itself. The existing state, knowing that the new state could not receive foreign military aid, would have more incentive to use overwhelming military force to subdue the new state.

Nevertheless, a more restrictive and asymmetrical approach to military intervention would seem to be necessary. In other words, the fact that an entity has a right of forceful secession does not automatically justify unilateral military intervention on behalf of that new state. Why this asymmetrical approach? First, the judgments involved in determining whether the conditions for remedial-right secession are met are qualitative and highly subjective. Second, while the strict criteria for remedial secession would significantly reduce the risk of infinite divisibility of multi-ethnic nation-states and endless wars of secession, instability remains an inherent risk when new states are created, and that risk escalates when foreign governments intervene militarily. Third, military intervention always carries some risk that foreign governments, especially but not only regional neighbors, will intervene for self-interested reasons and in ways that undermine the sovereignty of the new state they purport to support.

Given these concerns, an asymmetrical approach seems appropriate in which regional and global peace and security trump the right of collective defense of the new sovereign state. As a result, criteria similar to that used for humanitarian intervention would seem appropriate in cases of secession. Specifically, legitimate authority would be enhanced if the UN Security Council or at least the regional body the new state would join (e.g., the African Union or European Union) recognized the new state and authorized military intervention. Only in exceptional cases, when dysfunction within these bodies prevents them from fulfilling their proper roles, would collective defense be permitted. Even then, such intervention should enjoy broad support from a substantial part of the international community.

Another criterion for foreign military intervention is that it must be part of a broader *jus post bellum* strategy and peacebuilding ethic. At a minimum, any military intervention would have to avoid undermining that state- and nation-building. For example, military interventions would have to avoid any direct or tacit support for ethnic cleansing or other actions that would reinforce exclusivist forms of extreme nationalism. In addition to doing no harm, some degree of support for state- and nation-building is necessary. The risk that interveners would have to fill a governance void by de jure or de facto occupation, as is often the case with humanitarian interventions, should be lessened by the *uti possidetis* requirement that the secessionist be an existing and functional substate governmental entity. But intervention would still have to contribute to and be part of a comprehensive strategy that can help the new state strengthen its legal, political, economic, and cultural institutions; respect basic human and minority rights; and promote reconciliation among ethnic, religious, and national groups.

Conclusion

The moral framework for remedial secession and intervention outlined here flows out of a communitarian and cosmopolitan ethic built on the twin pillars of human dignity and human rights, and the national and global common good. Because it is human-centric, not state-centric, and considers sovereignty a qualified and instrumental norm, it presumes that the right of self-determination may be achieved short of full independence or through creative forms of shared sovereignty. In other words, the default position is achieving self-determination through less-than-sovereign alternatives. Secession is the exceptional remedy (not a right), available only as a last resort in cases of serious, systematic, and long-standing injustice, where there is an existing major substate government that has the capacity and will to fulfill the broad purposes of sovereignty and to contribute to the global common good.

Even in cases where remedial secession is justified, the strong presumption is that political dialogue, negotiation, and adherence to legal processes are essential. While the use of force could meet just war criteria in some cases, forceful secession challenges domestic and international peace, often involves indiscriminate and uncontrolled violence, and rarely resolves the underlying disputes. As a result, forceful secession is harder to justify than self-defense by an existing state against aggression. Foreign intervention on behalf of secession should not, in most cases, be treated simply as collective self-defense but rather should require broad international authorization, preferably by the UN Security Council or a regional body. The intervention should also be tied to a broader peacebuilding strategy that can contribute to state- and nation-building.

This framework is more permissive than the traditional rejection of forceful secession outside the colonial context, but it is significantly more restrictive than a broad, primary right to secession based on popular will and ethnic or national identity. It takes seriously the right to self-determination while reducing the risk of endless wars of secession. It should contribute to the larger peacebuilding project of preventing, managing, and recovering from the identity and secessionist conflicts that have necessitated so many humanitarian interventions around the world in recent decades.

CHAPTER 6

Torture, Terror, and Just War

ANNA FLOERKE SCHEID

Following the terrorist attacks unleashed against the United States on September 11, 2001, the subsequent initiation of what is routinely called the "war on terror," and the continuing rise of extremist groups around the world, discussions have arisen as to whether international law's prohibition of torture needs to be reconsidered to meet the challenges posed by terrorism in the twenty-first century. Terrorists have demonstrated their willingness to flout both the standards of human decency and the laws of war. Some may ask, is it fair or reasonable to require the US military to abide by ethical standards not respected by their enemies? If terrorists continue making plans to attack civilians, then shouldn't the US military have access to torture as a tool for trying to prevent future attacks? Aren't just war concerns regarding criteria such as right intention, proportionate means, and the humane treatment of detainees obsolete in the face of terrorists whose goal is to murder as many civilians as possible?

Daniel Bell has argued that instead of eroding the standards of the just war tradition (JWT), the war on terror demonstrates that we need them more than ever.[1] The just war criteria are meant to restrain our impulses toward excessive violence in warfare. Most Americans, Bell contends, have misunderstood the JWT, viewing it primarily as a tool to justify total warfare against their enemies when there is a just cause. In other words, we frequently reduce the idea of a just war to the single criterion of just cause; when our cause is just, we consider ourselves to have "permission to destroy enemy forces" and, indeed, in Bell's language, "annihilate" them.[2] This view of warfare emerges, Bell demonstrates, from French General Henri Jomini's understanding of war as "postpolitical" rather than from Carl von Clausewitz's

---

1. Daniel M. Bell, Jr., "Discriminating Force: Just War and Counterinsurgency," *Christian Century* 130, no. 16 (August 7, 2013): 22.

2. Ibid.

view of war as "politics by other means."[3] Building on Clausewitz's perspective as a corrective, Bell holds that just war is encompassed by overarching political aims—in particular to reestablish a just and secure peace—that are undermined by unrestrained warfare. The JWT, when it is not reduced to the criterion of just cause, places limits on the conduct of warfare so as to increase the probability of establishing the political goal of a just peace. Within this approach to just war, Bell rejects the use of drones, contending that drones violate the criteria of proportionality and noncombatant immunity since they cause an unacceptably high rate of civilian casualties. Drone warfare as currently practiced has more in common with Jomini's vision of total war to annihilate one's enemies than with the JWT, which envisions future reconciliation with them.

In this essay, I argue that Bell's point about the politically directed aims of a just war toward a just and secure peace can be extended beyond the question of drones to the issue of torture in the war on terror. The essay proceeds in three parts: I begin by defining torture and describing the George W. Bush administration's legal maneuverings in their attempt to legitimize "enhanced interrogation" of suspected terrorists. Policy changes made by the Bush administration led to a military culture that considered torture and the abuse of detainees permissible.[4] Second, I describe arguments surrounding the well-known "ticking-time-bomb" scenario that is often used to demonstrate an exception to the rule that torture is always wrong. This extreme case frequently arises in discussions about whether torture is a licit means of combating terrorism. I reject the efficacy of the ticking-time-bomb argument for dealing adequately with the moral issue of torture in the war on terror. Third, I argue against the use of torture in warfare on just war grounds.

Permitting Torture

Both US and international law prohibit torture, as well as cruel, inhumane, and degrading treatment. The Geneva Conventions prohibit "violence to life and person, in particular murder of all kinds, mutilation, cruel treatment and torture" as well as "outrages upon personal dignity, in particular humili-

---

3. Ibid., 23.

4. For a full argument narrating these events, see Scott R. Paeth, "'Dirty Hands' Revisited: Morality, Torture, and Abu Ghraib," *Journal of the Society of Christian Ethics* 28, no. 1 (2008): 163-81. See also Jonathan Rothchild, "Moral Consensus, the Rule of Law, and the Practice of Torture," *Journal of the Society of Christian Ethics* 26, no. 2 (2006): 125-56. See also PBS *Frontline*'s "The Torture Question" (2005), http://www.pbs.org.

ating and degrading treatment."[5] In addition, the United Nations Convention against Torture and Other Cruel, Inhuman, or Degrading Treatment or Punishment (CAT), which the United States ratified in 1994, defines torture as "any act by which severe pain or suffering, whether physical or mental, is intentionally inflicted on a person for such purposes as obtaining from him or a third person information or a confession, punishing him for an act he or a third person has committed or is suspected of having committed, or intimidating or coercing him."[6] The CAT's prohibition of torture is absolute: "No exceptional circumstances whatsoever, whether a state of war or a threat of war, internal political instability or any other public emergency may be invoked as a justification of torture."[7]

In the aftermath of 9/11, and the subsequent military engagement with Afghanistan's Taliban, questions arose as to how best to prevent future terrorist attacks. Despite the prohibitions in international and US law, the Bush administration began using tactics variously described by politicians and military personnel, ethicists, and the Red Cross as "enhanced interrogation techniques," "torture lite," or torture.[8] These practices—some of them explicitly approved by then Secretary of Defense Donald Rumsfeld—included sensory deprivation, nudity, the use of stress positions for extended periods of time, the use of dogs to threaten detainees, and waterboarding, or simulated drowning. In the climate of fear and insecurity following the 9/11 terrorist attacks, officials in the Bush administration sought actionable intelligence—in other words, crucial information that could be used to prevent future attacks. As prisoners from the war in Afghanistan were transferred to Guantanamo Bay (Gitmo), Deputy Assistant Attorney General John Yoo drafted a legal memo arguing that suspected members of al-Qaeda and the Taliban were "enemy combatants" not protected by the Geneva Conventions.[9] A subsequent memo written by Jay Bybee diminished the definition of torture as it is understood in international law, contending that torture involves only "extreme acts" that "must be of an intensity akin to that which

---

5. Third Geneva Convention, Article 3, http://www.icrc.org.

6. United Nations Convention against Torture and Other Cruel, Inhuman, or Degrading Treatment or Punishment, Part I, Article 1.1, http://www.un.org/.

7. United Nations Convention against Torture, Part I, Article 2.2.

8. The Red Cross affirmed that "enhanced interrogation" activities constitute torture in its 2007 report to the Central Intelligence Agency. International Committee of the Red Cross, "ICRC Report on the Treatment of Fourteen 'High Value' Detainees in CIA Custody" (2007), http://assets.nybooks.com.

9. Karen J. Greenberg and Joshua L. Dratel, eds., *The Torture Papers: The Road to Abu Ghraib* (New York: Cambridge University Press, 2005), 135; noted by Paeth, "'Dirty Hands' Revisited," 165.

accompanies serious physical injury such as death or organ failure."[10] Additional memos and documents signed by administration officials including John Ashcroft, Donald Rumsfeld, and Alberto Gonzalez created legal loopholes and policy changes that allowed for torture.

The military officer responsible for improving interrogation and obtaining actionable intelligence at Guantanamo was Major General Geoffrey Miller. Miller oversaw the use of "sleep deprivation, exposure to extremes of cold and heat, and placing prisoners in 'stress positions' for agonizing lengths of time."[11] However, despite the authorization of these new methods of interrogation, Guantanamo interrogators failed to obtain much in the way of actionable intelligence, most likely because prisoners had little information to give.[12] In August 2003, General Miller was transferred to Iraq's Abu Ghraib prison. "It was his recommendation that Abu Ghraib be 'Gitmo-ized,' that is, made to function more like Guantanamo Bay...."[13] Four months later, Sergeant Joseph Darby reported "examples of shocking violence" at Abu Ghraib,[14] and three months later the now infamous photographs of prisoner abuse at Abu Ghraib shook the world.

Those photos make clear that the primary motive for torture in the war on terror was no longer gaining actionable intelligence. Instead a culture now was in place wherein torture and the abuse of detainees had become permissible, frequent, and normalized.[15] Pictures of US service men and women grinning, pointing, and laughing at abused prisoners suggested that torture was less about American national security[16] and more about humiliating an enemy that many Americans felt justified in annihilating, to use Bell's language. Abu Ghraib confirmed William Cavanaugh's argument that torture is the ritual enactment of power on the bodies of those we consider

---

10. Greenberg and Dratel, *The Torture Papers*, 215; noted by Paeth, "'Dirty Hands' Revisited," 166.

11. Paeth, "'Dirty Hands' Revisited," 167.

12. Paeth reports that at least one CIA analyst was convinced that more than half of those prisoners held at Guantanamo ought not to have been there in the first place (ibid., 166).

13. Ibid., 167.

14. Rodney Clapp, "Soldiers against Torture," *Christian Century* 127, no. 2 (October 19, 2010): 69.

15. Indeed, the Senate Select Committee on Intelligence's *Study of the Central Intelligence Agency's Detention and Interrogation Program* attests to the prevalence and brutality of torture in the post-9/11 wars. The full report is available at http://www.intelligence.senate.gov.

16. The Senate report explicitly states that "the CIA's use of its enhanced interrogation techniques was not an effective means of acquiring intelligence or gaining cooperation from detainees" (9).

to be enemies.[17] At Abu Ghraib, the torturers appeared to be enjoying the act of dehumanizing prisoners, and the act of torture can be construed as an expression of collective revenge or punishment inflicted on the person being tortured.[18] Thus, policy changes at the highest levels of the president's administration filtered down through the military ranks, eroded the legal prohibitions against torture, and led to acceptance of torture as a permissible and acceptable way of treating prisoners.[19] Kenneth Himes explains this dynamic well: "There are . . . consequences to consider before adopting a torture policy. History has shown that torture spreads once a society accepts it. The proliferation of torture will then heighten the risk of using torture against innocent people."[20]

The Ticking Time Bomb

There are no moral arguments made to support a culture of torture or to rally around the use of torture for the purposes of revenge or humiliation. Ethicists generally agree that using torture for retaliatory or punitive purposes is wrong. Still, some scholars imagine scenarios in which torture could be used toward morally good ends, and might therefore by justifiable. In other words, they make moral arguments that reject the notion that torture should never be practiced under any circumstances. These arguments are typically utilitarian or consequentialist in nature, and often depend on a situation that has never actually occurred: the ticking-time-bomb scenario. This hypothetical scenario initially gained credibility through the work of political philosopher Michael Walzer. He argued that politicians must sometimes accrue "dirty hands" by engaging in acts that "may be exactly the right thing to do in utilitarian terms and yet leave the man who does it

---

17. See William T. Cavanaugh, "Taking Exception," *Christian Century* 122, no. 2 (January 25, 2005): 9.

18. It is also worth questioning whether those being tortured were victimized because of what they symbolized or represented to US military personnel. Rothchild quotes military psychiatrist Henry Nelson: "Soldiers were immersed in the Islamic culture, a culture that many were encountering for the first time. Clearly there are major differences in worship and beliefs, and there is an association of Muslims with terrorism. All these causes exaggerate difference and create misperceptions that can lead to fear or devaluation of a people" ("Moral Consensus," 135).

19. The connections made between Bush administration policies and the illicit activities at Abu Ghraib are presented in several places, most helpfully in Greenberg and Dratel's *The Torture Papers*, Paeth's "'Dirty Hands' Revisited," and PBS *Frontline*'s "The Torture Question."

20. Kenneth R. Himes, "The United States at War: Taking Stock," *Theological Studies* 71, no. 1 (March 2010): 200.

guilty of a moral wrong."[21] Walzer invents a situation in which law enforcement has in custody a prisoner "who knows or probably knows" where several bombs are hidden in residential areas of a major city." Law enforcement also knows that these bombs are "set to go off within the next twenty-four hours."[22] The ticking-time-bomb scenario—and its equivalent for the war on terror—is discussed again and again in arguments both for and against torture. In the context of the war on terror, the hypothetical situation suggests that US officials have a terrorist in custody who knows the location of a bomb, perhaps even a nuclear bomb, that will imminently explode and cause the deaths of thousands of civilians. There are at least three prevalent arguments regarding whether and how torture might be justified in the midst of a ticking-time-bomb scenario. First, Alan Dershowitz concludes that the ticking-time-bomb scenario calls for the legalization and regulation of torture.[23] The second argument suggests that civil disobedience is an alternative to legalizing torture to deal with a ticking-time-bomb scenario. Finally, some ethicists, myself included, reject the ticking-time-bomb situation as one that does not meaningfully address how and why torture is typically used in actual conflict situations.

Alan Dershowitz suggests that legalizing torture and subjecting it to regulation and government oversight offer the best way to deal with a ticking-time-bomb scenario. He argues that in such a situation, torture would inevitably be used. Therefore, when officials are faced with such a situation, they should be required to retrieve a warrant to torture those they suspect of having crucial information that will save lives. In this way torture would be limited, regulated, and controlled. It would also be transparent, used in the view of the public eye and thus less likely to be a matter of vengeance or humiliating the enemy. "If it is true that torture would in fact be used in [a ticking-time-bomb scenario], then the important question becomes: is it better to have such torture done under the table, off the books and below the radar screen—or in full view, with accountability and as part of our legal system?"[24] Dershowitz maintains that making torture legal and requiring a warrant to practice it would have the effect of decreasing the overall resort to torture—making it more clearly a last resort. Others have countered Dershowitz's contention, however, and suggested that torture warrants would give legal validity to torture and thus increase, not decrease

---

21. Michael Walzer, "Political Action: The Problem of Dirty Hands," *Philosophy and Public Affairs* 2, no. 2 (1973): 160-80.

22. Ibid., 167.

23. Alan Dershowitz, "The Case for Torture Warrants," http://www.alandershowitz.com.

24. Ibid.

it. Elaine Scarry has pointed out that judges very rarely deny requests for warrants,[25] prompting Kenneth Himes to remark, "All warrants will do is increase the number of torturers by giving some, who might not otherwise torture, approval to do so, along with those who torture illegally."[26]

Another response to the ticking-time-bomb scenario suggests that torture should remain illegal, but that politicians and interrogators faced with such a situation should commit civil disobedience and embrace the legal and political consequences of their actions. Two ethicists suggesting this position are Scott Paeth and Darrell Cole.

Paeth expresses particular concern with the legal and political efforts to evade responsibility for committing torture. He demonstrates the maneuvers of the Bush administration as it sought legal loopholes in crafting its interrogation policy. Paeth notes that these maneuvers were meant to help administration officials avoid the consequences for what it viewed as the necessary "enhanced interrogation" of detainees at Guantanamo Bay. Paeth concludes that "whatever case can be made for or against the use of torture, the actions of the George W. Bush administration have been morally culpable, because rather than accept responsibility for their actions, they have sought in bad faith to deflect that responsibility, under the cover of law and executive power."[27] Paeth appeals instead to Dietrich Bonhoeffer as a counter-example. Bonhoeffer was a Christian theologian and minister executed by the Nazis for his role in planning to assassinate Hitler. For Bonhoeffer, responsible action in a sinful world involves making ourselves complicit in the guilt of the world: "Because Jesus took the guilt of all human beings upon himself, everyone who acts responsibly becomes guilty. Those who in acting responsibly seek to avoid becoming guilty divorce themselves from the ultimate reality of human existence. . . ."[28] Paeth thus concludes, "The relationship between responsibility"—that is to say accepting the burden of committing torture in a ticking-time-bomb situation—"and guilt"—that is, accepting moral culpability for the act of torture that is deemed necessary—"is rooted for Bonhoeffer in an understanding that there are circumstances in this life that may bring us to the limit of that which is morally permissible."[29] Breaking both positive and moral law by committing torture,

---

25. Elaine Scarry, "Five Errors in the Reasoning of Alan Dershowitz," in *Torture: A Collection,* ed. Sanford Levinson (New York: Oxford University Press, 2004), 286.

26. Himes, "The United States at War," 201.

27. Paeth, "'Dirty Hands' Revisited," 164.

28. Dietrich Bonhoeffer, *Ethics* (Minneapolis, MN: Fortress Press, 2005), 275; quoted by Paeth, "'Dirty Hands' Revisited," 171.

29. Paeth, "'Dirty Hands' Revisited," 171.

even in a ticking-time-bomb scenario, can be justified only through Christian civil disobedience. Civil disobedience involves accepting the sanctions that come with violating a law, even when one judges that breaking the law is the right thing to do, either to rectify or give witness to a terrible situation. Likewise, those who truly believe that it is necessary to violate both the positive and the moral law by committing torture in order to save many lives should not, as the Bush administration has done, seek to evade responsibility but ought instead to accept it. For Paeth, acceptance of responsibility is the only way that one can "acknowledge both the evil done, and the good for which it was done."[30]

Darrell Cole appeals to the ticking-time-bomb scenario to even more forcefully argue that torture should not be considered an exceptionless moral wrong. At the same time, he argues that morality demands that torture remain illegal and, like Paeth, suggests that committing torture as an act of civil disobedience is the only moral response to the ticking-time-bomb scenario. In a complex argument Cole suggests that torture is morally permissible only in a situation that meets several criteria. There must be an imminent danger, in which the lives of many people are stake. In addition, we must have a terrorist in custody who has information that will lead to saving those lives. Moreover, because torture is ultimately immoral, it must be illegal in the state where the prisoner is held. This would exclude the practice of rendition of prisoners to nations that routinely torture. The interrogator ought to be an expert in noncoercive interrogation methods, but these must have failed to get the crucial information. The interrogator must be a person of high moral character who recognizes the value of human life and is thus morally opposed to torture. Nevertheless, the virtuous interrogator must view torture, in this case, as the only way to protect the value of human life he/she holds dear. In torturing, the interrogator must accept the responsibility for violating the law out of love of neighbor and be willing to give up the benefit of legal protections and become a prisoner him/herself. Finally, echoing the just war principle of proportionality, the interrogator must use no more torture than is necessary to obtain the crucial information.[31]

A third kind of response to the hypothetical ticking-time-bomb scenario involves pointing out its improbability as *too* perfect a scenario for debating the morality of torture as it has actually unfolded in the war on terror. In the same article in which he argues for a Bonhoeffer-like approach to ethics with respect to torture, Paeth acknowledges that the ticking-time-bomb

---

30. Ibid., 172.

31. See Darrell Cole, "Torture and Just War," *Journal of Religious Ethics* 40, no. 1 (2012): 26-51. Cole's conclusion at 47 summarizes these points.

scenario "stacks the deck in favor of the decision to torture"[32] by describing a grave and imminent situation in which many lives will be lost. The interrogator knows, with near certainty, that a prisoner he holds has information that can save these lives. Moreover, the ticking-time-bomb scenario presumes (against all evidence to the contrary) that torture will be effective in obtaining the crucial information.[33] The set of circumstances and intentions that proponents of the ticking-time-bomb scenario portray has simply never occurred in real life, nor is it likely to occur. Thus, discussions of whether or not to permit torture that base their reasoning primarily on the ticking-time-bomb scenario run the risk of opening the door to permitting torture despite the vast improbability that such an archetypal situation will ever occur. Moreover, these arguments pay less attention to the very real circumstances under which torture had become ubiquitous in the war on terror. As the Senate Intelligence Committee report attests, torture was more brutal and more widespread in the war on terror than any ticking-time-bomb scenario would suggest.

Echoing Paeth, Kenneth Himes makes at least four arguments[34] against the validity of the ticking-time-bomb scenario, confirming Henry Shue's assertion that "artificial cases make bad ethics."[35] First, Himes points out that it is unlikely that those who must do the torturing would possess all the necessary intelligence regarding a ticking-time-bomb except its location. The ticking-time-bomb scenario suggests that we have all but one crucial piece of information. If this unlikely scenario ever emerged, Himes asks, wouldn't officials have other, more promising, leads to pursue besides the torture of a prisoner? Second, the ticking-time-bomb scenario is based on knowledge of an imminent attack—we are led to believe that the bomb will explode *soon*. In Walzer's original scenario the time frame is sometime within 24 hours. Himes asks, how realistic is it that this bomb could be stopped even with the application of torture? Couldn't a prisoner simply give misinformation over the 24-hour period until attack occurs? And wouldn't this force authorities to pursue false leads, taking resources away from more promising ones? Third, Himes asks a question of proportionality. How many potential lives lost justify torture? Here, Himes points to the probability that if we justify torture in the case of a nuclear ticking time bomb that would kill thousands, this will likely lead to justifying it in the case of a car bomb "where

---

32. Paeth, "'Dirty Hands' Revisited," 169.
33. Ibid., 175.
34. Himes, "The United States at War," 199.
35. Henry Shue as quoted by Rothchild, "Moral Consensus," 142.

the loss of life is closer to single digits."[36] Finally, Himes notes that in order
to be prepared for a ticking-time-bomb scenario, we would need a class of
"professional torturers," pretrained to torture very effectively and stationed
around the world to deal with such emergency situations. He asks if we as a
nation are prepared to support a military system dedicated to torture.[37] Thus
Himes concludes, "The ticking-time-bomb is not really an argument for an
exception case; in reality it would entail the establishment of a torture system.... The alleged reasonableness of torture declines as one questions the
premises of the TTB [ticking-time-bomb scenario] and a more realistic picture of how torture will occur is presented."[38]

Torture and Just War: Right Intention and Discrimination

Indeed, the post-9/11 scramble for "actionable intelligence" devolved into
something much more like a torture system—or a culture that permitted
torture—not to defuse bombs and save lives but to humiliate and exercise power over those who were considered enemies. Both the photos and
accounts from Abu Ghraib and the recent Senate reports on torture have
provided for us a "more realistic picture," in Himes's language, of how torture functioned in the war on terror. Because of this, I suggest that Christian
ethicists must continue actively to reject the use of a hypothetical ticking-
time-bomb scenario to justify torture. This fictitious and improbable situation allows people to approve of torture while feeling morally superior for
purportedly keeping civilians safe and saving innocent lives. Instead, following the lead of other Christian social ethicists, I suggest that the JWT, which,
when properly understood, restrains excessive violence and impulses toward
total warfare, rules out the use of torture in the context of war in at least two
ways. First, the just war criterion of right intention mitigates against torture. Right intention to establish a just peace is undermined by torture, as is
right intention to reconcile after conflict. Second, torture violates the spirit
of noncombatant immunity, which has historically and in contemporary
international law included a prohibition on attacking defenseless prisoners
of war.

Torture mitigates against the right intention to reconcile with former
enemies following conflict. The US bishops extend the traditional notion

---

36. Himes, "The United States at War," 199.
37. Ibid.
38. Ibid.

of right intention as the intent to build a secure and just peace by asserting that "during the conflict, right intention means pursuit of peace and reconciliation, including avoiding unnecessarily destructive acts."[39] If a nation's actions in the midst of war detract without sufficient cause from the goal of postconflict reconciliation with former enemies, then they ought not be done. Torture, rather than making prospects for reconciliation more auspicious, lessens them. Instead, torture feeds the flames of terrorism and creates greater animosity between warring parties. Thus Himes remarks, "Many military leaders have noted that the news about Abu Ghraib was a recruiting bonanza for the insurgency in Iraq."[40] Torture increases hostility in warfare rather than restrains it, making postconflict reconciliation more difficult to facilitate. In this way, it demonstrates a wrong intention.

Torture emerges from and exacerbates the kinds of intentions that the JWT has held to be wrong. As we have seen above, torture in the war on terror has not been primarily motivated by a desire to protect innocent civilians from terror attacks. Instead, it seems to have been motivated by precisely those intentions St. Augustine rejected: "love of violence, revengeful cruelty, fierce and implacable enmity ... and the lust of power."[41] Thus, through its insistence that those who want to engage in war justly maintain a right intention, the JWT functions to restrain us from using torture as a tool of warfare.

Torture also violates the JWT's criterion of noncombatant immunity, or discrimination. Discrimination prohibits the intentional targeting of civilians in warfare, but James Turner Johnson has pointed out that the protected class of people envisioned by discrimination has historically also included prisoners of war. Those who have been captured or wounded and thus unable to continue to fight were to be immune from further attack on the grounds that they, as prisoners, are defenseless and at the mercy of those who detain them.[42] It is precisely for this reason that the United Nations' CAT prohibits torture for any reason. Thus, in examining Johnson's work, David Gushee explains, "Today's international law specifically includes prisoners of war as exempt from direct harm or 'further attack.' [James Turner] Johnson

---

39. National Conference of Catholic Bishops, *The Challenge of Peace: God's Promise and Our Response* (Washington, DC: United States Conference of Catholic Bishops, 1983), 95, http://www.usccb.org.

40. Himes, "The United States at War," 200.

41. Augustine, *Contra Faustum*, 22.74, http://www.newadvent.org/fathers/1406.htm.

42. James Turner Johnson, "Torture: A Just War Perspective," *Review of Faith and International Affairs* 5, no. 2 (2007): 29-31.

accepts this classification as legitimate and applies it without equivocation to the torture of those suspected of terrorism."[43]

Conclusion

The terrorist attacks of September 11, 2001, spurred the American government to propose a series of legal challenges to the Geneva Conventions and United Nations' policies prohibiting torture. Many American citizens, rightly horrified by 9/11 and also fearful of new waves of terrorism, have supported the idea that torture might be used to gain crucial intelligence that will prevent terrorist attacks. However, the ubiquitous use of torture against detainees makes clear that our use of torture has not been primarily directed toward the prevention of terrorism or the protection of civilians. Evidence instead points to a culture of permissiveness regarding torture in which torture has been used to humiliate and degrade those considered enemies and to ritually enact power upon them. In this way, the war on terror has revealed torture to be what it really is, a violation of human dignity. Christians believe that all human beings are created in *imago Dei,* as "the image of God." Torture dehumanizes both its victim and its perpetrator, as the torturer turns the tortured into an object on which to exercise his/her wrath, hatred, sense of power, and desire for revenge. Torture can never be reconciled with the Christian doctrine of the *imago Dei*. Indeed, torture should be especially repugnant to Christians. When we torture we reenact the dynamics of the crucifixion, attacking the image of God that is inscribed on the human being who is tortured. In the same way, the powers of the state were used to torture to death the one that Christians call God. The prevalence of an attitude of permissiveness toward torture in the United States has led David Gushee to suggest that US Christians have cultivated a kind of "historical amnesia" when it comes to torture.[44] We have forgotten that Jesus himself was a victim of "imperial torture," enduring beatings, flogging, spitting, and crucifixion, "all in the context of a purported interrogation by governmental authorities in the interest of national security."[45] Similarly, throughout Christian history disciples of Jesus have been subject to torture and execution at the hands of those who would have them recant their deeply held beliefs.

---

43. David P. Gushee, "The Contemporary U.S. Torture Debate in Christian Historical Perspective," *Journal of Religious Ethics* 39, no. 4 (2011): 595.

44. Ibid., 591.

45. Ibid., 592.

Christians ought to remember their history and firmly reject torture as a tool of state coercion. The Christian tradition has resources to help us in this task, including the JWT, which remains acutely relevant in the twenty-first century and in the context of the war on terror. Attention to the JWT reminds us of the political aims of just war—to establish a just peace; and in this way it corrects the intention with which we approach warfare. A just war is not oriented toward the annihilation of our enemies, regardless of war's cause. Instead, right intention requires that we pursue peace, even through warfare, and choose means in fighting that do not mitigate against ultimate reconciliation. Moreover, the JWT prohibits us from attacking defenseless people, including prisoners in our care. The JWT thus answers the question of whether torture is morally permissible in the context of the war on terror with an unreserved no. In this way it holds Christians accountable to respect the image of God, even in those we may be most tempted to view as less than human. In respecting the image of God present in our enemies, we maintain not only their dignity but also our own.

CHAPTER 7

Just War Theory and Environmental Destruction

LAURIE JOHNSTON

In our day, there is a growing awareness that world peace is threatened
not only by the arms race, regional conflicts and continued injustices
among peoples and nations, but also by a lack of due respect for nature.
—Pope John Paul II[1]

War always does grave harm to the environment . —Pope Francis[2]

The Environment and War

We hear in the words of several recent popes that war is "always a defeat
for humanity."[3] We may add that war is also a defeat for the natural environment. Human actions during war have long posed a threat to nature.
As Pope Francis wrote recently in *Laudato si'*, "The violence present in our
hearts, wounded by sin, is also reflected in the symptoms of sickness evident
in the soil, in the water, in the air and in all forms of life."[4] But this insight is
also an ancient one; Tacitus cited an ancient Celt's accusations that Roman
conquerors "make a desert and call it peace."[5] During the Third Punic War,
the victorious Romans are said to have salted the ground around Carthage
to make it impossible for that great city ever to revive itself. One might even

---

1. John Paul II, "Peace with God the Creator, Peace with All of Creation," World Day of
Peace Message, January 1, 1990, par. 1, http://w2.vatican.va.
2. Pope Francis, *Laudato si'*, May 24, 2015, par. 57, http://w2.vatican.va.
3. "Pope Francis: War Is Always a Defeat for Humanity," Vatican Information Service, September 7, 2013, http://www.news.va; Pope John Paul II, "Address to the Diplomatic Corps,"
January 13 2003, http://www.vatican.va.
4. *Laudato si'*, par. 2.
5. Tacitus, *Agricola*, ch. 30.

think of the fictional war in Shakespeare's *Macbeth*, in which the English army cuts down so many branches to use as camouflage that Birnam forest itself seems to be approaching Dunsinane.

Efforts to limit the environmental impact of war are also ancient; we read the following in the book of Deuteronomy:

> If you besiege a town for a long time, making war against it in order to take it, you must not destroy its trees by wielding an axe against them. Although you may take food from them, you must not cut them down. Are trees in the field human beings that they should come under siege from you? You may destroy only the trees that you know do not produce food; you may cut them down for use in building siege-works against the town that makes war with you, until it falls. (Deut 20:19- 20 NRSV)

A similar prohibition against the destruction of fruit trees also exists also in the widely cited "Ten Commands" of Abu Bakr, the first caliph after the death of the prophet Muhammad:

> Oh army, stop and I will order you [to do] ten [things]; learn them from me by heart . . . you shall kill neither a young child nor an old man nor a woman; you shall not fell palm trees or burn them; you shall not cut down [any] fruit-bearing tree; you shall not slaughter a sheep or a cow or a camel except for food.[6]

Thus, the idea that plants and animals ought to enjoy some protection from the effects of warfare—just like humans who are noncombatants—is an ancient one.

Modern warfare makes the problem of environmental impact much more serious, with the vastly greater potential destructiveness for both human and nonhuman environments. The actual use of both conventional and nuclear weapons poses major threats, but even preparations for war represent a major environmental problem. Mark Woods writes that "collectively the world's militaries are estimated to be the largest single polluter on Earth, accounting for as much as 20 percent of all global environmental degradation."[7] Further- more, environmental degradation in turn causes more warfare, as competi- tion for increasingly scarce natural resources heats up. The Pacific Institute

---

6. Al-Tabari, *The History of al-Tabari*. Vol. 10, *The Conquest of Arabia* (New York: SUNY Press, 1993), 16.

7. Mark Woods, "The Nature of War and Peace: Just War Thinking, Environmental Eth- ics, and Environmental Justice," in *Rethinking the Just War Tradition*, ed. Michael W. Brough, John W. Lango, and Harry van der Linden (New York: SUNY Press, 2007), 20.

has shown a fourfold increase in violent conflicts over water in the past decade.[8] Resource wars and climate refugees are appearing in the news more often, as "the human environment and the natural environment deteriorate together."[9] The intersecting dangers of warfare and environmental degradation command our urgent attention.

Recent Wars: Environmental Destruction and Legal Responses

Two major conflicts in the last century provoked particular discussion about the environmental consequences of warfare. The first was the Vietnam War, during which US forces sprayed more than 19 million gallons of Agent Orange and other herbicides to eliminate ground cover for enemy forces and to destroy the farms that supplied the enemy with food.[10] More than 10 percent of the territory of Vietnam was sprayed, resulting in long-term contamination, massive numbers of birth defects and cancers, and loss of biodiversity. Only in 2012 did the US government begin providing assistance in cleaning up contaminated soil in Vietnam.[11] The devastation caused by Agent Orange prompted the international community to adopt Protocol I, an amendment to the Geneva Conventions that forbids the use of weapons that "cause widespread, long-term, and severe damage to the natural environment."[12] Though ratified by most of the countries of the world since its drafting in 1977, Protocol I has never been ratified by the United States. Another international agreement prompted by the war in Vietnam is known as ENMOD, and forbids modifying the environment for military purposes in any ways that would have "widespread, long-lasting or severe effects."[13] This concern arose after the US military had attempted to manipulate the

---

8. Suzanne Goldenberg, "Why Global Water Shortages Pose Threat of Terror and War," *The Guardian,* February 8, 2014, http://www.theguardian.com.

9. Pope Francis, *Laudato si'*, par. 48.

10. "Facts about Herbicides," US Department of Veterans' Affairs, http://www.public health.va.gov.

11. Jessica King, "U.S. in First Effort to Clean Up Agent Orange in Vietnam," CNN, August 10, 2012, http://edition.cnn.com.

12. International Committee of the Red Cross, "Protocol Additional to the Geneva Conventions of 12 August 1949, and relating to the Protection of Victims of International Armed Conflicts (Protocol I), 8 June 1977," http://www.icrc.org.

13. United Nations General Assembly, "Convention on the Prohibition of Military or Any Other Hostile Use of Environmental Modification Techniques," May 18, 1977, http://www.undocuments.net/enmod.htm.

weather in Vietnam by cloud seeding in order to cause rain and make movement more difficult for the North Vietnamese troops. The United States
ultimately decided to back away from such tactics, and, with the Soviet
Union, drafted ENMOD, which was adopted by the UN General Assembly
in 1976 and ratified by the United States in 1980. These two measures in
international law are an important beginning, but legal scholars generally
agree that they are ultimately too vague and all too often go unenforced.[14]

Another recent conflict that provoked significant concern about war and
the environment was the first Gulf War, during which Saddam Hussein's
retreating forces set fire to Kuwaiti oil wells and engineered a massive oil
spill in the Persian Gulf, purportedly to make landing along the coast more
difficult. The result was an environmental catastrophe—the toxic smoke and
the oil together killed hundreds of thousands of birds and other animals, in
addition to the negative health effects on both soldiers and civilians.[15] The
more recent war in Iraq has not witnessed such dramatic individual events of
environmental destruction, but the cumulative effects of the conflict are also
very serious. Much of the impact remains to be determined, but there have
been a number of reports of increased levels of birth defects in some Iraqi
cities due to pollution from weapons that use depleted uranium and heavy
metals.[16] Similarly, Afghanistan today faces a serious environmental crisis as
a consequence of decades of conflict there.[17]

While this chapter focuses on environmental damage caused by war, it is
also important to acknowledge that war can also be good for the nonhuman
environment at times and in some limited ways. The no-man's land on the
border between North Korea and South Korea, untouched by humans, has
become a hotspot for biodiversity, but not a model of a harmonious environment as it remains full of landmines and other weaponry.[18] Still, the loss
of human life and freedom of movement that accompanies war may prove

---

14. See, e.g., Richard Falk, "The Inadequacy of the Existing Legal Approach to Environmental Protection in Wartime," or Adam Roberts, "The Law of War and Environmental Damage,"
both in *The Environmental Consequences of War: Legal, Economic, and Scientific Perspectives*, ed.
Jay E. Austin and Carl E. Bruch (Cambridge: Cambridge University Press, 2000).

15. United States Library of Congress, *The Environmental Aftermath of the Gulf War: A
Report* (Washington, DC: US G.P.O., 1992). See also Muhammad Sadiq and John C. McCain,
eds., *The Gulf War Aftermath: An Environmental Tragedy* (Dordrecht: Kluwer Academic Publishers, 1993).

16. Ross Caputi, "The Victims of Fallujah's Health Crisis Are Stifled by Western Silence," *The
Guardian,* October 25, 2012, http://www.theguardian.com.

17. Carlotta Gall, "War-Scarred Afghanistan in Environmental Crisis," *New York Times,*
January 30, 2003.

18. Nick Easen, "Korea's DMZ: The Thin Green Line," CNN, August 22, 2003, http://
edition.cnn.com.

very beneficial for the other members of an ecosystem. There are also circumstances in which efforts to preserve the environment can unwittingly contribute to sustaining violent conflict; for instance, in the Democratic Republic of the Congo, Mozambique, and other countries, nature preserves have sometimes provided shelter for violent guerilla movements. Nevertheless, in most cases of violent conflict, the fate of the natural environment and the fate of human lives are deeply intertwined and complementary. Human and environmental factors must be considered together in any assessment of the consequences of war, because "Peace, justice and the preservation of creation are three absolutely interconnected themes, which cannot be separated and treated individually."[19]

A Prescription for Just War Theorists

Given the devastating environmental impacts of modern war, damage to the environment ought to be explicitly considered by ethicists in any case where just war theory is being applied. When the principle of proportionality is invoked—traditionally part of both *ad bellum* and *in bello* considerations—potential environmental damage should be explicitly weighed as one of the harms of war to determine if such damage is in proportion to the goods that are sought by would-be just warriors. Such consideration can help to further limit the resort to war in the future and also minimize the environmental impact of wars that do take place.

In choosing to focus on proportionality, I do not wish to imply that an environmental ethic of war need not also rely on the other components of just war theory. In fact, just war theorists would do well to bring environmental considerations into their reasoning about *all* of the just war criteria. Gregory Reichberg and Henrik Syse have discussed the implications of a number of other principles of the just war theory. They note, for instance, that right intention with regard to the environment is important in limiting the impact of war: if one's intention is peace, then scorched-earth tactics or wanton destruction of the natural environment for revenge's sake would be ruled out.[20] They also argue that the criterion of competent authority comes into play. Because of the difficulty involved in making judgments about

---

19. Pope Francis, *Laudato si'*, par. 92, citing the Conference of Dominican Bishops, Pastoral Letter, "Sobre la relación del hombre con la naturaleza" (January 21, 1987).

20. Gregory Reichberg and Henrik Syse, "Protecting the Natural Environment in Wartime: Ethical Considerations from the Just War Tradition," *Journal of Peace Research* 27, no. 4 (2000): 460.

complex, ecologically vulnerable areas, Reichberg and Syse argue that "some decisions involving environmental destruction should never be taken solely by commanders in the field. . . . This would apply to situations where it needs to be decided whether or not to engage in military maneuvers in areas where natural items of great value (such as scarce ground water, fragile eco-systems, or endangered species) would likely be harmed."[21] They believe that a serious conversation is needed about who—if anyone—has the authority to give orders that will result in serious environmental collateral damage. A number of ethicists have also suggested applying the principle of discrimination to the environment—for example, are there some environmental hotspots that should be regarded as having noncombatant immunity? Recently, Pope Francis criticized an indiscriminate attitude toward the environment when he asked, "Isn't humanity committing suicide with this indiscriminate and tyrannical use of nature?"[22]

Most significant, perhaps, are the suggestions that just cause for war may include the duty to protect the environment itself from attack. Richard Miller, among others, has argued that just as humanitarian intervention may be necessary at times, "ecological interventions" could also be justified:

> The good of nature can generate both a presumption against war *and* a set of reasons for considering coercive measures. For example, it is not inconceivable that . . . the use of force or coercion in response to ecological terrorism or the profligate destruction of natural resources is warranted. Nature, like nations and people, deserves protection from oppression.[23]

Considerations such as these are important and useful, but we must always return to the principle of proportionality in order to apply these components of just war theory. To judge right intention, we still need to know whether someone is intending an activity that constitutes *wanton* destruction, or instead, making careful, sustainable use of natural resources. To know when to defer to higher competent authorities, we must know when there is a risk of disproportionate damage to fragile ecosystems. And even if we want to assign "noncombatant immunity" to fragile ecosystems, few of us would maintain that as an absolute principle if doing so comes

---

21. Ibid., 462.

22. "In latest interview, Pope Francis reveals top 10 secrets to happiness," http://ncronline. org.

23. Richard P. Miller, "Just-War Criteria and Theocentric Ethics," in *Christian Ethics: Problems and Prospects*, ed. Lisa Sowle Cahill and James F. Childress (Cleveland: Pilgrim Press, 1996), 339.

at a disproportionately high cost in terms of human lives. Proportionality, therefore, is constantly in play, and deserves particular attention in the conversation about war and the environment.

The Context of the Conversation

In 2010, the US Army published a 200-page field manual entitled "Environmental Considerations."[24] It contains striking passages such as the following:

> From every philosophical or moral perspective, environmental stewardship and sustainment is the right thing to do. As humans make more demands on the shrinking resource base, ethical issues become clearer. Senior leaders must create ethical climates in which subordinate leaders recognize that the natural resources of the earth are exhaustible, that the environment has an impact on human health, and that they must take responsibility to protect the environment. (Section 4-2)

The field manual offers detailed instructions to commanders about carrying out this responsibility. It addresses a wide range of matters, including preventing fuel spills or improper hazardous waste disposal, avoiding operations near bodies of water or important environmental resource areas, limiting noise, preventing erosion, and limiting the use of live plants as camouflage. It is clear from this manual that military planners are indeed considering at least some of the environmental implications of their activities. To be sure, these concerns are more often discussed in the context of "mission effectiveness" rather than focused on the intrinsic value of environmental resources. And some of the case examples are less than impressive: the first one describes a situation where army trucks tracked a good deal of mud onto a civilian roadway. We might wish that that were the only environmental damage caused by military operations! The manual also contains some unintentionally ironic statements: "Protecting natural resources and the facilities exploiting them are now major components of planning." Indeed, as we exploit natural resources for our own survival, we must also address the urgent need to protect those resources; still, those two competing priorities are rarely juxtaposed so closely. Of course, as a field manual, this document is not posing larger questions about the justice of our use of natural resources generally, or whether the particular operations carried out with environmen-

---

24. Available at http://armypubs.army.mil.

tal sensitivity are operations that should even be carried out in the first place. Still, it is heartening to see that such a field manual exists.

The greater question about environmental justice and its implications for choices about war, however, must be urgently addressed by those who shape policies on a larger scale. Yet in recent discussions about just war theory and its relevance for modern warfare, I find little attention to environmental damage as a possible reason that a war might be disproportionate and therefore unjust. In the debate that preceded the recent Iraq war, many reasons were offered as to why the war did not meet the criteria of a justified war. We might expect that, given that terrible environmental damage caused by the first Gulf War, opponents of a new war in Iraq would have raised further environmental damage as a possible negative consequence of President George W. Bush's proposed war. While I have not conducted an exhaustive survey, I have found little evidence that environmental concern played any role at all in the opposition to the war, apart from some warnings from environmental organizations such as the World Resources Institute. Of course, there were many other reasons to oppose the Iraq war, and it failed to meet several of the criteria of the just war theory—notably, I would argue, just cause. But even when the US Catholic bishops explicitly mentioned the principle of proportionality in their letter of objection published in November 2002, they included many possible disproportionately negative consequences but did not mention possible environmental damage.[25] This omission is, in some ways, understandable; they were addressing the US government and the general public. And how can the US military control or be responsible for the actions of an enemy leader who decides to destroy the environment, as Saddam Hussein did in the first Gulf War? Nevertheless, in war, one is responsible not just for the evils that one commits intentionally but in some way also for the evils that one unleashes.

---

25. *"Probability of success and proportionality.* The use of force must have 'serious prospects for success' and 'must not produce evils and disorders graver than the evil to be eliminated' (*Catechism*, #2309). We recognize that not taking military action could have its own negative consequences. We are concerned, however, that war against Iraq could have unpredictable consequences not only for Iraq but for peace and stability elsewhere in the Middle East. The use of force might provoke the very kind of attacks that it is intended to prevent, could impose terrible new burdens on an already long-suffering civilian population, and could lead to wider conflict and instability in the region. War against Iraq could also detract from the responsibility to help build a just and stable order in Afghanistan and could undermine broader efforts to stop terrorism," http://www.usccb.org/issues-and-action/human-life-and-dignity/global-issues/middle-east/statement-on-iraq.cfm.

Proportionality and Environmental Considerations

How, then, should consideration for the natural environment be incorporated into discussions of proportionality? I will first outline some of the challenges in such an endeavor before arguing for an approach that incorporates virtue ethics.

How should we understand proportionality? Proportionality is a criterion to be considered both *ad bellum* and *in bello*: Will the death, destruction, and harm brought about by this war be proportional to the good that can reasonably be anticipated? Or, when considering a particular course of action *in bello*, will the anticipated goods outweigh the actual harms? The criterion of proportionality forces us to count the costs of war as much as we humanly can. As Paul Ramsey has written, "The principle of proportion serves to jog us loose from notions that if the cause is right, there is no need to count the costs, or from the notion a political good can be secured without costs."[26] This is precisely what is needed when it comes to the environment and war: a focus on counting the costs, in part so that we may be very clear about the high cost of war.

The criterion of proportionality is, perhaps, the point at which those who believe in the possibility of a justified war depart most clearly from the viewpoints of both pacifists and political realists. What unites the pacifist and the realist is, in fact, a willingness to ignore costs—whether it is the realist who thinks anything is permissible when it comes to *raison d'état*, or the pacifist who believes one must avoid violence even at the cost of one's life and the lives of others. Proportionality, then, is about weighing costs and comparing values. But in that sense it becomes messy, and frequently leads to comparisons of value that seem impossible, or, at the very least, morally repugnant: How can one weigh life against life, or the extinction of a species against the genocide of a people? How can one even predict the effects of a complex and chaotic activity like warfare upon a complex entity like an ecosystem? This is why Paul Ramsey, the thinker most responsible for introducing the criterion of proportionality into modern just war theory, called it a test that is "open to the greatest uncertainty." Ramsey wrote,

> It can never be right to resort to war, no matter how just the cause, unless a proportionality can be established between military/political objectives and their price, or unless one has reason to believe that in the end more good will be done than undone or a greater measure of

---

26. Paul Ramsey, *The Just War: Force and Political Responsibility* (New York: Scribner's, 1968), 433.

evil prevented. But of all the tests for judging whether to resort to or participate in war, this one balancing an evil or good effect against another is open to the greatest uncertainty. This, therefore, establishes rather than removes the possibility of conscientious disagreement among prudent [people].[27]

Discussions of proportionality often get caught up in almost mathematical calculations of the positives and negatives of war, as if the justness of a war can be determined numerically. For instance, one philosopher writes,

Consider the coalition bombing campaign in the [First] Gulf War. It initially caused around 2,000 Iraqi civilian deaths, but many more followed from its aftereffects, especially the damage to Iraq's water filtration plants. Some of these later deaths were unavoidable, but others could have been prevented had the Iraqi government repaired the country's infrastructure more quickly, as it arguably had a moral duty to do. In assessing the bombing for proportionality, then, do we count all the civilian deaths that resulted given the Iraqi government's actual behavior, or only those that would have resulted had that government acted as it should?[28]

Clearly, when discussing the environmental impact of war, there is also endless scope for calculating the possible consequences of war, and we can easily become mired in the details. Nevertheless, the complexity of a moral judgment does not excuse us from attempting it.

It is important to note here that proportionality overlaps with and must be considered with other criteria. The justness and gravity of the cause, for instance, must be known in order to adequately evaluate proportionality. For instance, it would be appropriate to risk significant destruction to a fragile ecosystem in order to prevent a massive genocide or a nuclear war that would destroy the entire planet. There is also overlap with the principle of discrimination, of course. Reichberg and Syse urge us to consider how environmental considerations help reveal the interconnectedness of the criteria of proportionality and discrimination:

[Environmental] destruction with severe and/or long-term consequences may in some cases (albeit not in all) be deemed both proportionally wrong in connection with the projected military gains (not

---

27. Ibid., 195.
28. Thomas Hurka, "Proportionality and the Morality of War," *Philosophy and Public Affairs* 33, no. 1 (2005): 48.

least since the environmental consequences most likely outlast the military campaign) and indiscriminate, since the destruction threatens to eliminate vital natural resources upon which civilian life depends. In addition, such destruction may be condemnable insofar as it irreparably destabilizes ecosystems for which man [*sic*] can rightly be seen to be a sort of custodian.[29]

Thus, we must incorporate environmental concerns into discussions of proportionality not only because humans are a dependent part of ecosystems but also because humans bear a particular responsibility for the common good of all creation.

Applying the Principle of Proportionality

To help provide some clarity in understanding how to use the principle of proportionality, I want to turn to an essay by Chris Vogt in which he argues that, like the other components of the just war theory, proportionality cannot be applied in a vacuum. In order to help us arrive at an accurate prudential judgment, proportionality, like just cause, right intention, and other criteria, must be applied in the context of a broader approach to morality by those who are committed to certain values and are formed by the virtues. As Vogt explains,

> Stanley Hauerwas raised [this basic] point over a decade ago. Commenting on the use of the just-war tradition to defend the first American war in Iraq, Hauerwas called upon Christians to become more aware of the fact that just-war criteria are never used in the abstract, but rather always in context. His claim was that the moral validity of conclusions drawn from just-war criteria [is] heavily dependent upon the values of the persons employing them. For example, the application of just-war principles took on a Christian quality in the hands of Paul Ramsey who could embrace the just-war tradition only because he assumed that it would be applied according to various unspoken values that he regarded as essential (e.g., the inviolable sanctity of innocent human life). Likewise, in the hands of cynical political leaders who have only their nation's interests at heart, just-war criteria do not serve a discernible Christian moral purpose, but rather simply promote the interests of the state. Thus it is not enough to ask whether just-war

---

29. Reichberg and Syse, "Protecting the Natural Environment in Wartime," 464–65.

criteria have been applied. One must always ask *how* they have been applied; one must seek to reveal what comprehensive moral framework informed the moral deliberations of persons using the just-war framework.[30]

Thus, in order for us to describe how the principle of proportionality can help guide judgments about environmental damage, we must first ask, What is the underlying moral framework with regard to the environment? What are the values and virtues that must be in play if we are to choose wisely about how to weigh the costs of a potential war? What are the factors shaping us as we attempt to "understand the goods and harms in play and to reason well regarding their relative importance"?

Vogt suggests two primary virtues that must be in play for proportionality to be well understood. These he calls "respect for persons" and "compassion," and he notes that "the use of prudential reason in consideration of proportionality must entail an effort to know the costs of war at an emotional level." Vogt's article does not specifically address environmental damage when he speaks of the costs of war; he is primarily concerned with the deaths of humans that result from war. But his approach holds promise for considering the environmental costs of war as well. We must ask ourselves what underlying values and virtues with regard to the environment must be considered in evaluating proportionality. How can we become people who accurately perceive the costs of war, including on an emotional level, as they affect the environment?

Environmental Virtues and Vices

When it comes to valuing the environment, there is a long-standing debate among environmental ethicists about whether or not to regard the natural environment as having *intrinsic* or merely *instrumental* value. From a Catholic perspective, of course, the answer is both. But when there are conflicts of values—between, for instance, human communities who want to exploit certain resources and others who argue that those resources have important value (whether intrinsic or instrumental) and ought therefore to

---

30. Christopher Vogt, "Integrare la guerra giusta e le virtù per promuovere la pace: compassione, rispetto per le persone e misura della proporzionalità" ("Integrating Just War and the Virtues of Peacemaking: Compassion, Respect for Persons and the Measurement of Proportionality"), *Rassegna di Teologia* 47, no. 2 (2006): 195-218, citing Stanley Hauerwas, "Whose Just War? Which Peace?" in *But Was It Just? Reflections on the Morality of the Persian Gulf War*, ed. David E. DeCosse (New York: Doubleday, 1992), 86, 91-92.

be preserved—then we must have some way of evaluating such conflicts, by examining the virtues that should inform decision making about the environment. Such virtues are important in assessing questions about proportionality and just war.

One virtue ethicist, Thomas Hill, begins his discussion about environmental virtue by pointing to an example of something we might call environmental vice. Hill describes a wealthy man who purchased a house with a flourishing garden and promptly paved the entire garden over with asphalt. It was the man's legal right to do so, but Hill found himself asking, "What sort of a person would do a thing like that?"[31] In a similar vein, there are many acts of war that should lead us to ask what *sort* of a person would do "a thing like that" to the environment or to other humans. Such a question is focused on the individual, but it should also open up a line of questioning that is more systemic: What kind of an approach to security would allow for creating and maintaining weapons that threaten the very survival of life on this planet? What type of political system allows for environmental destruction to proceed unchecked? What type of global economic system is it that fails to account for the true costs of our economic activity? What are the cultural factors that prevent human communities from feeling appropriate horror at callous exploitation of natural resources and destruction of natural beauty?

Similarly, both individual and social forms of environmental virtue are needed for the assessment of proportionality in war. If there is any modern evil that merits a structural critique today, it is certainly war and our reliance on military force. With that in mind, I would like to point to two environmental virtues that seem particularly important in shaping our use of the just war theory: humility and solidarity.

Humility could be the classic "environmental virtue," since the word itself is etymologically related to the Latin *humus*, "earth" or "soil." It is the virtue that teaches us that we are creatures, part of creation and dependent on it. It is a virtue that helps us to respond to natural beauty with appropriate awe and even gratitude. Hill argues that it is precisely the virtue that was lacking in the man who paved over the beautiful garden:

Those who fully accept themselves as part of the natural world lack the common drive to disassociate themselves from nature by replacing

---

31. Thomas Hill, Jr., "Ideals of Human Excellence and Preserving Natural Environments," in *Environmental Virtue Ethics,* ed. Ronald Sandler and Philip Cafaro (Lanham, MD: Rowman & Littlefield, 2005), 47.

natural environments with artificial ones. . . . The person who is too ready to destroy the ancient redwoods may lack humility, not so much in the sense that he exaggerates his importance relative to others but, rather, in the sense that he tries to avoid seeing himself as one among many natural creatures.[32]

In other words, those who show a readiness to carry out disproportionate, unnecessary destruction of the natural environment reveal a type of hubris; they are making the assumption that they have the right to use nature in this way. And they neglect to notice their own dependence on the natural world. Humility reacquaints us with our own interdependence and "creatureliness" in a way that, Hill believes, helps us avoid a superior or merely instrumental attitude to nature. On a social level, humility lends itself to the cultivation of sustainable approaches to the natural world. Hill further argues that developing humility in relation to nature is closely connected to developing compassion for other humans: both require that we learn "to value things *for their own sake,* and to count what affects them important aside from their utility. . . . If a person views all nonsentient nature merely as a resource, then it seems unlikely that he has developed the capacity needed to overcome self-importance."[33] Reverence for the integrity of nature is deeply connected to respect for others' human dignity—and war is a threat to both. An attitude of humility teaches us to be careful about seeing either nature or other humans as merely a means to an end. And when it comes to warfare as a tool of justice, humility also reminds the just war thinker about the very real limitations of what war can accomplish. In its epistemological form, humility produces salutary caution about how much we can know or foresee about a particular situation that may call for the use of force. Finally, because humility is about accurately *valuing* both oneself and other creatures, it is vital for assessing proportionality in just war. Proportionality requires consideration of the values at stake—the relative importance of various competing goods or bads—and humility is an important aid in perceiving the weight of these things accurately.

Humility, however, can seem a rather passive virtue. The urgency of the present moment requires just war thinkers to consider a more active "environmental virtue" as well. For that purpose I propose solidarity, and particularly *cosmic* solidarity. Solidarity might be described as the virtue that prevents us from ever saying "that's not my problem" in relation to the

---

32. Ibid., 55.
33. Ibid., 54.

suffering of others or the wasteful destruction of the environment. While humility helps us understand our own limits and our own dependence on nature, solidarity helps us to embrace our own ability and responsibility to act on behalf of others and the environment. Solidarity teaches us, as Pope Francis has said, that "The climate is a common good, belonging to all and meant for all."[34] For Christians, cosmic solidarity is rooted in the idea that the salvation that Christ brings is a cosmic salvation that redeems all of nature from bondage; it is not only humans, but all of creation, that groans in anticipation of the salvation that has been promised, as Paul's letter to the Romans reminds us (Rom 8:19-22 NRSV). This sense of shared destiny is a key aspect of the virtue of solidarity.

On a more practical level, the growing consequences of global warming for both human lives and the environment must lead us to develop a greater capacity for both human and ecological solidarity. While there are certainly occasions when we must choose between protecting the environment and protecting human lives or livelihoods, I would contend that far more often it is possible to pursue the common good of both human and nonhuman nature. There are deep connections between ecological crises and human suffering, and the desperation that accompanies humanitarian crises frequently leads to damage to the natural environment as well. One need not choose between the instrumental and intrinsic value of nature; cosmic solidarity leads to an appreciation of both.

Conclusion

The idea that human sin has negative effects on the natural environment is as ancient as the book of Genesis. And from the Hebrew prophets to the book of Revelation, the hope for peace and justice that is expressed is not merely about humans but about peace in the natural world as well; the lion lies down with the lamb, a river flows with the water of life, and fruit trees flourish—and all the nations find unity. In the here and now, as humans seek the limited forms of peace and justice that we can achieve in a flawed world, such a vision of harmony can never be fully achieved. Nevertheless, such a vision serves as a powerful countertestimony to the horrors of war that the world witnesses; the deaths of humans and the destruction of the environment must shock the human conscience, even as we find that we can-

---

34. *Laudato si'*, par. 23.

not always prevent them. And as we live in this in-between time, the promise of the just war theory is precisely in its ability to help us think clearly and carefully about the destructiveness of warfare. Particularly in its criterion of proportionality, just war theory offers the best chance we have of ensuring that, in our attempts to pursue justice for our fellow creatures, we do not cause more harm than we prevent.

CHAPTER 8

Justice in War Preparations: A Just War Application to Nuclear Testing in the Marshall Islands

RACHEL HART WINTER

There are only 90,000 people out there. Who gives a damn?
—Henry Kissinger, 1969[1]

In 1946, the US government asked the citizens of the Republic of the Marshall Islands to allow the testing of atomic bombs on their atolls "for the good of mankind and to end all world wars."[2] Actually, it was good neither for the Marshallese nor the islands they inhabit, and although we have not experienced another world war, wars on the planet and against the planet rage on. The devastation and violence done in the Marshall Islands by the nuclear arms race was, and still is, disproportionate to the good sought in deterrence as a necessary step toward peace. The testing conducted there— which continues to impact innocent Marshallese lives—requires a renewed application of just war criteria vis-à-vis nuclear weapons. I argue that the just war theory must encompass more than *jus ad bellum, in bello,* and *post bellum* considerations, but also the preparations for war, including the testing of possible weapons of mass or long-term destruction.

Documents such as *Gaudium et spes,* written at Vatican II in 1965, the 1983 pastoral letter *The Challenge of Peace: God's Promise and Our Response,* and the 1993 pastoral letter *The Harvest of Justice Is Sown in Peace* present directives for nuclear disarmament. There has been a steady progression, from supporting deterrence in the 1950s toward recommendations for full

---

1. Quoted in Donald F. McHenry, *Micronesia: Trust Betrayed* (Washington, DC: Carnegie Endowment for International Peace, 1975).

2. Jack Niedenthal, *For the Good of Mankind: A History of the People of Bikini and Their Islands,* 2nd ed. (Majuro, Marshall Islands: Bravo Publications, 2001), 2.

disarmament today. In 2009, Pope Benedict invited us to strive for "progressive and concerted nuclear disarmament."[3] Pope Francis has made the end to nuclear weapons one of the top priorities of his papacy.[4] Seeking an end to the nuclear arms race is an important component of recent work by scholars to align the just war tradition (JWT) with pacifism, or nonviolence, as seen in the work of Glen Stassen in *Just Peacemaking* and David Carroll Cochran in *Catholic Realism and the Abolition of War.*[5] Some Catholic theologians have also suggested new angles for discourse and modern adaptations of the JWT. Scholars such as Tobias Winright, Mark Allman, and Eric Patterson have begun to discuss not only *jus post bellum* but also the concept of *jus ante bellum.*[6] The latter can be defined as "justice prior to war, which hopefully would minimize the likelihood of many wars from ever erupting in the first place."[7] I emphasize that this category must critically examine the injustices of the nuclear buildup and testing.

This essay begins by examining recent Catholic applications of the JWT. Next, I analyze the situation in the Marshall Islands, detailing snapshots from the history of the arms race. Then I apply three criteria of the JWT to the situation in the Marshalls. I argue that the same ethical guidelines that are used in just war must be used in the preparations for it, thus an application of *jus ante bellum*. To support my claims, I look again to some just war thinkers who offer relevant insights for our present context: Lisa Sowle Cahill, Tobias Winright, Mark Allman, and Michael Walzer. Finally, I present the necessary components of *jus ante bellum*, concluding that the preparation for war should never destroy a culture.

Just War Tradition: What Is Essential Today?

The ethical principles that comprise the JWT challenge the use of violence to arrive at peace. This tradition, present in Catholic thought for 1,500 years,

---

3. Benedict XVI, "Fighting Poverty to Build Peace," World Day of Peace Message, 2006, par. 13.

4. Elizabeth Dias, "Pope Francis' Latest Mission: Stopping Nuclear Weapons," *Time*, April 10, 2015, http://time.com/3817021/pope-francis-nuclear-disarmament/.

5. Glen Stassen, ed., *Just Peacemaking: The New Paradigm for the Ethics of Peace and War*, new ed. (Cleveland, OH: Pilgrim Press, 2008); David Carroll Cochran, *Catholic Realism and the Abolition of War* (Maryknoll, NY: Orbis Books, 2014).

6. See, e.g., Mark J. Allman and Tobias L. Winright, *After the Smoke Clears: The Just War Tradition and Post War Justice* (Maryknoll, NY: Orbis Books, 2010); Eric Patterson, ed., *Ethics Beyond Wars' End* (Washington, DC: Georgetown University Press, 2012).

7. Allman and Winright, *After the Smoke Clears*, 7.

continues to offer ethical guidelines impacting our moral imagination and strategic thinking today with regard to deadly force and war. However, our moral responses do not adapt easily to rapid changes in modern technology. As the bishops of Vatican II observed half a century ago, "The horror and perversity of war are immensely magnified by the multiplication of scientific weapons . . . [that] can inflict massive and indiscriminate destruction far exceeding the bounds of legitimate defense."[8] In view of this sign of the times, the council called for "an evaluation of war with an entirely new attitude," and today I believe we still need to reevaluate how the JWT applies in light of our new context. I develop more thoroughly a growing edge in the tradition, *jus ante bellum,* and argue that today with our military power we must always be aware of the great cost and destruction that exists not only when we are at war but also when we are preparing for a war (or even just in maintaining excessive military capabilities).[9] I look specifically at nuclear arms and the historically justified use of deterrence, an "interim ethic"[10] proposed by the US bishops in *The Challenge of Peace.* Today, however, we are aware that we may need a more permanent ethic demanding disarmament. Sustained discussion of the arms race and the lack of justice and safety therein must accompany recent statements from the Catholic Church calling for "banning of weapons that inflict excessively traumatic injury or that strike indiscriminately."[11]

Recent scholarship focuses on the concept that the tradition is living and growing, as evidenced by the new attention to and expansion of the criteria today. Historically, the JWT has had two categories: *jus ad bellum* and *jus in bello.* Now, several theorists recognize the need to expand it to include *jus post bellum* and *jus ante bellum.*[12] All of the principles of the JWT ought to apply to preparations for nuclear war; later, in what follows, I develop three that I see most essential: authority, proportionality, and discrimination.

---

8. *Gaudium et spes,* no. 80.

9. With regard to my use of "our" in this sentence, I write as a Catholic theologian who is a US citizen, but what I propose in this chapter is also relevant for Christians and citizens in other nations possessing or seeking to acquire nuclear weapons.

10. Laurie Johnston, "Nuclear Deterrence: When an Interim Ethic Reaches Its Expiration Date," *Political Theology Today* (May 9, 2014), http://www.politicaltheology.com.

11. *The Compendium of the Social Doctrine of the Church* (Washington, DC: United States Conference of Catholic Bishops, 2004), no. 510.

12. See, for example, Allman and Winright, *After the Smoke Clears;* Paul Dearey, "Catholicism and the Just War Tradition: The Experience of Moral Value in Warfare," in *Just War in Comparative Perspective,* ed. Paul Robinson (Hampshire, UK: Ashgate Publishing Limited, 2003), 24-61; James G. Murphy, *War's Ends: Human Rights, International Order, and the Ethics of Peace* (Washington, DC: Georgetown University Press, 2014).

The documentary tradition in the Catholic Church has articulated the need to nuance just war criteria, especially with the advent of nuclear power. The US Catholic bishops issued *The Challenge of Peace* in 1983 and acknowledged that "nuclear weaponry has drastically changed the nature of warfare, and [that] the arms race poses a threat to human life and human civilization which is without precedent."[13] The pastoral letter echoes similar significant statements from *Gaudium et spes*: "The arms race is an utterly treacherous trap for humanity, and one which injures the poor to an intolerable degree."[14] Therefore, any discussion of the arms race must realize that "any act of war aimed indiscriminately at the destruction of entire cities or extensive areas along with their populations is a crime against God and man himself."[15] *Gaudium et spes* affirmed that deterrence is not "a safe way to preserve a steady peace," nor is it "authentic peace."[16] This seems even more relevant today than it was in 1965.

In *The Challenge of Peace*, the bishops recognize the violence and destruction caused by nuclear arms, and they state their explicit *no* to this as "definitive and decisive."[17] They also argue that using nuclear weapons "to counter a conventional attack" is "morally unjustifiable."[18] Deterrence, which is understood as a "balance of forces," according to the bishops, is one of the most dangerous aspects of the arms race.[19] However, the bishops state that deterrence—in spite of the many complexities and paradoxes involved in the strategy—is a morally acceptable "step on the way toward progressive disarmament."[20] I argue that deterrence has not worked and, moreover, has caused more harm than good. Today, perhaps bishops might place greater emphasis on the toll that the arms race has already taken on our planet and people. More robust demands from Catholic voices to ban nuclear weapons and to continue to reduce stockpiles are imperative.[21] The case in the

---

13. National Conference of Catholic Bishops, *The Challenge of Peace: God's Promise and Our Response* (Washington, DC: US Catholic Conference, 1983), 80-81. Three decades later we can add another "threat to human life and human civilization which is without precedent," which Catholics are starting to take seriously, namely, climate change.

14. *Gaudium et spes*, no. 81.

15. Ibid., no. 80.

16. Ibid., nos. 80-81.

17. National Conference of Catholic Bishops, *Challenge of Peace*, 138.

18. Ibid., 153.

19. Ibid., 161; see also Richard B. Miller, "Introduction: The Advent of Nuclear Ethics," in *War in the Twentieth Century: Sources in Theological Ethics*, ed. Richard B. Miller (Louisville, KY: Westminster/John Knox Press, 1992), 234, for a clear explanation of deterrence.

20. National Conference of Catholic Bishops, *Challenge of Peace*, 175.

21. There is a robust history of Catholic voices, such as Dorothy Day, the cofounder of the Catholic Worker, calling for peace and an end to any type of violence. See, e.g., "*The Challenge of*

Marshall Islands, to which I turn next, underscores why deterrence is not a strategy for "authentic peace," nor has it proven to be a "step on the path to disarmament."

Case Study: Nuclear Weapons in the Republic of the Marshall Islands

In 1948 President Truman remarked that "the sacrifice of Hiroshima and Nagasaki was necessary for the future of both Japan and the Allied nations."[22] What about the other side of the story for the people of both Japan and the Marshall Islands? Certainly the victims did not actually experience the atomic bomb as necessary. I know that the Marshallese do not consider the twenty-three atomic and hydrogen bomb tests on their islands a necessity.[23] How can the JWT expand and embrace larger contexts, such as the *probable* destruction of a people and the land on which they depend merely for the purposes of military readiness for, or to deter, a *possible* conflict? Several scientists and politicians argued that Operation Crossroads, the name for the first series of tests in the islands, was excessive, unjust, and a flawed experiment from the start.[24] Hence, a more thorough *jus ante bellum* analysis of this case involving the atomic tests in the Marshall Islands and their disproportionate effects on the Marshallese and their land might influence concrete issues having to do with preparations for war today, such as our military budget and spending.

I met Jack Niedenthal in 2000, when I taught his son in the sixth grade in the Marshall Islands. Getting to know Jack, an American who had lived in the Marshall Islands for 30 years, and learning about the horrific nuclear testing that has occurred there have impacted me ever since. Niedenthal knew well many of the people who had been displaced from Bikini atoll (one of the twenty-nine coral atolls that comprise the Marshall Islands). Niedenthal's book, *For the Good of Mankind: A History of the People of*

Peace and the Catholic Peace Movement," in Marvin L. Krier Mich, *Catholic Social Teaching and Movements* (Mystic, CT: Twenty-Third Publications, 2003).

22. Dorothee Soelle, *The Arms Race Kills Even without War* (Philadelphia: Fortress Press, 1982), 102.

23. Jonathan M. Weisgall, *Operation Crossroads: The Atomic Tests at Bikini Atoll* (Annapolis, MD: Naval Institute Press, 1994), 315. When elders from Bikini returned to the atoll in 1988 for the beginning of the nuclear cleanup efforts, one of them shared: "We've learned to dry our tears of sorrow with dollar bills. . . . But money will never take the place of Bikini." This quote can be found in the *New York Times*, April 10, 1988, 4.

24. Weisgall, *Operation Crossroads*, 82-96.

Bikini and Their Islands, exposes this dark chapter in Marshallese history for two reasons: first, so that the Marshallese do not forget; and second, to remind humankind of the mistakes that have been made in the past. Niedenthal reveals to us who humans are and what we are capable of, both in our destructive powers and in our capacity for peace, and encourages us to move toward hope.[25] He offers a succinct overview of the history of a lack of *jus ante bellum* in Bikini:

> After promising that they would take care of the Bikinians as if they were their own children, the US government moved the islanders off their atoll; they bombed their homelands with the most powerful weaponry ever tested in the history of the world; they destroyed their culture and way of life; then they left them to starve on places that weren't—and still aren't—fit for human habitation.[26]

This Marshallese story must be told so that the ignored victims of radiation from US tests are reminded that they have dignity. The story also must be told since it demonstrates the flaws in the arms race: "The story of Bikini is the story of fear and destruction, the arrogance and ignorance of the atomic age."[27]

In 1946 Commodore Wyatt came to the people of Bikini and asked that they leave their island so that the United States could begin testing the effects of the atomic bomb at sea. The Bikinians went willingly and without great understanding of what these tests would entail—similar to the way in which there was no "informed consent" for the four hundred mostly poor, illiterate, African American sharecroppers who were enrolled and studied in the Tuskegee Syphilis Study conducted between 1932 and 1972.[28] Wyatt employed persuasive techniques, arriving to speak to the Bikinians on a Sunday after they had finished church services. He knew they viewed the Bible as authoritative, so Wyatt compared the Bikinians to the children of Israel.[29] The Bikinians left their land "believing that everything is in the hands of God."[30] However, everything was in the hands of the US government, and

---

25. Niedenthal, *For the Good of Mankind*, xviii.

26. Ibid., xvii.

27. Weisgall, *Operation Crossroads*, 3.

28. Ralph V. Katz et al., "The Tuskegee Legacy Project: Willingness of Minorities to Participate in Biomedical Research," *Journal of Health Care for the Poor and Underserved* 17 (2006): 698-715; James H. Jones, *Bad Blood: The Tuskegee Syphilis Experiment*, rev. ed. (New York: Free Press, 1993); and Fred D. Gray, *The Tuskegee Syphilis Study: The Real Story and Beyond* (Montgomery, AL: New South Books, 2002). Thanks to Tobias Winright for suggesting this comparison.

29. Weisgall, *Operation Crossroads*, 107-8.

30. Niedenthal, *For the Good of Mankind*, 2.

reverence for God and God's creation was not high on its agenda. The Bikinians were relocated to another atoll that was not sufficient for living and did not meet the dietary needs of the people. Within the year the people struggled with starvation. The food supply from the US government was not sufficient, and without the local foods as a supplement, the situation worsened. They were then moved to another island, where the problems only increased and starvation continued to afflict the people. The Bikinians were relocated for a third time within two years. The destructive impact on the islanders' health, their culture, their family life, and their emotional wellness, which began in 1946, continues today.[31]

Niedenthal describes the fear operating in the US government because of the Russian detonation of their own hydrogen bomb in 1952, leading to "paranoid politicians the world over."[32] On March 1, 1954, the bomb "Bravo" was detonated on a corner of Bikini atoll, even though several reports noted the unfavorable conditions of the wind. As a result of the wind, the nuclear fallout reached inhabited islands.[33] The Bikinians lost their island that day due to irradiation, and the people on the islands of Rongelap, located roughly one hundred miles from Bikini, also suffered from the effects of massive radiation. Jane Dibblin describes the horrific effects of the fallout from "Bravo" in her book *Day of Two Suns: U.S. Nuclear Testing and the Pacific Islanders.* "Bravo" used 17 megatons of TNT, making it 1,300 times as destructive as the bomb dropped on Hiroshima, and "was specifically designed to create a vast amount of lethal fallout."[34] The first test performed in 1946 used 23,000 tons of TNT, causing the temperature at the center of the blast to be 10,000 times greater than that of the sun's surface.[35] I find this to be disproportionate to whatever good may have resulted from the test because of the intentional harm caused to hundreds of people. Many atomic scientists did not support Operation Crossroads. The Federation of American Scientists went so far as to say, "Scientists are cooperating in these tests at the request of their country's armed forces, although they do so with heavy hearts, and without enthusiasm."[36] Critics noted that the tests were "simply educating would-be aggressors in atomic warfare."[37]

---

31. Ibid., 6.

32. Ibid., 7.

33. Ibid., 8.

34. Jane Dibblin, *Day of Two Suns: U.S. Nuclear Testing and the Pacific Islanders* (New York: New Amsterdam Books, 1990), 24.

35. Weisgall, *Operation Crossroads,* 2.

36. Ibid., 97.

37. Ibid., 102.

Not only were the tests necessarily excessive, the people directly affected were not adequately cared for or compensated.[38] In what could be called at best an egregious oversight, there was little attention to a plan for cleanup and treatment after the tests.[39] It was clear that in the wake of the underwater test that the "water near a recent surface explosion will be a witch's brew," with enough plutonium to "poison the combined armed forces of the United States at their highest wartime strength."[40] The US authorities knew that the fallout would harm the islanders, yet did not reschedule the "Bravo" test or relocate the people of Rongelap. Instead, the people of Rongelap were left there to watch and play in the nuclear fallout while the effects of radiation emerged within hours. Some people even thought that the fallout was snow. One islander, who was fourteen years old at the time, recounts her experience in the unknown white powder: "That night we couldn't sleep, our skin itched so much. On our feet were burns as if from hot water. Our hair fell out . . . we were frightened and sad."[41] It was two days before US officials came to rescue the islanders, even though they were close to Rongelap measuring the intensity of the radioactivity after the test.[42]

Although the people of Rongelap were told it was safe to return to their islands in 1957, the radioactivity remained above acceptable levels, leading to numerous health problems. The effects of the fallout continued as people ate radiated food and were exposed to radioactive elements throughout the island. Dibblin's personal interviews with the islanders in the 1980s reveal pieces of the tragic history. The rate of miscarriages after "Bravo" soared, and many women who did give birth had severely deformed babies, many of whom died.[43] Also on the rise were leukemia and various cancer-related tumors. Today, the high incidence of cancer in the Marshall Islands can still be traced to the nuclear testing done in the 1950s. Diabetes also became common among Marshallese people after the nuclear testing. Once the islands were radiated, the local food that had sustained the Marshallese diet for centuries was no longer healthy for them to eat. This necessitated a shift

---

38. Ibid., 227-34. For more on compensation, including reparations, after war, see Allman and Winright, *After the Smoke Clears*, 118-31.

39. Similarly, residents of Los Alamos, New Mexico, often referred to as the birthplace of the atomic bomb, were also not evacuated or even warned about the testing. Studies reveal today that these people were exposed to perhaps 10,000 times the normal radiation levels that the CDC recommends. See, e.g., http://www.science20.com.

40. Weisgall, *Operation Crossroads*, 216.

41. Dibblin, *Day of Two Suns*, 25.

42. Ibid., 26.

43. Ibid., 35.

from local foods to processed foods from the US government. Today they have one of the highest per-capita percentages of diabetes in the world.[44]

The US response to the conditions in the islands included "contradictory and even false statements and inaccurate studies both of the radioactivity levels and of the islanders' health problems."[45] This response is equally as disturbing as the medical effects. US reports from the Atomic Energy Commission after the "Bravo" test stated that "these individuals were unexpectedly exposed to some radioactivity," with "no burns," and all were reported "well."[46] Dibblin uncovers the lies in this statement and points to an official report from the Defense Nuclear Agency that confirms that the weather conditions before the "Bravo" test revealed "winds at 20,000 feet were headed toward Rongelap," so there would have been time to postpone the test for more favorable weather conditions.[47] Sadly, the Marshallese people still wonder if the United States "knowingly and consciously" allowed the people of Rongelap to be exposed to excessive radiation, thereby using them as "guinea pigs."[48] Like Niedenthal, Dibblin seeks to expose the truth too frequently ignored in US history. Both authors raise awareness of the destruction the arms race created and reveal the present struggle the Marshallese face on their journey toward justice and proper reparations.

After detailing the atomic bomb testing in the islands, Dibblin addresses the history of Kwajalein atoll, the site of the US Army base today and the location for long-range missile testing until recently. The tests for intercontinental ballistic missiles (ICBMs), which were launched from California, 4,800 miles away, occurred on Kwajalein.[49] This new wave of arms race buildup carried another set of problems for the Marshallese people. Once again, new sets of islanders were relocated from island to island so that they would be out of the flight path of the missiles. They also lost access to the rights of their lagoon, since they could no longer fish and use it for recreation because missiles were continually targeted toward it. While I spent time in Kwajalein in 2001, it was not uncommon to see protestors from Greenpeace sailing without permission in the lagoon in order to deter the missile tests. If anyone was found in the lagoon before a missile test it would have to be called off.

---

44. Ibid., 47.
45. Ibid., 58.
46. Ibid.
47. Ibid., 61.
48. Ibid., 62.
49. Ibid., 80.

While living in the islands from 2000 to 2002, I realized how this difficult history is now a part of the daily reality and struggle for survival for the islanders. I share pieces of the Marshallese reality to portray the devastating effects of the nuclear arms race. When the bishops, or anyone, claim that deterrence is a just use of nuclear weapons, world leaders must remember places like the Marshall Islands to argue for justice and peace in the arms race and increase efforts toward disarmament.[50] The Marshallese stories of ecological degradation and human injustice need special consideration when debating whether a nuclear arms race can ever be just.

Jus ante bellum: *Proposed Applicable Criteria*

Three criteria of the JWT most readily challenge the nuclear testing in the Marshall Islands. First, there must be a competent authority to engage in war or, as I argue, the preparation for war. Second, the supposed good that results from armed conflict must not have disproportionate costs. Finally, the principle of discrimination refers to the distinction between noncombatants and combatants.[51] Authority, proportionality, and discrimination are essential in this case because these principles are easily violated in the context of nuclear war or in the nuclear arms race.

Questions arise with regard to the authority of the US government here. Why was it just for the United States to declare that these tests must occur at a site "far away from the population centers in the United States," due to the "risk of radioactive contamination"?[52] Weisgall's account of the tests reveals that there was a great deal of argumentation and controversy between the Air Force and the Navy, which led many to see the tests as "silly and meaningless."[53] These tests, moreover, demonstrate a "breakdown of the wartime alliance between scientists and military."[54] The different groups involved in Operation Crossroads, mainly the atomic scientists and the US

---

50. See, e.g., *Pacem in terris*, nos. 112-13; *Gaudium et spes*, nos. 81-82; National Conference of Catholic Bishops, *Challenge of Peace*; United States Conference of Catholic Bishops, *The Harvest of Justice Is Sown in Peace*.

51. Mich, *Catholic Social Teaching and Movements*, 286-87; various authors refer to different categories; another helpful resource is found in Thomas Massaro, *Living Justice: Catholic Social Teaching in Action*, 2nd ed. (Lanham, MD: Rowman & Littlefield, 2012), 106-7.

52. Weisgall, *Operation Crossroads*, 31.

53. Ibid., 86.

54. Ibid., 82.

military, did not agree on implementation.[55] Who has the ultimate authority when there is a difference of opinion in matters such as these?

Second, proportionality is applicable based on the length and severity of the tests, which certainly outweighed the good sought in the end. In other words, the US government counterintuitively used destructive testing as a way to avoid destruction. Not only did the US government victimize the Marshallese, they also did not disclose the long-term health-related and ecological effects of these nuclear tests. Allman and Winright refer to nuclear bombs as "weapons of long-term destruction (WLTDs)" that "extend the pernicious effects of war well into the future."[56] The Bikinians believed they were leaving their island for a short time and would return before long to the graves of their ancestors and the homeland so deeply intertwined with their culture and identity.[57] The destruction from the testing was disproportionate to goods produced by the tests.

Finally, noncombatants were affected by the nuclear tests, and little was done to ensure their protection. The Marshallese were innocent victims in harm's way as the US government decided to utilize their land. It is helpful to remember the words of Pope Benedict XVI here: "In nuclear war there could be no victors, only victims."[58] Even though what happened on the Marshall Islands was only preparation for possible nuclear war, these tests, too, resulted in, as the pope emeritus puts it, "only victims." Likewise, Lisa Sowle Cahill states that the deterrence policy is "premised on an at least implicit threat to do that which it seeks to avoid as an irreducibly immoral violation of the immunity of noncombatants from direct attack."[59] The testing of nuclear bombs on the Marshall Islands presents a nondisputable case where US policy has harmed innocent lives.

A number of theologians, to whom I turn next to develop my claim, have contributed to the application of just war theory to our context today. Their

---

55. In connection with the Manhattan Project, scientists at Los Alamos, New Mexico, were discouraged from asking questions about what they were doing. J. Robert Oppenheimer encouraged them to trust the military and the government, telling them, "Once you know how to make the bomb it's not your business to figure out how not to use it" (quoted in Darrell J. Fasching, Dell Dechant, and David M. Lantigua, *Comparative Religious Ethics: A Narrative Approach to Global Ethics*, 2nd ed. [Malden, MA, and Oxford, UK: Wiley-Blackwell, 2011], 55). Thanks again to Tobias Winright for noting this.

56. Allman and Winright, *After the Smoke Clears*, 166. Other WLTDs include chemical and biological weapons, and antipersonnel land mines and cluster munitions.

57. Weisgall, *Operation Crossroads*, 109.

58. Benedict XVI, "Fighting Poverty to Build Peace," par. 13.

59. Lisa Sowle Cahill, *Love Your Enemies: Discipleship, Pacifism, and Just War Theory* (Minneapolis, MN: Fortress Press, 1994), 209.

hope is that we might move closer to strategies that embrace a just peace. In a 1946 speech before the Senate discussing Operation Crossroads, Ohio Senator James W. Huffman questioned, "Are we preparing for peace or war?"[60] If, Huffman went on to say, we are preparing for peace, "why indulge in this wanton destruction of property and display of atomic power?"[61] In her 1983 book, *The Arms Race Kills Even without War*, Dorothee Soelle prophetically asserted that the arms race perpetuates violence. We should keep her warning in mind even over thirty years later. Soelle considered that the arms race might "constitute a greater risk and danger for us than the peaceful third path we seek."[62]

Recent Extensions of the Just War Tradition

Michael Walzer presents a clear and convincing argument for both the uses and limitations of the just war theory for our context today in his classic text, *Just and Unjust Wars: A Moral Argument with Historical Illustrations.* Walzer claims that the strategy of deterrence is inadequate and based on an "immoral response" to an "immoral threat."[63] Walzer holds that "anyone committed to the distinction between combatants and noncombatants is bound to be appalled by the specter of destruction evoked, and purposely evoked, in deterrence theory."[64] The specter to which Walzer refers is, to say the least, apparent in the lasting devastation in the Marshall Islands.

In addition to exploring the counterintuitive nature of deterrence as a strategy, Walzer suggests that "nuclear weapons explode the theory of just war," since they will never "square with our understanding of justice in war."[65] Nuclear weapons can never be just within the formal limits of the JWT, such as "double effect, collateral damage, noncombatant immunity, and so on."[66] So while nuclear deterrence might allow for some calculation of justice along the "outer limits" of military justice, it is still "a bad way," and Walzer claims we must find "other ways" to prevent nuclear war.[67] Walzer's reflections invite us to consider the arms race and preparations for war when we

---

60. Weisgall, *Operation Crossroads*, 95.

61. Ibid.

62. Soelle, *The Arms Race,* 75.

63. Michael Walzer, *Just and Unjust Wars: A Moral Argument with Historical Illustrations,* 4th ed. (New York: Basic Books, 2006), 269.

64. Ibid., 270.

65. Ibid., 282.

66. Ibid., 283.

67. Ibid.

are evaluating the use of deterrence as a strategy. The excessive and dispro-portionate testing in the Marshall Islands was noted by several at the time, even called a "glorified experiment."[68] Adding a more robust evaluation of deterrence as a "bad way" to prevent nuclear war might eliminate so-called glorified experiments in the future.

Walzer sees nuclear weapons as "technological innovations that are simply not encompassable within the familiar moral world."[69] The creation of the atomic bomb was called "the greatest event in the history of mankind, except only the birth of Christ himself"[70]; however, it would be difficult to imagine two more different events for our moral horizon. Indeed, the first atomic bomb test occurred in the New Mexico desert at a location called "Trinity," and the dropping of the atomic bomb on Hiroshima happened less than a month later, on August 6, 1945, on the Feast of the Transfigura-tion, according to the Christian calendar. In the eyes of some ethicists, the life-giving meaning of these religious symbols was inverted, revealing instead "a power meant to produce total annihilation."[71] Not only are nuclear weap-ons not compatible with our moral world, they are not compatible with the birth of Christ and the tenets of the Christian faith that produced not only pacifism but also the JWT. Walzer concludes that "we must seek out ways to prevent [nuclear war], and because deterrence is a bad way, we must seek out others."[72] The growth of the arms race, however, has prevented us from seek-ing "other ways" toward the just peace to which Walzer refers. The situation in the Marshalls reminds us of how necessary "other ways" truly are.

In a 1994 article, "When the Shooting Stops: Missing Elements in Just War Theory," Michael Schuck recognizes the need for more robust cat-egories of ethical reflection not only before or during, but also after a war. Schuck presents three helpful considerations for *jus post bellum*: repentance, honorable surrender, and restoration. He argues that these principles not only expand the existing tradition but also may serve as a "litmus test for the sincerity of the just war claims made before and during the conflict."[73] Repentance and restoration certainly apply to the case in the Marshall Islands. Unfortunately, the United States has not shown great regret or suf-

---

68. Weisgall, *Operation Crossroads*, 77.
69. Walzer, *Just and Unjust Wars*, 282.
70. Weisgall, *Operation Crossroads*, 80.
71. Fasching, Dechant, and Lantigua, *Comparative Religious Ethics*, 44.
72. Walzer, *Just and Unjust Wars*, 283.
73. Michael Schuck, "When the Shooting Stops: Missing Elements in Just War Theory," *Christian Century* 111, no. 30 (October 26, 1994), 983.

ficient financial or structural help toward recovery for the people and land in the Marshalls.

Similarly, theologians Allman and Winright have sought to address the "growing edges of just war theory" and "broaden the scope" of the theory so as to include some of the "larger questions" that might surround a war.[74] Recognizing that war often has a "larger historical context" than just the present conflict helps create language and ethical guidelines for justice before, during, and after a war.[75] Allman and Winright propose a "more comprehensive and honest just war theory" that would close "the loop *ante, ad, in,* and *post bellum*," thereby being broad enough, in my view, to evaluate the testing in the islands and to create a better set of guidelines to minimize extensive destruction.[76]

Like the work of Allman and Winright, the essay of George Lucas, Jr., "*Jus ante* and *post bellum*: Completing the Circle, Breaking the Cycle," calls for a more comprehensive doctrine of just war. Lucas argues that when *jus ante bellum* and *jus post bellum* are added to the tradition, the "circle of relevant considerations" is completed.[77] This conceptual circle is a helpful tool and makes room for addressing the "general preparation for future war."[78] Ultimately what is gained here with this full-circle approach are more tools for ethical analysis and the hope that together these multiple criteria might help "avoid war's worst consequence in the future."[79]

Just War Tradition: Reimagined with Justice in the Arms Race

What does justice require for people, such as the Marshallese, who are affected by the arms race? What reparations are adequate to victims of nuclear testing? How must we continue to work toward disarmament? Can the Marshallese legacy help us challenge nuclear weapons and critically

---

74. Mark J. Allman and Tobias L. Winright, "Growing Edges of Just War Theory: *Jus ante bellum, jus post bellum*, and Imperfect Justice," *Journal of the Society of Christian Ethics* 32, no. 2 (Fall/Winter 2012): 174.

75. Ibid., 175.

76. Ibid., 180.

77. George R. Lucas, Jr., "*Jus ante* and *post bellum*: Completing the Circle, Breaking the Cycle," in *Ethics beyond Wars' End*, ed. Eric Patterson (Washington, DC: Georgetown University Press, 2012), 56.

78. Ibid.

79. Ibid., 60.

evaluate their destructive capacity even outside of war?[80] These are a few of the questions increasingly relevant and necessary for a discussion of justice in the nuclear arms race and in the broader context of *jus ante bellum*. Today, the US military budget might garner our attention in terms of preparation for war. At the beginning of 2015, it is estimated that the US inventory of nuclear warheads is 7,100, with projected spending on the maintenance and modernization of these warheads expected to be roughly $350 billion over the next decade.[81] Responding to this large financial figure, the US bishops, in a letter dated October 30, 2014, argue that this excessive spending "undermines the quest for nuclear disarmament."[82] Stephen Colecchi, director of USCCB's Office of International Justice and Peace, poignantly asks, "Are nations, including our own, serious about nuclear disarmament if they are modernizing their nuclear weapons systems?"[83]

I suggest that nuclear testing never occur at the expense of human lives. Human dignity is not honored when populations have to question if they were used as guinea pigs to further the knowledge of science. "The good of all mankind" that was promised to the Marshallese need truly be good for all humanity, especially those on the margins. The financial support for the arms race drains resources from other human needs.[84] If the Catholic Church continues to permit deterrence as an interim ethic, leaders must recognize the great cost of the arms race on scores of poor and developing nations.[85] The same just war principles that comprise the justice before, during, and after war must extend to the preparations for war.

---

80. See Holly M. Barker, *Bravo for the Marshallese: Regaining Control in a Post-Nuclear, Post-Colonial World (Case Studies on Contemporary Social Issues)*, 2nd ed. (Independence, KY: Cengage Learning, 2012).

81. See Hans M. Kristensen and Robert S. Norris, "US Nuclear Forces, 2015," *Bulletin of the Atomic Scientists*, 71, no 2.

82. See letter from Bishop Richard Pates (USCCB) to Dr. Ernest Moniz, secretary of energy, dated October 30, 2014, wherein he writes: "Excessive spending on nuclear weapons also undermines long-term initiatives to promote human security. The projected expenditure of $35.5 billion per year for nuclear weapons contrasts with the President's proposed 2015 budget of about $20 billion for poverty-focused international assistance, as identified by our Conference and Catholic Relief Services," http://www.usccb.org.

83. Dias, "Pope Francis' Latest Mission."

84. *Gaudium et spes,* no. 81.

85. In Pope Benedict's 2009 World Day of Peace Message he does call for nuclear disarmament and notes the "resources which would be saved could then be employed in projects of development capable of benefiting all their people, especially the poor." The devastation on the environment due to the arms race is an increasingly relevant topic today. The Marshalls were first displaced from their land because of the atomic bomb, and soon may be some of the globe's first climate refugees. See, in particular, "Losing Paradise: The People Displaced by Atomic Bombs, and Now Climate Change," March 9, 2015, in the *Guardian,* http://www.theguardian.com.

Deterrence has taken lives and has led to disproportionate suffering in the Marshall Islands.[86] If we take what several prominent voices have said around the morality of nuclear deterrence seriously and look to the situation in the Marshalls, it is apparent that new policies are needed to address the buildup of arms for the purpose of deterrence. Archbishop Bernedito Auza, the Holy See's ambassador to the United Nations, refers to the "peace of a sort" that has justified nuclear deterrence as "specious and illusory."[87] New applications of the just war tradition, like *jus ante bellum*, must include updated policies for justice in the arms race, and even perhaps a more concerted effort toward disarmament. This is the minimal change that will enable more dialogue and discussion in the process toward a just peace. The deterrence step on the way to disarmament that the bishops allowed for in 1983 needs to be reevaluated in light of just war principles *ante bellum* with an eye toward justice in all practices of the arms race for peace in our nuclear age. Pope Francis critiques the arms race as "a mistake and a misallocation of resources" that would be invested more prudently in areas of "integral human development, education, health and the fight against extreme poverty."[88]

A more recent example, which mirrors the testing in the Marshall Islands, can be found with the naval training conducted in Vieques, an island off the Puerto Rican coast. The US Navy began using the island after World War II and did not leave until 2003. Like the Marshallese, the people of Vieques are some of the poorest in Puerto Rico and sadly today report higher rates of infant mortality and cancer.[89] In 1999 a civilian was killed by a stray bomb—which began a large nonviolent protest calling for the Navy to leave.[90] The archbishop of Puerto Rico, Roberto Gonzalez, was one of the leading voices demanding justice and exposing the poor treatment of the local people.[91] Situations like those in Vieques and the Marshall Islands are receiving attention today as more voices call for new policies around war and

---

86. Beyond the scope of this paper, but worth mentioning, another similar case can be found in Australia. The British government performed similar tests in the Australian outback without properly warning the aboriginal people. Niedenthal's book details a delegation of Marshallese who went to visit the Australian people in 1988 to help share the story of lobbying to the US government to clean up the atomic waste and destruction. See Niedenthal, *For the Good of Mankind*, 100-104.

87. Dias, "Pope Francis' Latest Mission."

88. Ibid.

89. Katherine T. McCaffrey, "Social Struggle against the U.S. Navy in Vieques, Puerto Rico: Two Movements in History," *Latin American Perspectives* 33, no. 1 (January 2006): 85. Tobias Winright suggested Vieques as a possible related case.

90. Ibid., 84.

91. Michael Sean Winters, "25 Years a Bishop," *National Catholic Reporter* (October 3, 2013), http://ncronline.org.

the preparation for war. Last year the Marshall Islands presented a lawsuit at the International Court of Justice in The Hague suing "nine nuclear weapons possessors for failing to eliminate their nuclear arsenals."[92] Although this lawsuit may be seen as merely symbolic, it does reveal the growing awareness, as noted recently by Pope Francis, of the policies that tie "nuclear disarmament to humanitarian issues."[93] Prior to the tests in the Marshall Islands, Senator Scott Lucas of Illinois cautioned that we should "stop, look, listen, hesitate, and pause" before moving forward. Sadly, this advice has been ignored for too long, but perhaps we might pay attention to these cautionary recommendations more closely today.[94]

---

92. Avner Cohan and Lily Vacarro, "The Import of the Marshall Islands Nuclear Lawsuit," *Bulletin of the Atomic Scientists*, May 6, 2014, http://thebulletin.org.

93. Ibid.

94. Weisgall, *Operation Crossroads*, 74.

CHAPTER 9

Women in Combat, Civilian Immunity, and the Just War Tradition

CRISTINA RICHIE*

History attests to the fact that women around the world have acted in combatant roles. Indeed, some have been immortalized and celebrated. The Jewish heroine Judith[1] and the French warrior Joan of Arc come to mind as women who have subverted gender roles and fought for freedom. Other women have battled alongside men and been forgotten—written out of history as an aberration. But each culture has known what we would today call "women combatants." This essay contextualizes the presence of women in the military, briefly examines current challenges for women combatants, and introduces the concept of civilian immunity as a part of the just war tradition (JWT). Civilian immunity has historically depended on the distinction between men as combatants and women as civilians. But, in light of the admittance of women into combat roles, these assumptions need to be clarified by returning to the JWT's emphasis on war status instead of sex stereotypes.[2]

---

* In addition to this volume's editors, I want to thank Angelica Richie and Jen Lamson-Scribner for their helpful comments on earlier drafts of this essay.

1. Cristina Richie, "Judith: Heroine of the Israelites," *Mutuality Magazine* 17, no. 2 (2010): 11.

2. Many people use the terms "sex" and "gender" interchangeably; however, they are not the same. "Sex" refers to natural, biological, structural characteristics of any animal that is sexually dimorphic [both male and female]. "Gender" refers to emotional, mental, and personal characteristics that cultures assign to women and men. The idea that women are shy, that they should not wear pants, and that they are naturally peaceful are culturally constructed ideas that are not innate to the female sex, but rather relative to ideas about gender in particular societies during certain eras and geographical locations.

Female Fighters across the Globe

Women have been linked to war in various ways.[3] From Helen of Troy, whose face "launched a thousand ships," to the pejoratively titled "pin-up girls" who have consoled men in bunkers, and even to the Greek linkage between *eros* (sex) and *thanatos* (death),[4] women have been loosely tied to war, but they have also been directly linked to combat.

The ancient Greek philosopher Plato argued for the potential of women as warriors based on the capabilities and attributes of the individual woman rather than sweeping generalizations about womankind. Plato claimed that there were no essential mental or personal differences that separated all men from all women; therefore women should be trained in traditionally male pursuits such as music, gymnastics, and "the art of war."[5] A slice of Plato's vision for a nation where social role is assigned by aptitude—not sex—is evident in sex-inclusive militaries.

Across the modern world, women warriors are known, and are even sought out, as desirable in certain contexts. In the Middle East, for instance, there has been a tradition of women in combat roles. "While Muslim women, dressed as males, have in the past fought alongside Islamist militants, the creation of an all-female fighting force . . . dubbed the 'Burkha Brigade'"[6] highlights the extent to which some women will go to put themselves in harm's way for the sake of their beliefs. Governments aware of the tactical use of women have counterstrategies in place, which also rely on women to diffuse potentially violent situations. In one case, "Afghan special police now train females who are part of a unit to conduct searches when insurgents are suspected of using the women and children in the village to hide items such as weapons, drugs, and other devices such as cell phones and documents."[7] This is indispensable in cultures in which men and women are segregated in public and private; men cannot search women, and sometimes men cannot even enter the home of a woman who is alone.

In other military settings women train and serve in combatant functions. Prior to 2013, military forces in Australia, Canada, Denmark, France,

---

3. Thanks to Tobias Winright for pointing this out to me.

4. See Robert Emmet Meagher, *Killing from the Inside Out: Moral Injury and Just War* (Eugene, OR: Cascade Books, 2014), chap. 2.

5. Plato, *The Republic*, trans. Richard Sterling and William Scott (New York: W. W. Norton, 1985), 5.451e-452.

6. Frank Crimi, "Al-Qaeda's Female Suicide Bomber Death Cult," FrontPage Mag, November 6, 2012, http://frontpagemag.com.

7. Michael Ard, "Female Engagement Teams Foil Insurgent Tactics," *Defence Video and Imagery Distribution System,* November 25, 2011, http://www.dvidshub.net.

Germany, Israel, New Zealand, and Norway integrated women into combat training.[8] The United States is the ninth country to sanction women combatants.[9]

Women in the Armed Forces of the United States

In the United States, women have systematically permeated the previously all-male military. While women worked as nurses and administrators within the US armed forces prior to the modern era, previous bans on women combatants prevented capable and willing women from serving and protecting their country. Slowly, women have worked their way through the ranks, achieving top honors. At the same time, women remain a minority in the military, and some women in leadership seem to hold only token positions.

1980 was the first year that the US Air Force Academy admitted women, opening the door for gender equality in the military. Later, during the 1990-1991 Gulf War, a sizeable 40,000 women were among the armed forces.[10] In 2008, Army General Ann Dunwoody became the first female four-star general in US history.[11] Two years later, the US Navy lifted the ban on women submariners, placing three female officers in the crews of guided-missile attack submarines and ballistic missile submarines. The United States recorded 52,446 active-duty female naval officers in 2010.[12] Then, in 2013, the ban on women in land combat was lifted.

The US Department of Defense [DoD] indicated that as of March 31, 2014, women accounted for 14.69 percent of the total enlisted individuals in the US military. Within these ranks, 16.5 percent of all military officers were women, totaling 164,095 active-duty women in the United States serving across the four branches of Army, Navy, Marines, and Air Force. In addition to these enrolled women, 20.39 percent of all military academy cadets and midshipmen [*sic*] were women. When officers, enlisted persons, cadets, and midshipmen are taken as a whole, women accounted for a solid 15.05

---

8. Anna Mulrine, "8 Other Nations That Send Women to Combat," *National Geographic Daily News,* January 25, 2013, http://news.nationalgeographic.com.

9. Erin McClam, "'Valor Knows No Gender': Pentagon Lifts Ban on Women in Combat," *U.S. News,* January 24, 2013, http://usnews.nbcnews.com.

10. Charlotte Lindsey, *Women Facing War* (Geneva: International Committee of the Red Cross, 2001), 23.

11. Mark Thompson, "Female Generals: The Pentagon's First Pair of Four-Star Women," *Time,* August 13, 2012, http://nation.time.com.

12. Associated Press, "US Navy Lifts Ban on Women Submariners," *The Guardian,* April 29, 2010, http://www.theguardian.com.

percent of the armed forces, or 205,667 out of the 1,366,194 active-duty personnel in 2014.[13] Undeniably, the modern military landscape is changing as women and men fight side by side. Not everyone, however, has embraced the Platonic vision of combat based on capability instead of sex.

Challenges to Women in Combat

When women warriors were a hypothetical scenario rather than a reality, war strategists asked how the presence of women would alter unit cama-raderie, military safety, and soldiers' duties. Now that women are in com-bat units, a more complex picture of women and men at war is emerging. Sexual assault is a reality not only for women but also for men in the mili-tary. This intersex violence garnered considerable negative publicity in 2014 when Defense Secretary Chuck Hagel revealed that 5,000 service members "reported sexual assaults over the past year . . . up from about 3,400 the year before."[14] The presence of women has magnified the reality of sexual assault in the military, but not necessarily the prevalence.

Concern for the protection of female soldiers against male sexual aggres-sion has long been an argument against the integration of women in com-batant units. However, the reality is that sexual abuse occurs not only across gender lines as men assault women and women assault men,[15] but also as men sexually assault other men.[16] Sexual assault in the military continues to be among the most heinous of personal abuses and demands immedi-ate reformation. Other significant matters such as military training, living accommodations for soldiers, and postwar civilian reintegration remain.[17]

---

13. Department of Defense, "Active Duty Military Personnel by Rank/Grade," March 31, 2014, https://www.dmdc.osd.mil. Department of Defense, "Table of Active Duty Females by Rank/Grade and Service," March 2014, https://www.dmdc.osd.mil.

14. David Welna, "In Sex Assault Report, Pentagon Sees Progress—And a Long Way to Go," NPR, May 1, 2014, http://kuer.org.

15. Women have both raped men and been responsible for authorizing or assisting in rapes of women. In 2011, Pauline Nyiramasuhuko, the former Rwandan minister of family affairs, became the first woman found guilty of rape for her role in encouraging sexual assaults as a superior. See Dara Kay Cohen, "Female Combatants and the Perpetration of Violence: Wartime Rape in the Sierra Leone Civil War," *World Politics* 65, no. 3 (2013): 410.

16. James Dao, "In Debate over Military Sexual Assault, Men Are Overlooked Victims," *New York Times,* June 23, 2013, http://www.nytimes.com.

17. Women continue to be underserved in reintegration to civilian life. In addition to fighting against gender stereotypes while in the military, post-traumatic stress disorder (PTSD) diagnoses after service are increasing, as are the numbers of homeless among female veterans. The US Department of Veterans Affairs is also unequipped to meet the gynecological needs of

Yet these intramilitary quagmires are just outside the realm of the JWT, as it is traditionally understood. Instead, the JWT examines actions as they pertain to war and also poses challenges for the new military landscape of women combatants.

Just War and Women

The Christian just war tradition postdates the philosophy of Plato by nearly eight hundred years and is rooted in the writings of St. Augustine, among others. However, the JWT has been developed and critiqued by both Christians and non-Christians for many centuries. While Augustine primarily focused on the dimension of *jus ad bellum* (the criteria for initiating a just war),[18] other ethicists have developed guidelines for conduct in war (*jus in bello*) and conduct after war (*jus post bellum*). A millennium and a half after Augustine, the JWT houses a number of positions under one large tent, with the basic tenets of the theory firmly established. "It is now widely, if not universally, accepted that the legitimacy of war depends on the satisfaction of three sets of criteria: the traditional *jus ad bellum* and *jus in bello* criteria framing judgments about the decision to use force and the conduct of war respectively, and *jus post bellum* criteria concerning the legitimacy of the peace that follows it."[19] Perhaps not surprisingly for the long-standing and well-worn nature of the tradition, women combatants fit into and nuance historical just war theories on each point.

In *jus ad bellum*, the presence of women combatants and the legal framework for a draft that would include women might inhibit the impulse to go to war. The fear that a daughter or sister could be conscripted and return home on a stretcher or in a coffin might bolster the attitude that war is a "miserable necessity," thereby helping to ensure that embarking upon it is truly the last resort.[20]

---

female soldiers. See Committee on Health Care for Underserved Women, American College of Obstetricians and Gynecologists, "Committee Opinion no. 547: Health Care for Women in the Military and Women Veterans," *Obstetrics and Gynecology* 120, no. 6 (2012): 1538–42.

18. Augustine, "Reply to Faustus," in *Writings in Connection with the Manichean Heresy*, trans. Rev. Richard Stothert (Edinburgh: T. & T. Clark, 1877), 22.75.

19. Alex J. Bellamy, "The Responsibilities of Victory: *Jus post bellum* and the Just War," *Review of International Studies* 34, no. 4 (2008): 601. For a theological defense of *jus post bellum*, see Mark J. Allman and Tobias L. Winright, *After the Smoke Clears: The Just War Tradition and Post War Justice* (Maryknoll, NY: Orbis Books, 2010).

20. Cristina Richie, "Women Combatants and Just War Theory," *Political Theology Today*, January 17, 2014, http://www.politicaltheology.com.

In *jus post bellum,* women combatants might be appointed a special role in peacemaking[21] because they can be invited into homes where women are present,[22] establish rapport with other female soldiers no longer taking an active part in hostilities (*hors de combat*), and collaborate with female reporters, journalists, and photographers[23] to stabilize the recovering state. In crosscultural and crossreligious situations, sex-segregated public life is the norm; female soldiers are essential to supporting women in other countries as they move toward the rebuilding process.

Finally, in *jus in bello,* women combatants highlight and reiterate the need for discernment in determining who is a civilian and who is not. It is this category of the JWT that I address in what follows.

Jus in bello: *Civilian Immunity*

There are two basic criteria for *jus in bello,* or conduct in war, that determine the ethical acceptability of actions: discrimination and proportion. "The principle of discrimination is concerned with avoiding deliberate attacks on 'the innocent'; the idea that civilians should not excessively suffer in war. The principle of proportionality states that it is unjust to inflict greater harm than that which is unavoidable in order to achieve legitimate military objectives."[24] The concept of discrimination, or "civilian immunity," will be the focus of the remainder of this essay.

Precedent for civilian immunity comes from international law and the JWT. The Fourth Geneva Convention of 1949 declared "persons taking no active part in the hostilities, including members of armed forces who have laid down their arms and those placed *hors de combat* by sickness, wounds, detention, or any other cause, shall in all circumstances be treated humanely."[25] By contrast, individuals who are actively engaged in warfare are susceptible to attack, capture, and death. Individuals who are not directly engaged in actions of hostility, that is, "civilians," are considered innocent since they are not partaking in war.

---

21. Regional Command Southwest Press Room, "Female Engagement Team (USMC)," http://regionalcommandsouthwest.wordpress.com.

22. Ard, "Female Engagement Teams."

23. Aimee Baldridge, "War through a Woman's Eyes," *American Photo,* May 22, 2013, http://www.americanphotomag.com.

24. Lamber Royakkers and Rinie van Est, "The Cubicle Warrior: The Marionette of Digitized Warfare," *Ethics and Information Technology* 12, no. 3 (2010): 290.

25. Geneva Convention (IV), *Relative to the Protection of Civilian Persons in Time of War,* Geneva, August 12, 1949, art. 3 (1), http://www.icrc.org.

Even within these legal frameworks, just war ethicists debate the extent to which the principle of discrimination can be applied. For instance, if an army is camped outside a city and poses a clear and present danger of attempting to breach the city walls at dawn, would a preemptive nocturnal strike by the city's defenders against that army violate the principle of civilian immunity since those soldiers are not "actively" taking part in hostilities?[26] Furthermore, when engaged in a war and not simply a battle, it is unclear just how cooperative one has to be to qualify as a "combatant." Even civilians who are not taking up arms are implicated in war through supporting soldiers morally, providing them with food, manufacturing ammunition, and even allowing their taxes to finance the war. In this sense there are no "innocent" people in war—neither women nor children—thus muddling the line between civilians and combatants.[27]

Despite these gray areas, there is consensus that a "combatant" is an individual "who may legitimately be killed, according to whether or not they participate directly in hostilities," while "civilians [are individuals] whose lives must be spared, to be distinguished from combatants."[28]

The Historical Identifications of Woman as Civilian and Man as Combatant

Although it is not explicitly stated at the time of the Geneva Convention or during the development of *jus in bello* principles, all women were considered civilians since individual women were almost never combatants. In contrast, since battles and wars were fought by men, the term "combatant" became associated with men in general. "This distinction between combatants and non-combatants . . . has been constructed in part through gender binaries since its emergence during the Enlightenment."[29] These gender binaries led

---

26. Neta Crawford, "The Slippery Slope to Preventive War," *Ethics and International Affairs* 17, no. 1 (2003): 30-36; Whitley Kaufman, "What's Wrong with Preventive War?" *Ethics and International Affairs* 19, no. 3 (2005): 23-38.

27. For classic theological discussions surrounding these issues, see John Ford, "The Morality of Obliteration Bombing," *Theological Studies* 5, no. 3 (September 1944): 261-309; Karl Barth, *Church Dogmatics* III/4 ss. 55 Freedom for Life no. 2, "The Protection of Life," ed. G. W. Bromiley and T. F. Torrance (Edinburgh: T. & T. Clark, 1961), 451-70.

28. R. Charli Carpenter, "'Women, Children and Other Vulnerable Groups': Gender, Strategic Frames and the Protection of Civilians as Transnational Issue," *International Studies Quarterly* 49, no. 2 (2005): 296.

29. Ibid., 302.

to generalizations about both men and women, making all women "innocent civilians" and all men potential (or actual) "combatants."

The changing contours of the JWT and unforeseeable changes to the composition of the military have led to an imperfect application of *jus in bello* in the modern era. With the integration of women into the military, determining who is a citizen and who is a combatant can no longer be conflated with sex, as some women are combatants and some men are civilians. While protection of citizens is often touted as a political aim of *jus in bello*, couching protection agendas in gender essentialism terms "reproduce[s] the traditional notion that 'women and children' (but not adult men) are 'innocent.'"[30] This dichotomy reduces the effectiveness of protecting civilians, usually to the detriment of men.

When civilians are categorized by their sex and not their role in combat, all women are seen as innocent noncombatants, even though they might be involved in war. In contradistinction, all males of adult age are seen as combatants. The lingering effect of this ideology on historical military operations is summed up in the phrase "military age male" (MAM): any man who is approximately 18 to 65 years old, regardless of war status. There is no corresponding term "military age female,"[31] reiterating the false idea that men fight wars and women do not.

Although it is expedient to assess a person's involvement in war based on traditional sex roles, the laxness of stereotyping violates *jus in bello* standards. Blanket assessment of civilian or combatant status may appear harmless, especially when the benefit of the doubt is given to women, but just war theorists can no longer maintain these labels. Women in combat prompt us to return to classic just war demarcations based on *active military involvement*. Failure to do so results in a violation of the principle of discrimination because (1) female soldiers are not held responsible for war crimes and their moral agency is denied; and (2) male civilians are unfairly seen as targets of war, leaving them without protection. I will explain both of these consequences briefly, before concluding the essay.

---

30. Ibid., 296.

31. One also notes the sex-exclusive language of "unmanned" vehicles. While it would have been etymologically correct to use this term in an era when only men manipulated vehicles, now it is undeniably an excluding term. The use of the phrase "unmanned" aircraft/plane/etc. reiterates the dominant thinking that war and bellicose actions are primarily male. Instead, "unpersoned" aircraft, though it is inelegant, must be used to reiterate the nature of war as bigendered. Note that the *New Oxford American Dictionary* has more linguistic accuracy and gender inclusivity by defining "drone" as "a remote-controlled pilotless aircraft or missile." This is a semantic step forward.

Female Soldiers Are Not Held Responsible for War Crimes

Framing the discussion of civilians and combatants by using gender essential-ist categories incorrectly presents fully grown, morally autonomous women as immature, intellectually dependent quasi adults—that is, as innocent civilians who cannot act of their own volition. The phrase "women and chil-dren" sums up this thought precisely. In contrast, adult males are bestowed with responsibility, autonomy, and rationality as soldiers.

The implications of ignoring women as responsible parties are bleak when women transition from being civilian to combatant. If women—when they are combatants—are seen as civilians, then they would not be culpable for the deaths of other human beings under laws of war. Around the world, according to Dara Kay Cohen, "despite substantial involvement in armed groups . . . women's participation is marginalized; female fighters are often dismissively called 'females associated with the war,'"[32] and they therefore often fly under the radar of legal repercussions. As of 2011 there were 40 women "being investigated for war crimes in Bosnia, [but] not a single woman had been tried."[33] It took nearly a decade to bring a woman to trial and convict her for a war crime.[34] Some have traced this delay in justice to a general reluctance to sentence women,[35] but unless all combatants are held to the standards of *jus in bello*, justice cannot be served.

The role of women in war crimes was highlighted by the Abu Ghraib tor-ture case. Private First Class Lynndie R. England denied that she had full agency in her role in abusing captive prisoners, claiming "that she posed in the infamous photographs because her lover encouraged her," as if she had no will of her own and was subject to the desires of a man. Even her lawyers painted her "as a young, impressionable soldier."[36] While both men and women who were accused of torture at Abu Ghraib claimed that they were "just submitting to orders," the language of being impressionable and weak willed is accepted more readily from women who make these claims, perpetuating the stereotype that women are naturally submissive and not fully capable of considering their actions. Pleading partial responsibility for one's actions may lead to reduced sentencing in war tribunals, benefiting the

---

32. Cohen, "Female Combatants," 405-6.

33. Ibid., 410.

34. "Bosnian War Crimes Court Jails First Woman," *Reuters,* April 30, 2012, http://www.reuters.com.

35. Merima Husejnovic, "Bosnian War's Wicked Women Get Off Lightly," *Balkan Trans-national Justice,* February 7, 2011, http://www.balkaninsight.com.

36. Josh White, "Reservist Sentenced to 3 Years for Abu Ghraib Abuse," *Washington Post,* September 28, 2005, http://www.washingtonpost.com.

individual woman, but it corrupts the view of women as morally responsible. Just war theorists should not give mentally competent adult women a pass on morality. Any person—woman or man—who commits war atrocities should be liable for the consequences.

To safeguard the rights of civilians and to ensure justice when civilians are killed or tortured, all countries must recognize women's full moral agency by enforcing justice if and when women soldiers kill and torture. We must be aware that "gender imagery proves a potent cultural resource in terms of agenda setting, precisely because it resonates with pre-existing gender discourses, but since this gender essentialism is fundamentally misleading, it distorts the civilian immunity norm it is intended to promote."[37] With the addition of women to the battlefields, the lines between civilian and soldier are no longer drawn by sex. This leads to the second violation of the principle of discrimination.

Male Civilians Are Unfairly Seen as Targets of War

With the entrance of women into combat, a twofold problem for male civilians emerges. First, they may not be afforded the same protection as female civilians when their country is attacked. Second, they may be overlooked in humanitarian relief services presented to the public. The vulnerabilities of male civilians were highlighted clearly in 2012 when President Barack Obama reinscribed the definition of "combatant" during US drone attacks, a move many thought to be a violation of the principle of civilian immunity.

Through a change of semantics, the Obama administration "embraced a disputed method for counting civilian casualties [which] . . . in effect counts all military-age males in a strike zone as combatants."[38] Instead of the traditional definition of a combatant as one actively engaged in armed conflict, this definition placed sex and location as the primary determinates of combatant status and changed one of the central tenets of *jus in bello* through manipulating the definition of "civilian" and thus the concept of civilian immunity.

This approach permitted the Obama administration to continue to mount drone attacks and other strikes under the guise that "no civilians were killed" or that "the numbers [of casualties] are in the single digits," thus saving face. Yet this unilateral change in policy contradicted the JWT, which is meant as a rigorous standard for initiating, engaging, or concluding a war. Basing combatant status on sex neglects an essential principle of the JWT, evades account-

---

37. Carpenter, "'Women, Children,'" 312.

38. Jo Becker and Scott Shane, "Secret 'Kill List' Proves a Test of Obama's Principles and Will," *New York Times*, May 29, 2012, http://www.nytimes.com.

ability for male civilian deaths, and reinforces the image of man as belligerent, thus making the public indifferent toward the vulnerabilities of men.

R. Charli Carpenter noted that "the same year that nearly 8,000 unarmed men and boys were executed at Srebrenica, the ICRC [International Committee of the Red Cross] published a brief entitled 'Civilians in War,' featuring sections on 'women' and 'children' . . . but contained no images of un-uniformed adult men and failed to discuss endemic patterns of attack against civilian males."[39] While female civilians are afforded protection and given relief services based on their sex, susceptible male civilians are ignored on the same basis. This issue stretches across the JWT and is a humanitarian concern.

The stereotype of men as not only willing but also able to defend themselves places them at a disadvantage as they are at once seen as able to forestall their own deaths (though they are not), and at the same time seen as legitimate targets of war (though they have not taken up arms). When all men are seen as combatants—because of the historical precedent for a predominantly male army—male civilians are killed without repercussion. As Robert Sparrow notes, "Ensuring that someone can be held responsible for each death caused in war is an important requirement of *jus in bello*."[40] Although there are moral and legal sanctions against killing a civilian, the deaths of civilian men are often absorbed into the public perception as deaths of combatants.

While viewing all men as combatants is far more convenient for those determining military policy and for those safe at home, it is not true to *jus in bello* guidelines. Yet, "when asked about whether to highlight civilian men and boys as a 'vulnerable group,' participants at the ICRC's Seminar on the Protection of Special Categories of Civilian responded . . . 'If you suggest a program for "vulnerable men" no one will fund it.'"[41] Given the pressing reality of a sex-integrated military, civilian immunity is complicated. Women combatants highlight the mixture of gender roles in war as they increasingly act as warriors, while men are protected if and when they are civilians. The JWT clearly responds to each of these demands.

Conclusion

Simplistic definitions of all women as innocent civilians and all males as combatants no longer hold in present military operations. With the addition of

---

39. Carpenter, "'Women, Children,'" 304.
40. Robert Sparrow, "Killer Robots," *Journal of Applied Philosophy* 24, no. 1 (2007): 67.
41. Carpenter, "'Women, Children,'" 320.

women in combat, classic understandings of *jus in bello* are nuanced; women combatants reify the need for discrimination in determining who is a civilian and who may be attacked ethically and legally. This has a twofold purpose of protecting civilians and safeguarding that fatalities in battle are only of combatants. Though strenuous, the purpose of *jus in bello* is not simple policies but moral actions in the face of the less-than-ideal situation of war.

Daniel M. Bell, Jr., writes, "the discipline of just war asks ... [for] the fortitude to embrace the political dimensions of war.... It calls for a people dedicated to the harder right instead of the easier wrong."[42] This is no easy task. It is much simpler to assume that all men of a certain age are suspect and that all women are innocent, but this glosses over the intricacy of warfare in an age of women combatants and male innocents.

To do justice to the people who are in the midst of a war, civilians must be protected based on the role they are or are not playing, not by generalization about their sex. This means a nuanced mode of discrimination: attention to the individual and not the group, and a detailed bank of information in cases where the war status of the individual is unclear. "Intelligence gathering" cannot rely on stereotypes of men or women, though it is easier to link civilian or combatant status with sex. *Post-hoc* policies that assume combatant status unless, as the Obama administration says, "there is explicit intelligence posthumously proving them innocent,"[43] cannot be endorsed.

It will take diligence and effort to separate the soldier from the civilian in this era of remote battlefields and women warriors, but this is the purpose of the parameters of a *just* war. The homogenous model of using sex to indicate war status breaches the ethical principles of *jus in bello*, but delineating between civilian and combatant based on bellicose action satisfies both international law and the JWT. In the twenty-first century we cannot rely on generalizations or become slack in our determination of civilian status. Women have tenaciously challenged sex stereotypes as they have entered the military in the United States and other countries. Now women as combatants highlight the need for discrimination in war as the gendered image of the soldier is inverted, even as the image of the civilian is reinvented, once again breaking down barriers and building up new ones.

---

42. Daniel M. Bell, Jr., "Discriminating Force: Just War and Counterinsurgency," *Christian Century* 130, no. 16 (August 7, 2013): 35.

43. Becker and Shane, "Secret 'Kill List.'"

CHAPTER 10

Just War and Its Implications for African Conflicts

ELIAS O. OPONGO

An analysis of the application of the moral considerations and the principles of the just war tradition on African conflicts has to take into account the trends and character of the African conflicts. The just war tradition (JWT) has developed in international relations as a war ethics limiting interstate conflicts, whereas conflicts in Africa have largely been intrastate. Hence, for these conflicts, the moral evaluation of the justifiability of conditions before going to war and the conduct of the combatants in war have to be analyzed within the framework of nonconventional wars. What then would be the relevance of applying the JWT to intrastate African conflicts?

The intrastate conflicts within Africa are often between the government and a rebel group. This poses two major challenges. First, international law favors governments as the sole legitimate authority that can authorize and declare war. While a rebel group could have a just cause, it is unlikely to be recognized as a legitimate authority with the capacity to declare war. The second challenge is that, whereas a government is bound by international law to observe minimum moral standards in the conduct of war, a similar imperative could not be imposed on a rebel group nor would the rebel group feel obliged to observe the required standards, unless such a rebel group had solid international backing.

Therefore, a discourse on the application of the JWT to African conflicts will have to be based both on internal analysis of the justifiability of the conflicts and exploration of alternative mechanisms, and external analysis of the justifiability of humanitarian military intervention within the framework of the responsibility to protect. This chapter will examine these two analytical approaches while discussing the extent of the relevance of the JWT in African civil wars.

Conflicts in Africa

The JWT has for centuries guided how governments should respond to the threat of potential armed conflicts. To a great extent, the JWT has been used to limit wars and to provide principles that guide the recourse to wars. The justifiability before war, *jus ad bellum,* has to be in line with the just war principles, which include just cause, right intention, proportionality, legitimate authority, public declaration of war, reasonable hope of success, and last resort. On the other hand, the conditions guiding the conduct of war, *jus in bello,* include noncombatant immunity and fair treatment of prisoners of war. In recent years, there have been considerations for responsibilities for postconflict peacebuilding, *jus post bellum.* To what extent then can these principles be applicable to the Africa context?

The Peace of Westphalia, which in 1648 ended different wars between nations and recognized the sovereignty of the states in central Europe, may be viewed as a key moment in history leading to the recognition of sovereignty. In this connection, the JWT has been understood within the framework of international relations, in which nations have the obligation to respect the internal sovereignty of every other nation. In other words, the JWT has mainly been applied to potential and existing conflicts between states. To a great extent, states have been responsible for mass killings of civilians. According to Rummel,[1] states have largely been responsible for deaths of civilians leading to what he refers to as *democide.* He points out that in the twentieth century more than 150 million people have died in "mega-murders" as a result of the unchecked totalitarian power of states. As such, the powers of the states need to be regularly under international law. The JWT plays a pivotal role in ensuring that the states are held accountable for the choices they make before, during, and after the war.

However, the end of the Cold War saw an increase in internal conflicts and the fragmentation of a number of states into "failed states." Within Africa there are currently eight live conflicts: South Sudan, Sudan (Darfur), Mali, Central Africa Republic (CAR), Chad, Democratic Republic of the Congo (DRC), Libya, and Somalia. These conflicts have largely been between the state and specific militia groups.[2] The causes of these conflicts include eco-

---

1. R. J. Rummel, *Never Again: Ending War, Democide, & Famine through Democratic Freedom* (Coral Springs, FL: Llumina Press, 2005).

2. Thomas G. Weiss, *Humanitarian Intervention: Ideas in Action* (Malden, MA: Polity, 2007), 78. Weiss identifies three types of nonstate actors as (1) armed groups fighting the state for whatever grievances; (2) groups that use violence for economic gains; and (3) "spoilers," who are a result of a hybrid of both military and economic motivators to violence. This last category

nomic and political marginalization of certain sectors of the country, social-ethnic discrimination, political persecutions of certain groups, autocratic rule, the imposition of presidency on the people, and more.

There are other bubbling conflicts that are transnational in nature, such as the separatist rebels in the Cassamance region in Senegal, the Islamic jihadists in northern Mali, Al Shabaab in Somalia, and Boko Haram in Nigeria. These last three have been able to recruit their militia from across countries and continents. Some of these groups have used terrorist tactics, often targeting unarmed civilians. Other than the war in the DRC, which has involved different nations, the rest of the conflicts have mainly been internal.

There have been discussions in Africa on the application of humanitarian military intervention as a means of protecting civilians against the tyranny of the state. A number of cases in Africa have attracted external intervention. These include Mali, Libya, Sierra Leone, DRC, and Sudan. Since the 1994 genocide in Rwanda, in which more than 800,000 people were killed, there has been an increased awareness of the need to intervene rapidly in situations that threaten the lives of civilians. The African Union has thus endeavored to establish standby forces that can swiftly respond to such situations.

I will highlight here three African conflicts for analysis in the light of the JWT. These also represent three categories of conflicts in Africa: internal wars between government and militia groups, internal conflicts that degenerate into external wars that attract other nations into the conflict, and state conflicts that necessitate external humanitarian military intervention.

Internal Wars between Government and Militias

The first category includes the conflicts in Sudan and South Sudan, which are representative of most civil conflicts in Africa in the sense that they are characterized by political marginalization, military aggression against civilians by both government and militia forces, and the use of nonconventional war tactics against the opponent. African conflicts falling under this category include the northern Uganda conflict between the government and the Lord's Resistance Army (LRA) and conflicts experienced in Sierra Leone, Côte d'Ivoire, Liberia, and, recently, Mali, among others.

The conflict in South Sudan, the world's newest nation, is one of the most recent conflicts in Africa. The conflict broke out in February 2013 between two government military factions, one led by President Salvar Kiir and another by Riek Machar, the former vice president. This conflict has led to

---

includes mercenaries, private military companies, etc. The spoilers use violence to deliberately undermine peace processes or cause post-accord achievements to fail.

more than 100,000 deaths and 2 million people displaced. The peace agreement signed on August 26, 2015, may fail to bring peace to the young nation because of the potential pitfalls in the agreement likely to exacerbate the conflict. The current peace negotiations taking place in Addis Ababa, Ethiopia, have not borne any fruit. It is important to note that, before the secession of South Sudan from Sudan in 2011, there had been internal conflict for more than twenty-two years between the government of Sudan and the Sudan People's Liberation Army. The initiatives by various regional bodies and governments finally led to a Comprehensive Peace Agreement (CPA) in January 2005. The Intergovernmental Authority on Development (IGAD), in collaboration with governments from African, Europe, and the United States, was able to convince the two parties to end the conflict.

Sudan has also known other internal conflicts. For example, in the Darfur region, conflict has been going on since 2003 between the Sudanese government and the non-Arab Sudan Liberation Movement/Army (SLM/A) and Justice and Equality Movement (JEM). The rebel groups claim that the government of Sudan has been marginalizing the non-Arab population in Darfur. The government has reacted with aggressive military offensives and ethnic-cleansing activities that have caused thousands of deaths. This led to the indictment of President Omar al-Bashir for genocide and crimes against humanity by the International Criminal Court (ICC).

In the oil-rich Abyei region there has been conflict between Sudanese military forces and the Sudan Revolutionary Front (SRF), which is mainly supported by the Sudan People's Liberation Movement-North (SPLM-N), an affiliate of the Sudan People's Liberation Movement/Army in South Sudan. The struggle for the control of the oil resources has led to the protracted nature of the conflict.

Internal Wars with External Interventions

The second category includes the DRC conflict, which is one of the most complex conflicts in Africa, and the only one that joined seven African countries in one conflict. The DRC conflict has also been the epicenter of what is commonly referred to as the "Great Lakes conflict," affecting Rwanda, Uganda, Tanzania, Kenya, and Burundi. The conflict erupted in 1996 when the political tensions in the eastern part of the country led to the expulsion of the Banyamulenge to Rwanda. (The Banyamulenge are Congolese citizens of Rwandan origin, going back to the seventeenth century.) At the time, eastern Congo had more than 1 million refugees following the genocide in Rwanda in 1994. The refugee camps were largely controlled by military from the former Rwandan government. This situation was seen as a security threat by Rwanda, and in 1996 both Rwanda and Uganda led a military attack against Mobutu Sese Seko's government, replacing him with Laurent Kabila. However, there was later a falling out between Kabila and his backers (Rwanda and Uganda) when he allowed the Hutu militias in eastern DRC to arm themselves. This led to yet another attack by Rwanda and Uganda on the DRC in 1998. However, Angola, Namibia, and Zimbabwe came to the rescue of the DRC, leading to what is commonly referred to as the first Great African War. The war went on for five years, between 1998 and 2003. In between, Kabila was assassinated in 2001 and his son Joseph Kabila took over as president. Joseph managed to negotiate a peace agreement that led to the withdrawal of both Ugandan and Rwandan forces from the DRC. However, militia groups multiplied, and the internal wars have continued over the years, particularly in eastern parts of the country, causing close to 6 million deaths.[3] The United Nations deployed the largest peacekeeping contingent in the world to prevent further conflicts and maintain peace. Despite these efforts, there has been limited progress in pacifying the affected regions in the country.

Sectarian Conflicts

The third representative category includes the sectarian conflicts that have been experienced in Rwanda, leading to genocide and indiscriminate killings. Countries that have experienced sectarian conflicts include Libya, Mali, Côte d'Ivoire, Kenya, South Africa, and Liberia, among others. However, in recent years, Rwanda and Libya stood out as clear cases requiring humanitarian military intervention. The conflict between Hutu, who form the majority 84 percent, and Tutsi, who are 15 percent of Rwanda's population of 7 million, began right before independence in 1959 and culminated in sporadic attacks and counterattacks between the two groups, political and economic marginalization, and violation of human rights against the citizens. The colonial Belgian government favored the Tutsi elite to rule over the majority Hutu. As a result, in 1959 the Hutu conducted genocide against the Tutsi, and more than 20,000 people were killed. This propelled what was later known as the "Hutu Peasant Revolution," or "social revolution," lasting from 1959 to 1961. By the time of independence in 1962, more than 100,000 people, mainly Tutsi, had fled the country and become refugees in neighboring countries. The Hutu dominated the government. There

---

3. Godfrey Mwakikagile, *Post-Colonial Africa: A General Survey* (Dar es Salaam, Tanzania: New Africa Press, 2014).

were further intermittent and retaliatory attacks between the two groups, leading to further deaths and displacement of persons.

In 1988, the Tutsi formed a militia and political group known as the Rwanda Patriotic Front (RPF), composed mainly of about six thousand refugees living in neighboring countries, particularly Uganda. The main agenda of the RPF was to secure the safe return of the thousands of Tutsi living as refugees as well as to bring an end to the marginalization of the Tutsi. The Arusha peace accord between the RPF and Rwandan government and the establishment of the United Nations Assistance Mission for Rwanda (UNAMIR) increased the hope for peace, but tensions continued. The death of President Juvenal Habyarimana of Rwanda in a plane crash in April 1994 led to the climax of the protracted Rwanda conflict. The Hutu-led government orchestrated genocide against the minority Tutsi, leading to the death of more than 800,000 persons, mostly Tutsi and moderate Hutu. With the help of the Ugandan military, the RPF managed to end the genocide in 1994 and took over the government.

The Application of the Just War Tradition

Looking at the above conflicts, how would one apply the JWT? Obviously the conflicts are different and have diverse backgrounds. The JWT restricts the use of force, and only permits it as a last resort. Under International Humanitarian Law (IHL), the United Nations Charter permits the use of force only under Chapter 7. Article 39 of the charter limits the use of force to humanitarian intervention, authorized by the Security Council. Further, Article 51 allows for individual or collective self-defense: "Nothing in the present Charter shall impair the inherent right of individual or collective self-defense if an armed attack occurs against a Member of the United Nations, until the Security Council has taken measures necessary to maintain international peace and security." However, the charter is particularly focused on nation-states and not individuals or groups.

To what extent, then, is the use of force justified to settle grievances and disputes; end political, ethnic, and economic marginalization; and prevent genocide? This is an important question with reference to the civil conflicts in Africa. For example, in Sudan and South Sudan the conflicts seemed to have emerged sporadically, and as such there was no clear period during which to explore the *jus ad bellum* principles. The justification for the war was based on the immoral acts meted out by one party against the other. In the case of Darfur, both the SLM/A and JEM held the position that the non-Arab Africans had been socially and economically marginalized.

In addition, the Sudanese government sponsored a militia group known as Janjaweed to conduct a proxy war. This complicates any analysis of the application of the JWT. Should the moral evaluation be limited to the conduct of Janjaweed or that of the Sudanese government? Does the Sudanese government have the legitimate authority to declare war or has this authority been subcontracted to the rebel group? The principles of the JWT do not envision proxy wars. In such situations, the moral evaluation ought to be directed to the sponsoring government. Thus, the Sudanese government ought to take full responsibility for the actions of the Janjaweed. However, one of the major challenges would be to establish the fact that the rebel group is a proxy entity of a government. For example, for a long time the M23 rebel group in eastern DRC has been accused of being a proxy militia group for both Rwanda and Uganda. However, both countries have denied these allegations, which makes it difficult to hold them morally responsible for acts of crime against humanity conducted by the M23. The conflict between North Sudan and South Sudan for many years was based on the plea for social, economic, and political recognition by the northern Sudanese government. In the postindependence era, the conflict in South Sudan has taken on ethnic characteristics, particularly between the Dinka, President Salvar Kiir's ethnic group, and the Nuer, the former vice president's ethnic group. These two ethnic groups are the largest in the country and the most dominant in the army.

How would one evaluate whether the intention for going to war was right? In the case of Sudan, would the intention of SLM/A and JEM in Darfur be mainly to correct the existing wrongs by protesting militarily or fighting for secession so that they can manage their own affairs independently? Studies conducted and shared by Frances Stewart[4] have shown that horizontal inequalities and discrimination against groups—whether ethnic, social, religious, or political—can in many cases lead to conflict. For example, when the shared common good of the nation is wrongly distributed, there could be grievances leading to conflict.[5] This was evident in the case of Rwanda, where the colonial Belgian government favored the Tutsi against the Hutu, and later the Hutu government marginalized the Tutsi population. Similarly, in the case of Darfur, there was a just cause for war, yet in the JWT, a just cause is in itself not a good enough reason to justify war. All other means have to be exhausted first.

---

4. Frances Stewart, ed., *Horizontal Inequalities and Conflict: Understanding Group Violence in Multiethnic Societies* (Basingstoke, UK: Palgrave Macmillan, 2010).

5. James K. Boyce, *The Political Economy of the Environment* (Cheltenham, UK: E. Elgar Publishing, 2002).

In the DRC there have been many nonstate actors fighting with the government and among themselves. Rwanda and Uganda have both been accused of fighting proxy wars in Congo by sponsoring specific rebel groups. The Congo war has also been motivated by the looting of natural resources for sale on the black as well as the official market. The intention of the belligerents in that conflict ought to be evaluated according to the "greed and grievance" framework. Collier and Hoeffler,[6] in their study of 79 different conflicts between 1960 and 1999, concluded that the reasons behind the conflict could be greed and grievance, and less on the motivations that drive the insurgencies. In other words, it is important to identify the conflict triggers. Once there is clarity on key triggers, then peace negotiations or any form of military intervention can be morally evaluated. It is important to take into account the fact that the conflict triggers are often propelled by the latent or obvious grievances within a framework of unmet expectations.

In addition, the JWT puts emphasis on the legitimate authority that should authorize war. International law recognizes only the government as a legal entity. This means that in the case of civil conflicts, nonstate actors such as militia or rebel groups would not be recognized. In such a case, the evaluation of the legality of the authority behind the conflict should be based on a different moral discourse. The equation becomes even more complex when the former rebel group takes over power from the incumbent government. Such situations have been seen in Rwanda, the DRC, Angola, Sierra Leone, and Uganda, among others. The legitimacy of the authority of the former militia group could be questioned under international law. However, if the circumstances were such that the social, economic, and political grievances had reached a justifiable level for a military solution, then I would suggest that the militia group would have a morally justifiable cause. The moral evaluation should thus be based on the gravity of the matter of dispute, the extent of human suffering involved, and the urgency of the curtailment of the threat to human life and property. However, there ought to be evidence that there were clear attempts by both parties to resolve the conflict amicably. The use of military force should come as a last resort.

The determination of the point at which one could conclude that all other means have been exhausted and that a war has to be fought as a last resort can be a difficult task, even in conventional wars. The recourse to war is often marred by political and economic interests both within and outside the affected state. The conflict in both Sudan and South Sudan was closely

---

6. Paul Collier and Anke Hoeffler, "Greed and Grievance in Civil War," *Oxford Economic Papers* 56 (2004): 563-95.

monitored by the neighboring countries under the IGAD. These countries intervened to bring an end to the conflict. Similarly, there were attempts at peace negotiation in Rwanda, Somalia, the DRC, Burundi, and Côte d'Ivoire, among others. Peace negotiations are important because they can be gatekeepers to war or to peace and stability. However, peace negotiations do not necessarily guarantee peace. In Africa, a number of countries have experienced war in the postaccord period, particularly when the major grievances have not been addressed and the road map to peace and stability was not well designed.

The militarization of peace and conflict has unfortunately become the norm for peacebuilding. Conflicts within the African continent have been heavily militarized. The largest and most protracted conflict in the DRC has been sustained in large part by the proliferation of and easy access to small arms. The UN has taken a military option through peacekeeping troops that have been unable to quell the conflict despite their large presence on the ground. The UN Assistance Mission for Rwanda (UNAMIR) could have prevented the war from escalating, but they had very limited military presence on the ground. In the DRC, the 1996 invasion by Rwanda and Uganda was definitely against just war principles, particularly the consideration of war as a last resort, lack of a legitimate international authority that should have authorized the war as justifiable, and observance of noncombatant immunity (given the large number of people who died during the invasion). There were no direct negotiations between the then Zaire government under Mobutu Sese Seko and the Rwanda/Uganda block. The purpose of the war seemed to have been the dismantling of the military activities along the border between Rwanda and the DRC. However, this aim was further extended to the removal of President Mobutu. Within the framework of international law, both Rwanda and Uganda had violated the sovereignty of the Congolese government. In addition, Congo had not been militarily aggressive against either of the countries.

What then could be the alternative to the militarization of peace and conflict? Joseph S. Nye advocates for the complementary use of *soft power* (moral influence) as opposed to *hard power* (military coercion).[7] He observes that "soft power" is based on "the ability to shape the preferences of others."[8] In political terms, this would mean presenting "attractive" values such as human rights, peacebuilding, and democracy, which have the

---

7. J. S. Nye, "The Place of Soft Power in State-Based Conflict Management," in *Leashing the Dogs of War: Conflict Management in a Divided World*, ed. C. A. Crocker, F. O. Hampson, and P. R. Aall (Washington, DC: United States Institute of Peace Press, 2007).

8. Ibid., 291.

potential to change the society.[9] Nye acknowledges the limitations of soft power but fails to acknowledge the hegemonic assumptions that a society would be attracted to externally proposed values. Besides, public perceptions of soft and hard power are not as distinct as he claims. The complexities of the African conflicts further imply that the application of soft power will have to be complemented by peace negotiations, regional interventions, and effective sanctions. There is therefore need for reconceptualization of a better framework that would reevaluate the crucial link between a just cause, right intention, and last resort. However, in situations of gross violation of human rights, an international humanitarian military intervention could be justified under the framework of international law.

Humanitarian Military Intervention

Global criticisms of inaction by the international community to end the genocide in Rwanda, mass killings in the DRC and Darfur, and internal conflicts in South Sudan have shifted the debate from the evaluation of moral and legitimate justifications for military intervention to debates on whether interventions should be carried out in extreme cases of human rights violations. Thus, in recent years, there have been discussions on the moral authority of the state, its responsibility to its citizens, and the integrity of its leadership as a sovereign nation. If the state fails to protect its own citizens and instead becomes a predator upon civilians, then the civilians have the moral right to defend themselves while waiting for international diplomatic and military assistance to end the conflict. In situations where such resistance cannot be conducted internally, then it would be justifiable for the international community and regional bodies to intervene to save human lives.

Sovereignty has been closely tied to responsibility to govern the state in such a manner that civilians feel safe and experience the provision of basic needs such as security, food, housing, medical care, infrastructure, and other social amenities. Whenever a population is threatened by a state through the gross violation of human rights, then it is the responsibility of the international community to prevent further loss of lives and property. The increased incidence of civil conflicts in the world has meant that "conflict prevention, humanitarian interventions and post conflict peacebuilding" have become part of an international policy of global management in the

---

9. Ibid., 391-93.

post–Cold War period.[10] Kofi Annan, the former UN secretary-general, asserted that "the internal violation of human rights within a nation warrants humanitarian intervention by the United Nations."[11] The 2004 doctrine of the responsibility to protect (R2P), put forward by the International Commission of Intervention and State Sovereignty (ICISS), placed the moral obligation on states to stop gross violations of human rights. Since then there have been initiatives to articulate the moral imperative to bring accountability to state sovereignty. For example, Kofi Annan, as the UN secretary-general, produced a report entitled *In Larger Freedom: Towards Development, Security and Human Rights for All.*[12] Likewise, a UN high-level panel[13] issued a report entitled "Threats, Challenges and Change, A More Secure World: Our Shared Responsibility." Both of these reports call the world's attention to the changing nature of the conflicts, from interstate to intrastate. The former report proposes the formation of a "peacebuilding commission" to address the gap in the UN response to interstate wars. This discourse has led to the reimagination of humanitarian intervention as a moral responsibility.

The legality of humanitarian intervention is limited by the principle of nonintervention. This principle operates under a logical imperative of international law that upholds the sovereignty of states. The question of intervention challenges a "vestigial uneasiness about crossing the sovereignty line,"[14] and yet, inaction in clear cases of human rights violations is inexcusable. Hence, military intervention today is characterized by a conflict of values that often falls between two opposing poles: the state's sovereignty and its responsibility for the suffering citizens, on one end, and the world community's concern for the suffering masses, on the other. Stanley Hoffman argues that the *empirical revolution* of interdependence and globalization that subjects states to the global order, on the one hand, and the *normative revolution* that puts checks on sovereignty and restricts a state's right to independent internal operation, on the other, have brought accountability

---

10. Neclâ Tschirgi, *Post-conflict Peacebuilding Revisited: Achievements, Limitations, Challenges* (New York: International Peace Academy, 2004), 4.

11. Kofi Annan, "The Two Concepts of Sovereignty," *The Economist,* September 18, 1999.

12. Kofi Annan, *In Larger Freedom: Towards Development, Security and Human Rights for All (A/59/2005)* (New York: United Nations, 2005).

13. African Union Protocol (2004), Protocol Relating to the Establishment of the Peace and Security Council of the African Union, www.africa-union.org.

14. Chester A. Crocker, "Intervention: Toward Best Practices and a Holistic View," in *Turbulent Peace: The Challenges of Managing International Conflict,* ed. A. Crocker et al. (Lansing, MI: United States Institute of Peace Press, 2001), 231.

to sovereignty.[15] Thus, the acknowledged moral good of sovereignty must yield to superior imperatives of global peace.

J. Bryan Hehir reiterates that from the normative perspective we can identify two characteristics of intervention.[16] First, the ethic of the use of force has had as its major concern the conduct of states in relation to other states. Thus, this turns out to be the ethic of war and not of intervention. This would probably be the case with the situation in the DRC, where Rwanda and Uganda justified their attack on the DRC in 1997 based on the fact that the latter was harboring rebels who were a danger to the former states' stability. Such an intervention, whether justified or not, is an act of war and not necessarily a humanitarian intervention. Second, Hehir observes that within the framework of the existing policy debate on military intervention, neither the moral nor the legal tradition's view of intervention has the full capacity to change dominant political trends. In most cases, politics tends to dominate over moral influence.

In the post–September 11 era, moral justifications for intervention have been hamstrung by unilateral military interventions based on national interest. Prior to 9/11, in the case of Rwanda, the UN and the United States failed to stop the genocide, despite the fact that they had information about the planned genocide and had the military resources to intervene. However, because of the political interests and the fear of yet another failure similar to the US military defeat in Somalia in 1992, the world watched while Rwanda was burning. However, in the case of Libya, President Muammar Gaddafi was in 2011 accused of sectarian violence, and the UN Security Council hastily passed a resolution to intervene militarily under the principle of responsibility to protect. Through a combined military action, the UN-led military force managed to remove Gaddafi from power. However, the situation in Libya has remained unstable with increased violence. Similarly, the military intervention in Iraq has failed to bring about a sustainable peace.

The cases of Libya and Iraq have demonstrated that interventions have in some cases ignored the local dynamics of conflict and the risk factors involved in militarized operations. The re-creation of a state is a long-term process that cannot be achieved simply through militarized peacebuilding. Taking into account the historical, cultural, ethnic, religious, and social aspects of conflict is vital for the transition to peace and stability.

---

15. Stanley Hoffman, "The Politics and Ethics of Military Intervention," *Survival* 37, no. 4 (Winter 1995–1996): 29-51.

16. Bryan Hehir, "Military Intervention and National Sovereignty: Recasting the Relationship," in *Hard Choices: Moral Dilemmas in Humanitarian Intervention*, ed. J. Moore (Lanham, MD: Rowman & Littlefield, 1998), 29-52.

As an attempt to limit hegemonic initiatives that do not reflect the comprehension of contextual complexities, security has been organized at regional levels. This process attempts to devolve the responsibility for global peace to regional bodies that are much closer to the issues at stake. Chapter VIII of the UN Charter allows regional bodies to monitor and resolve conflicts peacefully. Michael C. Pugh asserts that the regionalization of security is based on "'partnership' involving respect for the UN Charter but allowing variable geometry in a range of peace operations and conflict resolution activities."[17] Pugh further adds that the UN is the peacebuilding coordinator because of its political status, but lacks the field presence that regional bodies have.

An example of a regional security initiative is the African Union (AU) Peace and Security Council (PSC), founded in March 2004. The council, consisting of fifteen member states of the African Union, is tasked with effecting a collective security for the AU members while instituting early-warning mechanisms aimed at ensuring rapid response to conflict situations in Africa. The PSC is also supported by the Commission of the AU through the Chairperson and the Commissioner for Peace and Security and the Directorate for Peace and Security—a five-member Panel of the Wise consisting of recognized and respected African personalities who are selected with a three-year term limit on the basis of regional representation. Their task is to mediate African conflicts as well as to act as a conflict-prevention team: the Continental Early Warning System (CEWS) monitors conflict and issues early warnings as a prevention mechanism; an African Standby Force (ASF) and Special Fund, collectively referred to as the African Peace and Security Architecture (APSA) is composed of five regional brigades with the objective of intervening in regional conflicts.[18]

According to the 2010 Strategic Survey,[19] the AU made concerted diplomatic efforts to intervene against "coup leaders in Guinea, Guinea-Bissau, Niger, Madagascar and Mauritania. Unexpected rapprochements between Rwanda and the Democratic Republic of the Congo (DRC) and between Chad and Sudan also improved intra-regional dynamics in the Great Lakes and Horn of Africa regions."

---

17. M. Pugh, "The World Order Politics of Regionalization," in *The United Nations and Regional Security: Europe and Beyond*, ed. M. Pugh and W. P. S. Sidhu (London: Lynne Rienner Publishers, 2003), 37.

18. African Union Protocol (2004).

19. International Institute of Strategic Studies, "Africa," Strategic Survey, *The Annual Review of World Affairs* 110, no. 1 (2010): 259-94.

The PSC is still in its infancy and presents a great opportunity for the continent to manage its own conflict. The commitment of the PSC to adhere to the principles of R2P should put more emphasis on institutional reforms of the structures of governance of the member countries as a means of conflict management and prevention. Along the same lines as the PSC, the R2P has three main responsibilities: to prevent conflicts, to react to conflict situations, and to reconstruct countries coming out of conflict. A good number of civil conflicts in Africa are low intensity, perennial or seasonal, with high aggregate numbers of civilian casualties. Given the low intensity characteristic of these conflicts, they often do not attract an immediate intervention from either the PSC or the UN Security Council, despite their cumulatively grievous nature. Such grievances include, among others, periodic constitutional manipulations to favor those in power, disregard for postconflict reconstruction priorities, and triggering perennial ethnic and religious conflicts. These situations often reflect weakness in institutions of governance marked by the concentration of power in the hands of a few, limited democratic participation of citizens, and inequitable distribution of national and natural resources. On the other hand, the historical evidence of military intervention indicates that there are limited success stories to demonstrate their effectiveness.

Whichever way states seek to achieve and enforce human rights, it is important to take into account a wider perspective based on "central issues of context, timing, sequencing, the link between force and diplomacy, and deciding what works where."[20] A broader approach curtails interventionism and unilateralism.

Conclusion

The application of the JWT principles to African conflicts remains relevant but ought to be done within a much broader framework that takes into account the complexities of the intrastate wars. A moral evaluation is largely limited by the lack of clarity on the factors leading to war, the external actors that give financial and political support to either the government or the rebels, the question of the legitimacy of the rebel groups fighting against a government or a rebel group that takes over a government, and the lack of infrastructure for peace intervention. Gradually, the AU has made efforts to lay down structures that can analyze conflicts at early stages and put into place

---

20. Crocker, "Intervention," 229.

mechanisms to prevent them from happening. However, the structures are yet to be effective on the ground because of financial, personnel, and logistical challenges.

In situations of extreme violation of human rights, it is morally permissible to intervene in order to stop human suffering. Such has been the case in Rwanda, Libya, Sierra Leone, and Mali, among others. However, while human rights violations could be a just cause for humanitarian military intervention, it would be important to apply military force only as a last resort. The gravity of the violations ought to be thoroughly examined whenever possible. Other means of intervention should be considered, such as negotiations and sanctions. Peacemaking could be applied by creating a buffer zone that would stop the escalation of violence. For example, while the situation in Zimbabwe has deteriorated because of poor governance, civil rights suppression, and economic crisis, it does not warrant immediate military intervention. It would be important to attempt other means such as diplomatic interventions and persuasion, economic and political sanctions targeting the political elite, etc. Humanitarian military intervention should therefore be undertaken as a last resort, with reasonable hope of success. In other words, it is vital to weigh the cost of military intervention against the values being defended. Thus, the reasons for an intervention would be put to the test by examining the means used and the hope for success, which should go beyond simply stopping the violence to ensuring a sustainable peace.

CHAPTER 11

Civilian Vulnerability in Contemporary War: Lessons from the War in the Democratic Republic of the Congo

JOHN KIESS

Nearly half a century ago, Paul Ramsey observed, "'Modern war' is not nuclear war. Instead the possibility of nuclear war has made the world safe for wars of insurgency.... This will remain the military situation for decades to come."[1] How right he was. The vast majority of armed conflicts since Ramsey's time have been internal armed conflicts. Going back to 1946, nearly three-quarters of all armed conflicts have been internal wars.[2] Of the 128 conflicts that took place between 1989 and 2009, only eight were interstate wars.[3] While the total number of wars has decreased significantly since the early 1990s, the percentage of internal wars has remained high; in 2013, all 36 registered conflicts were fought within states.[4] As Ramsey well understood, the burden of these wars is borne disproportionately by civilians. Whereas the civilian toll for World War I was only about 10 percent, it has been as high as 90 percent in some recent civil wars.[5]

For Ramsey, the key moral dilemma of civil war and internationalized-internal armed conflict was how to defeat insurgencies without directly

---

1. Paul Ramsey, *The Just War: Force and Political Responsibility* (Lanham, MD: Rowman & Littlefield, 1968), 427-28.

2. Lotta Harbom and Peter Wallensteen, "Armed Conflicts 1946–2009," *Journal of Peace Research* 47, no. 4 (July 2010): 501-9. See also Nils Petter Gleditsch et al., "Armed Conflict 1946–2001: A New Dataset," *Journal of Peace Research* 39, no. 5 (September 2002): 615-37.

3. Lotta Harbom and Peter Wallensteen, "Armed Conflicts, 1946–2008," *Journal of Peace Research* 46, no. 4 (July 2009): 578.

4. Lotta Themnér and Peter Wallensteen, "Armed Conflicts, 1946–2013," *Journal of Peace Research* 51, no. 4 (July 2014): 542. Nine of these conflicts were internationalized (meaning an external state supports one or two parties to the conflict).

5. P. W. Singer, *Children at War* (Berkeley: University of California Press, 2006), 4.

intending the death of civilian lives already endangered by insurgent tactics. The urgent moral question was, in his words, "How is it possible, if indeed it is possible, to mount a morally acceptable counter-insurgency operation?"[6] Writing more recently, and with the advantage of hindsight that Ramsey did not enjoy, Oliver O'Donovan points out that there is a second, no less important question at stake in insurgency warfare and internal armed conflict more broadly. This concerns the actions of insurgents themselves: "Can the conduct of counter-insurgency be conducted in such a way as to persuade insurgents to abide by the principle of discrimination?"[7] O'Donovan's willingness to ask this question reflects a significant shift in moral and legal thought that has occurred since Ramsey's day, as ethicists and international lawyers, chastened by the brutality of the civil wars of the early 1990s, have found themselves more willing to extend the rights and duties of war to non-state actors in the hopes of restraining violence against civilians. With the development of legal instruments such as the ad-hoc tribunals for the conflicts in Rwanda and ex-Yugoslavia and the recently launched International Criminal Court, there are now institutional structures for enforcing humanitarian law across the board. O'Donovan argues that the moral compromise of providing nonstate combatants with such privileges as POW status in exchange for more discriminate conduct is more than worth it in terms of civilian lives saved.

Common to both Ramsey's and O'Donovan's approach to the moral challenges of internal armed conflict is a focus on the vulnerability of civilians to direct or indirect military attack. The relevant moral actors in both accounts are combatants, and the morally urgent task is getting these actors to fight discriminately. Recent analysis of armed conflict suggests that this focus on military conduct, while rightly addressing the problem of indiscriminate violence, may focus the relevant moral questions too narrowly to the field of battle. As Gerald Schlabach and John Paul Lederach remind us, battle-related civilian deaths in many civil wars actually represent a small percentage of total war deaths, in some cases as little as 10 percent.[8] Most

---

6. Ramsey, *The Just War*, 428.

7. Oliver O'Donovan, *The Just War Revisited* (Cambridge: Cambridge University Press, 2003), 64.

8. Gerald W. Schlabach, ed., *Just Policing, Not War: An Alternative Response to World Violence* (Collegeville, MN: Liturgical Press, 2007). See Lederach's essay, "The Doables: Just Policing on the Ground," in Schlabach, *Just Policing*, 175-91. For more on the ways that the indirect costs of war challenge conventional just war theory, see Todd D. Whitmore, "Peacebuilding and Its Challenging Partners: Justice, Human Rights, Development, and Solidary," in Robert J. Schreiter, R. Scott Appleby, and Gerard F. Powers, eds., *Peacebuilding: Catholic Theology, Ethics, and Praxis* (Maryknoll, NY: Orbis Books, 2010), 155-89.

civilians in civil wars in fact die from indirect effects, such as malnutrition, starvation, and disease. These may be the result of violence and displacement, but they are also related to broader, conflict-related dynamics: the abandonment of subsistence farming, the rush to boom-and-bust industries controlled by rebel actors, and the weakening of the state and the consequent loss or diversion of public revenue that would otherwise fund health care, schools, and other social services. While these considerations by no means take away from the importance of stressing discriminate military conduct (in fact, more restraint would go a long way toward mitigating these indirect costs), they point to another, largely overlooked interface of civilian vulnerability. As the Human Security Centre suggests, "attempting to assess the impact of war by counting only those who die as a direct result of violence grossly underestimates the real human costs of conflict—particularly in poor countries."[9]

Nowhere has the indirect effect of war been more deadly than the Democratic Republic of the Congo (DRC), where the International Rescue Committee (IRC) estimates that nearly 5 million people have died from a series of wars that began in 1998 and continue in some parts of the country today.[10] During the first three years of the conflict, the IRC recorded 2.5 million total war deaths, but only 145,000 (or 6 percent) were battle related.[11] The proportion has remained steady in subsequent years.[12] Public infrastructure was already devastated through two decades of state collapse under the longtime dictator Mobutu; the situation only worsened as the war expanded to include several African states, numerous regional rebel movements, and countless local defense forces. While neighboring states have since departed, numerous insurgencies have continued to destabilize the eastern part of the country for much of the past decade. Compounding the problem in the DRC has been the widely reported illegal exploitation of natural resources, which has provided an independent funding stream for many of the armed groups that remain active. When combined with the destruction of infrastructure, mass displacement, and the continuing deprivation of any state services, the crisis has had a devastating impact on livelihood. But it has not

---

9. Human Security Centre, *Human Security Report 2005: War and Peace in the 21st Century* (New York: Oxford University Press, 2006), 134.

10. Benjamin Coghlan et al., "Mortality in the Democratic Republic of Congo: A Nationwide Survey," *The Lancet* 367 (January 7, 2006): 44-51.

11. Bethany Lacina and Nils Petter Gleditsch, "Monitoring Trends in Global Combat: A New Dataset of Battle Deaths" (Oslo: Centre for the Study of Civil War, 2004).

12. International Rescue Committee, *Mortality in the Democratic Republic of Congo: An Ongoing Crisis* (2008), http://www.rescue.org.

simply destroyed livelihoods. It has transformed them, introducing new economic imperatives and opening different opportunities for entry into regional and global markets.

In an age when civilian vulnerability in war is more than a matter of indiscriminate military conduct, the question of how to protect the innocent now demands a much broader approach, one that takes into account the indirect costs of war and their multiple sources. To adapt the language of Ramsey and O'Donovan, we might formulate a further moral question this way: "How is it possible to address the indirect costs of war without endangering the lives of those such strategies are meant to protect?" This, as the case of the DRC shows, is no small challenge, where the attempt to address the specific impact of the war economy upon civilians has had several unintended consequences. In what follows, I use the issue of illegal resource exploitation as a way to focus both the perils and possibilities of addressing the indirect costs of war today. I begin by providing a broad overview of the conflict economy and its impact on civilian livelihood. I then review recent strategies that have been developed to address it, including the controversial 2010 Dodd-Frank Act, which required corporations to disclose the origin of their minerals and certify whether they were conflict free, inadvertently prompting a crisis in the mining sector and causing several companies to leave the country. I consider the lessons that this approach offers and reflect on ways that such strategies can be improved to meet the broader range of challenges that drive conflict and endanger civilians. Such lessons will no doubt be crucial in addressing these challenges in the future, where more wars are likely to resemble the one in the DRC, with similarly grave risks for civilians.

The Conflict Economy and Its Impact on Civilians

The crisis in the DRC is familiar to most Western observers through the much-publicized role that illegal resource exploitation has played in exacerbating conflict in the region. Instead of "blood diamonds," attention in the DRC has focused upon "blood tantalum," a conductor used in cell phones and other electronics equipment.[13] Colin Kinniburgh reports that at one point earlier in this century, "the DRC was supplying some 20 to 30 per-

---

13. For more on resource exploitation in the DRC, see David Renton, David Seddon, and Leo Zelig, *The Congo: Plunder and Resistance* (New York: Zed Books, 2007); Global Witness, "'Faced with a Gun, What Can You Do?' War and the Militarization of Mining in Eastern Congo" (July 2009), www.globalwitness.org; and Michael Nest, *Coltan* (Cambridge: Polity, 2011), 66-104.

cent of the world's tantalum."[14] Many other resources have been exploited as well, from tin to tungsten and gold. It is important to stress at the outset that while such minerals have played a significant role in sustaining a number of armed movements, they have not been the primary source of conflict in the DRC. The instability in the country has much deeper roots in divisions over citizenship, land, and identity, as well as the complicated legacy of the Rwandan genocide, whose impact still reverberates throughout the region.[15] We will return to the dangers of focusing on conflict minerals in isolation from these other issues when we discuss responses to the conflict economy below.

Reports of illegal resource exploitation surfaced soon after the 1998 war began. The UN dispatched a team of investigators that uncovered systematic exploitation not only by Rwanda and Uganda, the two main state parties fighting against the Congolese government, but also rebel movements and local defense forces known as "Mai Mai."[16] In the beginning of the war, all sides generated revenue by looting existing stocks of cassiterite, diamonds, coltan, and timber. When these stocks were exhausted, actors began to engage in direct exploitation and trade. The Rwandan government, in partnership with its proxy rebel group, the Rally for Congolese Democracy (RCD), set up several companies that controlled the trade of minerals in the occupied region of North and South Kivu. These resources were extracted, shipped to Rwanda, and then exported to the global market. Uganda's involvement was less systematic, as individual officers of the Uganda People's Defense Force (UPDF) worked with a small group of businessmen in northeastern Congo to smuggle exports across the border into Uganda. Flights that carried resources in one direction often carried arms in the other. The panel reported that Rwanda's and Uganda's official exports of diamonds and coltan (resources that neither country produces) significantly increased during the war years, and went on to name some eighty companies that traded in minerals sourced in the DRC.[17]

---

14. Colin Kinniburgh, "Beyond 'Conflict Minerals': The Congo's Resource Curse Lives On," *Dissent* 61, no. 2 (Spring 2014): 64.

15. For more on the sources of conflict, see Séverine Autesserre, *The Trouble with the Congo: Local Violence and the Failure of International Peacebuilding* (Cambridge: Cambridge University Press, 2010).

16. The panel produced four reports from 1999 to 2003. For a detailed account of resource exploitation during the war, see United Nations Security Council, *Report of the Panel of Experts on the Illegal Exploitation of Natural Resources and Other Forms of Wealth of the Democratic Republic of Congo* (S/2001/357).

17. UN Security Council, *Final Report of the Panel of Experts* (S/2002/1146), Annex III, 7-10.

When the war began to wind down in 2002 and Rwanda and Uganda eventually withdrew, many armed groups remained active in the east and continued to exploit resources. In the Ituri province, Hema and Lendu groups jostled for control of gold mines in a conflict that killed over 60,000 people and displaced hundreds of thousands.[18] The longest residing rebel group in the DRC, the Democratic Forces for the Liberation of Rwanda (FDLR), exercised a veritable fiefdom over gold and cassiterite mines in North and South Kivu during the course of its ongoing struggle against government forces. In 2007-2008, Laurent Nkunda's National Congress for the Defense of the People (CNDP) oversaw a lucrative tax system on mining activities at checkpoints and border crossings throughout its territory.[19] In addition to the larger rebel movements, local Mai Mai groups have controlled numerous mining sites as well. To cite one recent example, the Raia Mutomboki group presently controls over 20 mines in the territory of Kimbli, charging diggers a fee to access the mines and taking a percentage of their yield.[20] Resource exploitation, however, has not been limited to nonstate groups. For years, soldiers in the Armed Forces of the Democratic Republic of the Congo (FARDC) have illegally participated in the mining industry as well, taxing miners, siphoning off minerals, and smuggling them across borders, sometimes working in collaboration with rebel groups themselves.[21]

How has the conflict economy impacted civilians? We can assess this impact at multiple levels. The most direct impact of this activity is the violence that it sustains against civilians, from systematic attacks, theft, and abduction to the widely reported use of rape against women. The impact of these revenue streams can be felt in every destroyed home, burnt-out building, and impassible road, in the hundreds of thousands of civilians who have been displaced as refugees cut off from their traditional sources of livelihood. The alarmingly high death toll in the DRC is attributable to precisely this kind of disruption, leaving civilians exposed to malnutrition and disease, among many other dangers.

Yet the exploitation of resources has had just as profound an impact at the level of the broader economy, transforming the mining industry and opening new, precarious livelihood options for civilians. In a study of the coltan industry during its boom years of 2000 and 2001, Stephen Jackson describes how a large sector of the population in North and South Kivu shifted from

---

18. Human Rights Watch, *The Curse of Gold* (2005), http://www.hrw.org.

19. Global Witness, "'Faced with a Gun,'" 48-49.

20. Sudarsan Raghavan, "How a Well-Intentioned U.S. Law Left Congolese Miners Jobless," *Washington Post*, November 30, 2014.

21. Global Witness, "'Faced with a Gun,'" 43-47.

rural, subsistence farming to mining, in some cases converting land formerly used for agriculture and cattle grazing into artisanal mining sites.[22] Initially, when global prices for coltan increased tenfold, many civilians benefitted, but when prices dropped precipitously in 2001, these same civilians were left exposed, no longer able to farm or to sustain their families on mining activities. Making matters worse, the price drop led armed actors to eliminate intermediaries and engage more directly in the selling and exporting of the mineral themselves, further narrowing entry points for civilians. Timothy Raeymaekers and Koen Vlassenroot describe similar dynamics in the gold mining industry in South Kivu, noting a broader shift from rural to urban modes of livelihood.[23] In the process, modest income-earning opportunities have arisen through such activities as truck and taxi transport, packaging, money changing, and smuggling. Not everyone, however, enters the conflict economy at the same level. Patience Kabamba has shown that to keep their lucrative hold on the import trade in Butembo, Nande businessmen have provided funding for local Mai Mai militias, which in turn has given them a more stable foothold in the economy relative to the more volatile position of artisanal miners.[24]

The impact of this broader shift in the economy can be felt in many ways. In addition to the abandonment of traditional modes of livelihood and urban migration, it has led to the breakup of families and tribal bonds, weakening the two strongest safety nets that civilians formerly fell back on. The growth of the shadow economy has also deprived the already weak Congolese state of the public revenue that it would have collected through concession rights and export duties. Instead of being used to repair roads, health facilities, and schools, such funds have been diverted into the private sector or out of the country altogether. Wages in mines are notoriously poor, and in some cases labor is forced. Kinniburgh notes that children account for some 40 percent of the mining population, observing, "Like the other miners, many of them are exposed to mercury, uranium, and other heavy metals; all of them lift heavy loads, breathe in toxic dust, and wade in murky water, leaving them vulnerable to a predictable assortment

---

22. Stephen Jackson, "Fortunes of War: The Coltan Trade in the Kivus," in *Power, Livelihoods and Conflict: Case Studies in Political Economy Analysis for Humanitarian Action*, ed. Sarah Collinson (Humanitarian Policy Group Report 13; London: Overseas Development Institute, 2003), 21-36.

23. Timothy Raeymaekers and Koen Vlassenroot, eds., *Conflict and Social Transformation in Eastern DR Congo* (Ghent: Academia Press, 2004).

24. Patience S. Kabamba, "Trading on War: New Forms of Life in the Debris of the State," (Ph.D. diss., Columbia University, 2008).

of health problems. Protective equipment and medical services are scarce."[25] If conditions are brutal, such opportunities represent for many the only remaining livelihood strategies left.

Responses to the Conflict Economy

The conflict in the DRC is hardly the first in which illegal resource exploitation has played a significant role.[26] The issue came to prominence in the early 1990s through the conflicts in Sierra Leone, Côte d'Ivoire, and Angola. This prompted a number of international initiatives to rein in the illegal trade of conflict diamonds, including most notably the Kimberly Process, which required participating countries to certify the source of their exports and corporations to trade in certified diamonds. A number of countries and multinational corporations also agreed to stricter Organization for Economic Cooperation and Development (OECD) guidelines, nonbinding codes of ethics aimed at increasing transparency and corporate responsibility. Neither had much of an impact in the DRC, where exploitation was not limited to diamonds, government oversight was nonexistent, and armed actors could easily smuggle resources across the border. The reports of the UN Panel of Experts from 1999 to 2003 brought important international attention to the issue and prompted several major corporations to withdraw or amend their practices. Yet illegal exploitation and trade continued.

American-based advocacy groups such as the Enough Project began lobbying the US government to take a stand and hold its own companies accountable. In 2010, the US Congress passed the Dodd-Frank Wall Street Reform and Consumer Protection Act, which included a provision (Section 1502) requiring companies trading on the stock exchange to disclose annually whether any of their minerals originated in the DRC, and, if so, to certify whether they were conflict free.[27] The president of the DRC, Joseph Kabila, followed the bill by banning mineral exports from several eastern provinces for six months. Taken together, both measures constituted the most aggressive attempts since the conflict began to bleed armed movements of their

---

25. Kinniburgh, "Beyond 'Conflict Minerals,'" 64.

26. See Karen Ballentine and Jake Sherman, eds., *The Political Economy of Armed Conflict: Beyond Greed and Grievance* (Boulder, CO: Lynne Rienner Publishers, 2003).

27. According to the Act, "DRC conflict free" means that products "do not contain minerals that directly or indirectly finance or benefit armed groups in the Democratic Republic of the Congo or an adjoining country." See Dodd-Frank Wall Street Reform and Consumer Protection Act, H.R. 4173, sec. 1502 (2010).

funding. And according to the Enough Project, rebel activity immediately decreased in three of the four mining sectors (tantalum, tungsten, and tin).[28]

Yet these early successes were overshadowed by the law's unintended and far-reaching impact on civilians.[29] The Dodd-Frank bill demanded that companies certify that their minerals were conflict free, but the Joint Assessment Teams charged with certifying minerals were only able to reach a few of the mines by the time the law came into effect. In fact, by June 2014, only 11 of 900 mines in South Kivu were producing certifiably conflict-free minerals.[30] Rather than have their brands tarnished with possible association with noncertified minerals, many corporations decided to pull out of the country altogether, leading to what critics of the bill have called a "*de facto* boycott" of the country.[31] The best-known case is that of the Malaysia Smelting Corporation (MSC), which had purchased nearly 80 percent of eastern Congolese tin prior to the bill.[32] After it withdrew its business, sales of tin from North Kivu fell 90 percent.[33] Prices of tin dropped as well, from $7 per kilogram before the bill to $4 after, even as the global price for the metal rose during the same time.[34] While the ban on mining was eventually lifted in 2011, the gates of many mines remained closed. Writing in the *New York Times*, David Aronson painted this bleak picture:

> Children are dropping out of school because parents can't pay the fees. Remote mining towns are virtually cut off from the outside world because the planes that once provisioned them no longer land. Most worrying, a crop disease periodically decimates the region's staple, cassava. Villagers who relied on their mining income to buy food when harvests failed are beginning to go hungry.[35]

---

28. David Smith, "Congo Mines No Longer in Grip of Warlords and Militias, Says Report," *The Guardian*, June 11, 2014.

29. For more on the impact of the Dodd-Frank Act, see David Aronson, "How Congress Devastated Congo," *New York Times*, August 7, 2011; Laura Seay, "What's Wrong with Dodd-Frank 1502? Conflict Minerals, Civilian Livelihoods, and the Unintended Consequences of Western Advocacy," Center for Global Development Working Paper 284 (January 5, 2012), www.cgdev.org; Sudarsan Raghavan, "How a Well-Intentioned U.S. Law Left Congolese Miners Jobless," *Washington Post*, November 30, 2014; and Lauren Wolfe, "How Dodd-Frank Is Failing Congo," *Foreign Policy*, February 2, 2015, www.foreignpolicy.com.

30. Raghavan, "How a Well-Intentioned U.S. Law."

31. Wolfe, "How Dodd-Frank Is Failing Congo."

32. Seay, "What's Wrong with Dodd-Frank 1502?" 14.

33. Michael J. Kavanaugh, "Congo Tin Sales Tumble 90% as Companies Avoid 'Conflict Minerals,'" *Bloomberg News*, May 23, 2011.

34. Wolfe, "How Dodd-Frank Is Failing Congo."

35. Aronson, "How Congress Devastated Congo."

In a mining industry that supports a staggering 8 to 10 million Congolese, or one-sixth of the total population, the impact of the ban on trading was devastating. Laura Seay estimates that at least 1 million workers were left unemployed, and she suspects that a large majority remains either out of work or is turning to the gold industry, "where smuggling is easy and sales continue."[36] Some youth are said to be joining militias as a last livelihood option.

On the matter of the militias, critics of the bill wonder if it has really had much of an impact on their activities. Groups such as Raia Mutumboki have increased their grip over mines in their territories, while new "gold laundering" schemes have opened between the DRC and Burundi, which sends gold to destinations as far as Dubai.[37] But the deeper issue, as the critics see it, is that many of the most powerful armed groups were never as dependent on resources as defenders of the bill made it seem. Seay points out that the M23 movement, one of the most formidable of the recent armed groups, never controlled any mines.[38] It drew most of its support from the Rwandan government and from taxation and predation on the civilian population. In cases where militias have been weakened, observers suggest it was not due to Dodd-Frank, but to a more aggressive UN peacekeeping strategy and diplomatic efforts to hold neighboring state sponsors more accountable. Meanwhile, no one seems to have benefitted more from the bill than the FARDC, which continues to smuggle resources out of the country, sometimes from the very mines where the new certification processes are in effect.[39]

So it seems a bill that was intended to help civilians has hurt them, while only minimally impacting the armed groups it intended to weaken. What should we make of all of this?

Lessons Learned and Future Trajectories

The issue of illegal resource exploitation in the DRC raises perennial questions in the ethics of war: how to defend the innocent in a way that abides by the principles of discrimination and proportionality, how to distinguish between the intended and unintended ends of action, and how to discern the line between the foreseeable and unforeseeable consequences of such

---

36. Seay, "What's Wrong with Dodd-Frank 1502?" 15.

37. Global Witness, "Putting Principles into Practice: Risks and Opportunities for Conflict-Free Sourcing in Eastern Congo" (May 2013), 2, www.globalwitness.org.

38. Laura Seay, "Did Cutting Access to Mineral Wealth Reduce Violence in the DRC?" *Washington Post*, March 25, 2014.

39. Global Witness, "Putting Principles into Practice," 3.

actions. Yet it does so in a sphere of war that often goes unnoticed, one that exists on the fringes of conflict: in gold and tantalum mines, in crowded city centers, in the farms and homes of civilians, and in the offices of NGOs. As trends in armed conflict continue to move away from the interstate wars of the past, and as the lines between war and peace continue to blur in places such as Congo, we overlook the moral stakes of this sphere only at the risk of further jeopardizing civilian lives. In closing, I want to return to the specific question posed at the outset of the chapter, "How is it possible to address the indirect costs of war without endangering the lives of those such strategies are meant to protect?"

In light of the fallout over the Dodd-Frank bill, a cynical response might be that it is not possible. Efforts to cut off the funding supply of armed actors inevitably hurt civilians the most; instead, we should make do with the current economy because it provides an already desperate population with the only livelihood they know. But this would be the wrong lesson to draw. The lesson, which can be heard among both Dodd-Frank's champions and critics, is that such measures need to be more discriminating, both in terms of the sources of civilian vulnerability and the response that such vulnerability demands.

On the sources of civilian vulnerability, no one disputes that Dodd-Frank identifies one of the most important. It is estimated that the hills of the DRC contain over $24 trillion of minerals, and yet Congo remains one of the poorest countries on earth.[40] The illegal exploitation and trade of resources increases civilian vulnerability not only because it sustains armed activity, but also because it prevents a stable, fair, and sound mineral industry from developing, one in which miners can work in safe conditions, enjoy job security, and receive a decent wage. But to create that economy, there are other sources of conflict that need to be addressed. Two specific points are worth mentioning in this regard. First, while armed groups benefit from resource exploitation, it is clearly not their only source of income. As the events following the passage of Dodd-Frank have shown, rebels can be drained of resource income and still find other ways to survive, whether it is through palm oil, charcoal, and other natural resources, or, more significantly, the patronage of neighboring state benefactors.[41] The role of the latter reminds us of the limits of an economic strategy that focuses on the action of multinational companies alone. As the effectiveness of recent US pressure on the Rwandan government shows, demanding higher accountability from

---

40. Kinniburgh, "Beyond 'Conflict Minerals,'" 66.
41. Wolfe, "How Dodd-Frank Is Failing Congo."

neighboring states is essential to the creation of an environment in which rebel movements can no longer thrive. Second, while the financial gains of resource exploitation certainly represent a draw for armed groups, and even represent an attractive form of livelihood, they are not the primary reason why such groups fight. The FDLR has been active in Congo since the Rwandan genocide because fundamental issues of citizenship and repatriation have remained unresolved; rebel groups such as the CNDP and M23 Movement continue to form because Congolese of Rwandan descent remain doubtful that there is a home for minorities in the DRC; and Mai Mai militias continue to remain active not only because they seek to defend themselves against these rebel movements, but because they have their own grievances over long-standing land claims. These are the deeper issues that have made conflict so intractable, for which strictly economic solutions will not suffice. It largely falls to the Congolese and neighboring governments to finally give these issues the attention they deserve.

To emphasize other sources of conflict is not to dismiss the need for the reform of the mining sector, which remains an urgent one. While much criticism has concentrated on the Dodd-Frank bill, the recent crisis was a combination of at least three factors. First, the bill presented laudably high industry standards for corporations, but it proposed an unrealistic timetable for compliance. It did not foresee how long the certification process would take or anticipate the kind of resources that its own compliance standards would require. An earlier draft of the legislation included $20 million in support funds that was regrettably stricken from the final bill.[42] Such funds would not have averted the crisis, but they would have helped create enforcement mechanisms that matched the bill's legislative objectives. This connects to a second issue concerning coordination. The US and Congolese governments pursued strategies that undermined each other's efforts at multiple points in the crisis. The Congolese ban on exports is the most obvious example, which, far from preparing for the bill's successful implementation, exacerbated the situation by depriving civilians of employment and worsening an already deteriorating investment landscape for foreign companies. The bill would have benefited not only from a more heavily funded certification process, but more coherent collaboration between the governments, as well as more input from members of the artisanal mining community and other civil society actors. Third, there is a certain irony in the fact that a bill designed to instill higher corporate accountability resulted in

---

42. Ibid.

companies deciding to run away from the problem. This reveals the limits of the simplistic moral narrative that has emerged in recent years that equates corporate responsibility with compliance with conflict-free certification. Surely there is something to be said for the company that elects to stay the course and create lasting, decent-waged jobs in a difficult, insecure environment, even if it means there may be a transitional period when their operations are not yet in full compliance with mineral regulations. Corporate responsibility has been whittled down to something thin indeed if merely being "conflict free" is all that we aspire to. If we are to address civilian vulnerability in the years to come, in a future in which more wars look like the war in the Congo, then we will need our companies to aspire to something greater, something far more constructive: building an economy that builds up the people who till and mine the earth, a sustainable economy that makes for peace instead of war.

CHAPTER 12

Combat and Confession: Just War and Moral Injury

TOBIAS WINRIGHT AND E. ANN JESCHKE

> If also penance is good for anything, consideration should be given to reviving the requirement of forty days' penance following participation in any war.
>
> —Paul Ramsey[1]

Hoping to authenticate his scholarship on the martial virtues, West Point graduate and military ethicist US Army Colonel Theodore Westhusing left his family behind and boarded a plane for Iraq. Later, only weeks before the end of his deployment, on the afternoon of June 5, 2005, at a military base near Baghdad airport, Westhusing returned to a room in his trailer after meeting with private contractors and some colleagues to pen the following note:

> Thanks for telling me it was a good day until I briefed you. [Redacted name]—You are only interested in your career and provide no support to your staff—no msn [mission] support and you don't care. I cannot support a msn that leads to corruption, human rights abuses and liars. I am sullied—no more. I didn't volunteer to support corrupt, money grubbing contractors, nor work for commanders only interested in themselves. I came to serve honorably and feel dishonored. I trust no Iraqi. I cannot live this way. All my love to my family, my wife and my precious children. I love you and trust you only. Death before being dishonored any more. Trust is essential—I don't know who trust anymore [*sic*]. Why serve when you cannot accomplish the mission, when you no longer believe in the cause, when your every effort and breath

---

1. Paul Ramsey, *War and the Christian Conscience: How Shall Modern War Be Conducted Justly?* (Durham, NC: Duke University Press, 1961), 133.

to succeed meets with lies, lack of support, and selfishness? No more. Reevaluate yourselves, cdrs [commanders]. You are not what you think you are and I know it. . . . Life needs trust. Trust is no more for me here in Iraq.

—Colonel Ted Westhusing[2]

Then this devout Catholic man took his 9 mm pistol and killed himself. The military psychological reports stated that Westhusing was too attached to his moral convictions, causing him to be unable to harmonize his notion of just war with the simple reality that warfare is a business operation.[3]

After his death, Peter Fosl, a fellow philosopher, asked whether or not viewing Westhusing's suicide as a psychological reaction to the moral horrors of war was too narrow a scope for understanding his reaction to the complex realities warriors are asked to negotiate when deployed. Fosl suggested that the better angle of approach is to view Westhusing's suicide within the moral context of his scholarship on honor and other martial virtues. In particular, Fosl concluded that Westhusing's suicide may be the result of an unacknowledged form of despair that cannot be captured within the medical tradition.[4]

This experience has been named "moral injury," a term first coined by psychologist Jonathan Shay as part of his work with Vietnam veterans.[5] And now, following the terrorist attacks on September 11, 2001, with some 2.5 million men and women having been deployed by the United States to Afghanistan and Iraq, many of them, too, are having this experience. Not to be directly equated with post-traumatic stress disorder (PTSD), which is based in a fear response to a traumatic experience in combat, moral injury is a debilitating sense of shame and guilt that soldiers experience because of

2. Greg Mitchell, "General Petraeus's Link to a Troubling Suicide in Iraq: The Ted Westhusing Story," *The Nation*, June 27, 2011, http://www.thenation.com.

3. Peter A. French, *War and Moral Dissonance* (New York: Cambridge University Press, 2010), 42-43, 47.

4. Peter S. Fosl, "American Despair in an Age of Hope," *Salmagundi Magazine* 176 (Fall/Winter 2012): 99-126.

5. Jonathan Shay, *Achilles in Vietnam: Combat Trauma and the Undoing of Character* (New York: Scribner, 1995). The term "moral injury" has gained traction in public awareness and discourse due to articles in popular media. See, e.g., David Wood's three-part report on moral injury in the Huffington Post: "The Grunts: Damned If They Kill, Damned If They Don't," March 18, 2014, http://projects.huffingtonpost.com; "The Recruits: When Right and Wrong Are Hard to Tell Apart," March 19, 2014, http://projects.huffingtonpost.com; and "Healing: Can We Treat Moral Wounds?" March 20, 2014, http://projects.huffingtonpost.com. Also, Amanda Taub, "Moral Injury—The Quiet Epidemic of Soldiers Haunted by What They Did during Wartime," *Vox*, May 7, 2015, http://www.vox.com. For a recent academic book about moral injury, see Georgetown University philosopher Nancy Sherman's *Afterwar: Healing the Moral Wounds of Our Soldiers* (New York: Oxford University Press, 2015).

actions they have done or observed in war. Indeed, moral injury has been described as "a bruise on the soul, akin to grief or sorrow."[6] It does not occur only among warriors who feel like they have done or participated in something wrong, but it also occurs among warriors who have done things they regard as morally justified. For instance, when Army infantryman Alex Horton saw two men running across a street toward other US soldiers, Horton believed they were a threat; thus, he fired his weapon, shooting one of the men, who then stumbled and fell, out of sight, behind a building. Horton was not certain whether the man was a threat; nor did he know whether or not the man died. However, now, upon reflecting on his action, Horton believes the man was probably a civilian rather than an insurgent, but he adds, "That's not how good people act. But I did it, because I had to."[7] In his view, what he did was morally justified, but it still was not "good." And, with many warriors struggling to return to, and reintegrate with, civilian life, this dissonance produces the sense of shame or guilt now labeled "moral injury." As US Air Force Chief Master Sergeant Harry Marsters remarks, "It was very difficult to get adjusted—like you were in a different world."[8]

To date, efforts to address moral injury have been undertaken by psychologists and psychiatrists, as well as other medical professionals. While important, these efforts seem insufficient. For Marsters, for example, in addition to counseling and medication, his "involvement in his faith community," including "church functions, homeless outreach ministry, and board activities," has helpfully "sustained him through his time of difficulty."[9] According to Robert Emmet Meagher, however, the church, which indeed has a responsibility to returning warriors—to listen to them, be present to them, and "to go there with them" in their dark night of the soul—has failed to do so, instead "blessing" war and participating in the shallow "support the troops" catchphrases that are part of the American myth of war and the "hero."[10] In his recent book, *Killing from the Inside Out: Moral Injury and Just War*, Meagher, who is a humanities professor, argues that moral injury is an indictment of the just war tradition (JWT). In his estimation, the JWT has "blessed" killing and war as "a positive good" rather than "the lesser of two evils."[11] In reality, though, war not only rains destruction and death on

---

6. Wood, "The Grunts."

7. Taub, "Moral Injury."

8. Gregg Brekke, "Wounded Souls," *Sojourners* 43, no. 4 (April 2014): 24.

9. Ibid.

10. Robert Emmet Meagher, *Killing from the Inside Out: Moral Injury and Just War* (Eugene, OR: Cascade Books, 2014), 141.

11. Ibid., xv.

one's enemies, including not only combatants but also civilians, but war also does something to those doing the killing and fighting. Furthermore, rather than limiting the violence of war, the JWT has been used as a smokescreen for war. These two serious problems with the JWT, Meagher maintains, give rise to moral injury, which he also regards as requiring something more than counseling and medications can offer.

To be sure, these are serious charges against the JWT, which in this chapter we seek to explore, address, and challenge. While we agree with Meagher about the need for a better prescription for healing moral injury, we argue that he wrongly attributes moral injury to the JWT when the problem, in our view, is actually the version of just war theory that has become the dominant one in recent centuries, namely, the one that views just war, as Meagher notes, as a positive good. However, Meagher fails to do justice to another version of just war theory that held sway in the past and has been revived in recent decades, which acknowledged the evils of war and recognized the need for "moral grief" as a virtue that deals with moral injury and impels a warrior to move toward reconciliation within himself and the community.[12] In what follows, we address moral injury from a Christian justified-war perspective that views wars, including so-called just wars, as involving evils; and we call upon the church, as an element of *jus post bellum*, to revive its past prescription of penance for returning warriors and to explore similar "medicinal" or "healing" practices that may help those returning from war.

This essay proceeds in four parts. First, we provide an overview of how moral injury has been described in recent clinical literature. Second, we suggest how these dominant approaches to understanding and addressing moral injury fall short. Third, we turn to the question of sin in war, including in justified war, which we think resonates with the experience of morally injured soldiers and offers helpful contours for understanding it. Finally, we propose the recovery of penance and other similar rituals or practices to be made available to even just warriors.

Moral Injury in the Literature

Currently, definitions of and the literature about moral injury are predominantly found in medical journals. The psychological literature on moral injury defines morals as a tacit or explicit set of shared rules based on fam-

---

12. Mark A. Wilson, "Moral Grief and Reflective Virtue," in *Virtue and the Moral Life: Theological and Philosophical Perspectives*, ed. William Werpehowski and Kathryn Getek Soltis (Lanham, MD: Lexington Books, 2014), 57.

ily, culture, society, and legal codes that reinforce appropriate social behavior. Accordingly, moral behaviors are primate drives and instincts that are functional to the cohesion of a group or flourishing of a culture. To violate the moral code could be viewed as destructive to the group.[13] Moral emotions are also functional in promoting a moral code. These special types of emotion—such as embarrassment, shame, or guilt—are effective in prompting individuals to act in ways to win inclusion or approval within a group. Within the corpus of this literature, moral injury is viewed as a wound that disrupts the warrior's appropriate expression of moral emotion and gives rise to maladaptive social behavior.

Three main mechanisms of moral injury have been forwarded within the psychological literature. First, moral injury occurs when a warrior violates a deeply held moral belief.[14] Second, moral injury happens when the warrior witnesses or learns about acts that transgress deeply held moral beliefs.[15] Third, moral injury follows when the warrior is betrayed by someone who holds legitimate authority; this third way was how Shay understood moral injury in his work with Vietnam veterans.[16] Common to all three mechanisms is how moral injury occurs because of a breach of a moral contract and leads to a mental injury in the warrior with the following symptoms: disruption in a warrior's ability to behave in an ethical manner; self-harming behaviors; demoralization resulting in feelings of bewilderment, futility, hopelessness, and self-loathing; negative association with self and others; reexperiencing the morally injurious episode; intrusive thoughts; emotional numbing; and avoidance of social interactions.[17] It is, moreover, important to note that these feelings of shame and guilt can be associated not only with an act that violates a warrior's moral principles, such as killing a civilian, but also the failure to act, such as not shooting someone who then kills a fellow soldier. In other words, the violating act can be one of commission or omission. Also, it is noteworthy that although the mechanism of moral injury is different from that of PTSD, the constellation of symptoms is strikingly similar.

---

13. Brett T. Litz, "Resilience in the Aftermath of War Trauma: A Critical Review and Commentary," *Interface Focus* 4, no. 5 (August 26, 2014): 1-10.

14. Ibid.

15. Rita Nakashima Brock and Gabriella Lettini, *Soul Repair: Recovering from Moral Injury after War* (Boston: Beacon Press, 2013).

16. Shay, *Achilles in Vietnam*.

17. Kent D. Drescher et al., "An Exploration of the Viability and Usefulness of the Construct of Moral Injury in War Veterans," *Traumatology* 17, no. 1 (March 2011): 8-13.

All of the aforementioned conceptualizations of moral injury consider it an emotional-mental injury that results in long-term psychosocial consequences. The emotional distress typified by moral injury leads to strong feelings of shame and guilt resulting in perpetual negative beliefs about life or individual worth upon returning home from deployment.[18] Since the symptoms of moral injury parallel those of PTSD, treatment methods are generally the same as those used in PTSD: particularly, cognitive behavioral therapy, emotional processing therapy, exposure therapy. In addition, treatment focuses on forgiveness as a means of alleviating the warrior's toxic personal thoughts and maladaptive beliefs about the world and others. For our part, though, we follow Mark A. Wilson's description of moral injury as "the sort of suffering that is reported by well-meaning individuals who did their best to abide by the laws of war and who nevertheless experience forms of guilt, shame, regret, and remorse over their actions or inactions in war."[19]

How the Clinical Approaches Fall Short

The medical model defines moral injury as a cognitive injury and assumes that emotions of guilt and shame negatively influence how the warrior thinks, perceives, and interacts in the world. As such, moral injury is steeped in psychological methods that seek to eliminate feelings of guilt and shame because they are negative emotions that cause a warrior to be incapable of appropriately engaging reality. As Meagher critically quips, the pain that combat veterans experience "is supposedly 'in their heads,' or more precisely in their brains, and there are on offer perfectly good drugs to deal with that."[20] This conceptualization of moral injury is passive and assumes, for the most part, that injury happens to the warrior. In other words, the warrior is psychologically broken from his experience of the morally nefarious context of warfare. The warrior is basically labeled as a victim.

However, during a research interview conducted by E. Ann Jeschke, Joshua Hines shared the following story concerning a difficult moral situation with which he had to grapple during one of his deployments. He did not describe his experience of the moral complexity of war fighting as injurious or traumatizing; instead, he talked about the waste of resources and loss of focus on the bigger picture. There was no blatant violation of moral norms but a greater understanding that somehow a proper orientation

---

18. Litz, "Resilience."
19. Wilson, "Moral Grief and Reflective Virtue," 58.
20. Meagher, *Killing from the Inside Out*, xv.

toward creation, humanity, and a greater sense of respect for the value of life was lost during this mission.

> The thing that finally drove it home for me was when we went and got this mid-level Taliban dude.... We dedicated all these resources to go get this guy.... We end up dropping a bomb, and it didn't hit him, but it hit, something like 16 women and children in this tent.... I went back to my room and cried. I cried not just because of the loss of life, don't get me wrong, that's something to be worried about, I'm not condoning it, but what mostly pissed me off was for a couple of weeks we literally dedicated all these resources.... I was not seeing any progress in terms of what we were doing. You saw countless people in the military whose lives, not just from combat or wounds or anything, but so much of their lives have been spent in these last two wars.[21]

The medical model's approach to moral injury fails to understand the contextual realities of the warrior. As Meagher notes, some caregivers "have begun to question whether they truly grasp the source and extent or even the nature of their patients' suffering."[22]

Many warriors, like Hines, are deeply distressed by the circumstances in which they find themselves, but the reality does not fit nicely into the medical etiology of moral injury. That medical definition does not address the simple realities of dwelling in a morally ambiguous situation for years on end. Furthermore, it does not account for the warrior's extensive training, which forms a warrior ethos, which does not advocate passive victimization. These warriors are also shaped—in how they eat and hydrate, how they march, how they pull a trigger, and how they feel, think, and react while doing much more—so their character is deeply affected. As a result, therapeutic approaches to moral injury, which tend to be reductionist, overly cognitive, and mechanical, fail to address adequately the whole person who has experienced moral injury. They fail to capture the feelings of impurity that result from a just warrior encountering irresolvable moral dilemmas and being forced to make the best possible decision in order to move forward with his mission. Although the warrior may not see himself as passively injured by the realities of warfare, being present to destruction and violence does leave its mark on warriors and calls for healing.

---

21. Joshua Hines, Interview Two, October 23, 2014, lines 1364-89. This interview and others are included in Erica Ann Jeschke, "The Body Beatific: Total Force Fitness and Social Reintegration/Rehabilitation of America's Warriors" (Ph.D. diss., Saint Louis University, 2015).

22. Meagher, *Killing from the Inside Out*, 3.

Louis Iasiello, a retired admiral and a US Navy chaplain, succinctly distinguishes between the contrasting anthropologies (understanding of the human person) of the dominant medical model and the thicker theological view (which undergirds the JWT, rightly understood), writing,

> Combatants are not amoral agents or machines. . . . Warriors are persons—they are body-mind-spirit. They are complex moral agents who must live and fight within the context of military protocol and duty. . . . While warriors submit to the authority of their superiors, they never submit so completely that they surrender or forfeit their moral personhood. . . . Warriors are soldiers, marines, sailors, and airmen who must kill when legally ordered to do so, but must live with those decisions the rest of their lives.[23]

The standard clinical approach does not view soldiers as persons who are "body-mind-spirit." This holistic anthropology is, however, the way that the Christian tradition of medicine and health has viewed the human person. As Catholic medical ethicists Kevin O'Rourke, OP, and Philip J. Boyle have articulated it, "From a Christian perspective, then, health envisions optimal functioning of the human person to meet physiological, psychological, social, and spiritual needs in an integrated manner."[24] This, as Iasiello suggests, should include the person who is a warrior, too.

Unfortunately, theological, religious, and other philosophical perspectives to date have not attempted to address moral injury, leaving it to the medical literature to fill this void. There are a handful of exceptions, however. Writing two decades ago with Vietnam veterans in mind, Bernard J. Verkamp laments how the "therapeutic" society of the West, with its reductionist concentration on psychological treatment, has lost the "moral sensibility" that is "derived from a uniquely religious teleology."[25] More recently, psychiatrist and moral theologian Warren Kinghorn similarly writes that moral injury refers to "something that modern clinical disciplines structurally cannot provide, something like a moral theology, embodied in specific communities with specific contextually formed practices."[26] Therefore, a

---

23. Louis V. Iasiello, "*Jus post bellum*: The Moral Responsibilities of Victors in War," *Naval War College Review* 57, nos. 3/4 (Summer/Autumn 2004): 45.

24. Kevin D. O'Rourke, OP, and Philip J. Boyle, *Medical Ethics: Sources of Catholic Teachings*, 4th ed. (Washington, DC: Georgetown University Press, 2011), 7.

25. Bernard J. Verkamp, *The Moral Treatment of Returning Warriors in Early Medieval and Modern Times* (Scranton, PA: University of Scranton Press, 1993), 11-12.

26. Warren Kinghorn, "Combat Trauma and Moral Fragmentation: A Theological Account of Moral Injury," *Journal of the Society of Christian Ethics* 32, no. 2 (Fall/Winter 2012): 59.

more "capacious" understanding, as Wilson puts it, of moral injury requires a more holistic response, and the church should witness to how that is done.[27] Before delving into that, though, we turn now to how a proper understanding of the JWT should support such a capacious response to moral injury.

Evil and Sin in War, Including in Justified War

There is an older version of moral grief that emerged from within the Augustinian JWT and predates this Freudian psychology that views negative feelings as maladaptive. In that approach to just war, the moral emotions of guilt and shame were viewed as positive expressions of good character rather than maladaptive mental assessments of self, others, or the world. These moral emotions were the catalyst that emerged from a warrior's sense of love lost and also impelled a warrior to move toward reconciliation and restoration in the aftermath of combat. This Augustinian conception of moral grief took into account the complex reality of warfare. Furthermore, it presented mournfulness as an active and noble good that does not label the warrior as a passive victim, but as an active participant who both suffers from the stains of sin and desires to act in a morally upright manner.

We believe that the JWT offers insights that are relevant and should be retrieved for efforts seeking to address moral injury. Of course, admittedly, there are rival versions of just war theory circulating today, as Meagher notes on occasion, although we think he incorrectly emphasizes the prominence, at least on the part of most just war theorists (if not most US citizens and Christians in the pews), of the view that just war is a positive good rather than a lesser evil. Indeed, in recent years debate has transpired about whether just war is a "lesser evil" or a "lesser good," with most theological ethicists leaning away from the latter.

As for ourselves, we do not believe that war can ever be perfectly just. Indeed, one would be hard pressed to come up with an example of a perfectly just war, which would mean that all of the *jus ad bellum* criteria, justifying embarking upon war, and *jus in bello* criteria, governing and constraining its conduct—as well as the recently developed *jus post bellum* criteria and practices toward promoting a just and lasting peace in the wake of the war—would have been fully adhered to and satisfied.[28] At present, a number of attempts are circulating to articulate how just war is a lesser evil.

---

27. Wilson, "Moral Grief and Reflective Virtue," 60.

28. Mark J. Allman and Tobias L. Winright, "Growing Edges of Just War Theory: *Jus ante bellum, jus post bellum*, and Imperfect Justice," *Journal of the Society of Christian Ethics* 32, no. 2 (Fall/Winter 2012): 173-91.

Twentieth-century Protestant ethicist Reinhold Niebuhr realistically reminded us that perfect justice is unattainable in history due to human finitude and sinfulness.[29] For Niebuhr, war is a "tragic" event even when it is "necessary," and even wars possessing a "righteous cause" are always tainted by sin. Niebuhr stopped short of calling a war "just" and instead considered it a "necessary evil" or the "lesser of two evils."[30] It is an evil, but not as evil as an unjust war or as allowing unjust aggression to go unchecked.

The language of "lesser evil" is found not only among Niebuhr and his theological heirs; interestingly, it also surfaces in the Eastern Orthodox moral tradition, which offers a somewhat ambivalent approach to the ethics of war and peace.[31] Orthodoxy rejects any view that regards war as good, a lesser good, or as virtuous. Soon after the end of the Persian Gulf War, the Holy Synod of Bishops of the Orthodox Church in America (OCA) issued a statement noting that "just war theory . . . does not reflect our theological tradition," because war may never be "theologically justified"; yet, at the same time, the bishops added that "a lesser evil must sometimes be chosen to resist a greater evil."[32] Similarly, Fr. Stanley Harakas writes that Eastern Orthodox churches "cannot speak of a 'good war,' or even a 'just war.'"[33] Yet, he notes that "sometimes" war is a "necessary evil" to defend the innocent from an aggressor.[34] Reluctant to call war "just" because of the many evils that are its consequence, the Orthodox tradition nevertheless does not expect pacifism, which would rule out participating in fighting wars altogether. "And one may well call such involvement 'inevitable' and even 'right,' albeit tragically," Peter C. Bouteneff writes, "however this does not mitigate the fact that the totality of the dynamic that leads to such conflicts is evil, not just within the generalized dynamic of human brokenness, but as a particular series of death-dealing decisions and failures of creativity and wisdom—failures of

---

29. Reinhold Niebuhr, "When Will Christians Stop Fooling Themselves," in *Love and Justice: Selections from the Shorter Writings of Reinhold Niebuhr*, ed. D. B. Robertson (Louisville, KY: Westminster John Knox, 1992): 40-46.

30. Niebuhr, *Love and Justice*, 219, 221, 223, 268, 282, 285.

31. Alexandros K. Kyrou and Elizabeth H. Prodromou, "Debates on Just War, Holy War, and Peace: Orthodox Christian Thought and Byzantine Imperial Attitudes towards War," in *Orthodox Christian Perspectives on War*, ed. Perry T. Hamalis and Valerie A. Karras (Notre Dame, IN: University of Notre Dame Press, forthcoming).

32. Complete text in *The Orthodox Church* 27, nos. 5-6 (May-June 1991): 4.

33. Stanley S. Harakas, *Wholeness of Faith and Life: Orthodox Christian Ethics: Part One— Patristic Ethics* (Brookline, MA: Holy Cross Orthodox Press, 1999), 154-55, 157.

34. Stanley S. Harakas, "Thinking about Peace and War as Orthodox Christians," *Praxis* 3, no. 1 (January 2002): 28-29.

communion with God."[35] Likewise, Aristotle Papanikolaou sees war—even with its moments of "loyalty, sacrifice, and even love"—as "a space saturated with violence" and destructive, even "unsacramental" practices.[36] War's violence does something, not only to those upon whom it is inflicted but also to those who inflict it. As such, Orthodox moral theology does not provide, Philip LeMasters observes, "theoretical justification for war as a good endeavor, let alone pronouncements that war is holy."[37]

The "lesser of two evils" approach to war has been criticized by Methodist theologian Daniel M. Bell, Jr. Although he notes its connection with Orthodoxy, Bell targets Niebuhrians, alleging that "there is the practical problem that the logic of the lesser evil actually undercuts the moral force of the just war tradition."[38] It is a version of just war "without teeth." That is, just as the logic of the lesser evil sets aside Jesus's teachings on love of enemy as impossible to apply in this life, so too might this logic suspend the just war teaching, for instance, on noncombatant immunity in order to stop a greater evil. In contrast, Bell argues for just war to be viewed and practiced as a "faithful form of discipleship."[39] Drawing on Saints Ambrose and Augustine, as well as Paul Ramsey, Bell anchors Christian just war in the imperative to love the neighbor. It is also an expression of love, or "kind harshness," for the enemy. In Bell's view, sanctifying, enabling grace should help just warriors to act in accordance with virtues such as justice and charity rather than to be tempted to bend or set aside the rules as a "lesser evil." While we agree with Bell's account of just war as Christian discipleship and we take Bell's concerns about viewing just war as a "lesser evil" to heart, we worry, though, that a more positive approach may problematically contribute to viewing just war as a good, relaxing its constraints, and thereby mirroring the willingness to loosen or override the rules that he criticizes Niebuhrian "lesser evil" just war proponents for doing.

---

35. Peter C. Bouteneff, "War and Peace: Providence and the Interim," in *Orthodox Christian Perspectives on War*, ed. Perry T. Hamalis and Valerie A. Karras (Notre Dame, IN: University of Notre Dame Press, forthcoming).

36. Aristotle Papanikolaou, "The Ascetics of War: The Undoing and Redoing of Virtue," in *Orthodox Christian Perspectives on War*, ed. Perry T. Hamalis and Valerie A. Karras (Notre Dame, IN: University of Notre Dame Press, forthcoming).

37. Philip LeMasters, "Orthodox Perspectives on Peace, War and Violence," *Ecumenical Review* 63, no. 1 (March 2011): 59.

38. Daniel M. Bell, Jr., *Just War as Christian Discipleship: Recentering the Tradition in the Church Rather Than the State* (Grand Rapids, MI: Brazos Press, 2009), 34.

39. Ibid., 36.

Indeed, Darrell Cole does precisely this by calling just wars "good." He contends that the killing in a just war is not a necessary evil that is regretfully tolerated, but a good because it is a form of cooperation with God and "an act of love when it seeks to resemble God's use of force."[40] Similarly, Orthodox theologian Fr. Alexander Webster attempts to argue that just war is not a "lesser evil" but a "lesser good," and he alleges, incredibly, that those Eastern Orthodox theologians and bishops who view war as a "lesser evil" have been unduly influenced by Niebuhr.[41] Again, while we agree with Bell's critique of the "lesser evil" approach's willingness to set aside serious adherence to just war criteria, we are also worried that Cole's and Webster's depiction of just war as a "good" veers dangerously in the direction of a self-righteous crusading approach to just war—the version of the JWT that Meagher rightly criticizes, even though he wrongly attributes it to most just war theorists—in which there is less incentive to adhere strictly to the just war criteria.

Instead, we think the Catholic moral tradition, which has also sometimes spoken the language of "lesser evil" in connection with just war, may help steer a course that avoids these dangerous pitfalls. For example, the early-twentieth-century Benedictine monk Virgil Michel refers to war, including just war, as an evil. In his book *The Christian in the World*, Michel offers several pages on "the evil of war."[42] Beginning with quotes from scripture and the Eucharistic liturgy, he emphasizes how peace is "the particular legacy of Christ to the world" that Christians should imitate.[43] Michel then refers to war, in contrast, as "a most terrible evil when viewed in the light of Christian truth," especially when one considers its sinful causes (e.g., "the lust for power over men, or of conquest for its own sake, or the lust for riches and material possessions") and its dire effects (e.g., "apathy and callousness in regard to the inflicting of physical sufferings and death," "disregard of the command not to steal and disrespect in general for human property," "rapine and plunder, and an extreme development of sexual immorality," and "the open fostering of the so-called art of lying, etc."). Writing in the decades following the devastation of World War I, when Christians from opposing European nations killed one another, Michel declares, "For the member of Christ war is always a tearing asunder of the mystical body of Christ."[44]

---

40. Darrell Cole, "Good Wars," *First Things* 116 (October 2001): 31.

41. Andrew F. C. Webster, "Justifiable War as a 'Lesser Good' in Eastern Orthodox Moral Tradition," *St. Vladimir's Theological Quarterly* 47, no. 1 (2003): 3-57.

42. Virgil Michel, O.S.B., *The Christian in the World* (Collegeville, MN: Liturgical Press, 1939), 178-88.

43. Ibid., 179.

44. Ibid., 180, 181; see also 186.

Therefore, nearly a century ago anticipating Cardinal Ratzinger's question, Michel writes, "*the question has arisen anew* in our century, *whether there can be any moral justification for a nation to enter upon a war today* or for the individual citizens to take active part in it."[45] For him, there is a strong presumption against war, and after enumerating ten criteria for just war, he notes that right intent involves righting the injustice that was committed and that "the aim of reestablishing peace must be uppermost" throughout the prosecution of the war.[46]

Still, while admitting the possibility of a just war, the aforementioned evils accompanying modern war force Michel to say that "even a legitimate war of self-defense must be considered a great evil (even if not a *moral* evil, or a *sin*)."[47] This distinction is important to keep in mind in the next line, where he writes, "*The choice of war is therefore always a choice between two evils*, one being that of the injustices being committed against a nation by an unjust aggressor, and the other being the evils accompanying the morally just action of legitimate self-defense of national peace and security."[48] Michel does not mean the weighing of two moral evils; rather, he tries to hold together the view that all war is evil, though unjust war is morally evil, while just war is morally justified even though it is accompanied by many foreseeable evils (death, destruction, suffering). Nuancing things even more, Michel observes that it is possible for there to be lingering "doubts about the *complete* justice of a specific war" given that determining guilt for aggression is "not so clear-cut," since wars "have roots and causes going back into history, and they are due to influences that often remain hidden for a long time to come."[49] In our view, Michel offers a helpful, more nuanced, and stricter account of just war that neither views it as a "good" or "virtuous" activity, nor regards it as completely morally evil, both of which may dangerously open the door for bending the rules when "necessary."

The US Catholic bishops in their 1983 pastoral letter *The Challenge of Peace* raise similar points in their explanation of "comparative justice," the *jus ad bellum* criterion that asks two critical questions: "Which side is sufficiently 'right' in a dispute, and are the values at stake critical enough to override the presumption against war?"[50] On the first, the bishops write that

---

45. Ibid., 181 (emphasis original).
46. Ibid., 182.
47. Ibid., 183 (emphasis added).
48. Ibid. (emphasis original).
49. Ibid., 183-84 (emphasis added).
50. National Conference of Catholic Bishops, *The Challenge of Peace: God's Promise and Our Response* (Washington, DC: United States Catholic Conference, 1983), par. 92.

"no state should act on the basis that it has 'absolute justice' on its side."[51] Also, on that point, the bishops appear to be calling into question whether a just war can be absolutely or totally just. For the bishops, comparative justice is intended to rein in the strong impulse toward self-righteous crusades. The other critical question that comparative justice asks, according to the bishops, has to do with the presumption against war. War requires justification because "war, by definition, involves violence, destruction, suffering, and death."[52] As the bishops note, "the possibility of taking even one human life is a prospect we should consider in fear and trembling,"[53] and thus "even the most justifiable defensive war" is to be regarded "only as a sad necessity."[54]

The bishops' language here is strikingly similar to that of the above Orthodox bishops and theologians; however, it seems to move in the direction of Michel's distinguishing between moral and nonmoral evils, a distinction that has been highlighted in recent Catholic moral theology, which refers to death as a pre- or nonmoral evil (also sometimes referred to as "ontic" evil), though killing is not necessarily a moral evil.[55] The killing of an unjust aggressor is a nonmoral evil, because all death is something to be mourned; such killing is not necessarily a moral evil, however, because it is morally justified. Even so, a killing that is morally justified still affects the just warrior. As Catholic moral philosopher John Finnis explains, there is a transitive effect, the death of the enemy, but there are intransitive effects on the character of the person who kills an aggressor.[56] On the one hand, the just warrior has acted in accordance with justice, thereby reinforcing (in addition to expressing) that virtue; on the other hand, killing someone (and all of the suffering, death, and destruction witnessed in war by that soldier) certainly affects the killer, too. Or, as Meagher puts it, "all killing kills something in the killer and . . . there is no such thing as killing without dying."[57]

We have in mind here, moreover, what Orthodox theologians mean when they use the language of "wound" and "sickness" to talk about sin, including in particular the notion of "involuntary sin." For example, LeMasters writes that "the church merely tolerates war as a sometimes tragically necessary or unavoidable endeavor for which repentance for 'involuntary sin' is

---

51. Ibid., par. 93 (emphasis original).

52. Ibid., par. 92.

53. Ibid., par. 80.

54. Ibid., par. 83.

55. James T. Bretzke, *A Morally Complex World: Engaging Contemporary Moral Theology* (Collegeville, MN: Liturgical Press, 2004), 75.

56. John Finnis, *Fundamentals of Ethics* (Washington, DC: Georgetown University Press, 1983), 139.

57. Meagher, *Killing from the Inside Out*, xviii.

appropriate."[58] This seems to suggest that the moral/nonmoral evil distinction might be overly simplistic, neglecting a sense of sin that has more to do with being and character. In the West, this notion of involuntary sin has not been emphasized as much as in the Orthodox tradition. Focusing on acts, we view sin as something freely chosen. There are sins of commission and sins of omission. Other than some lingering references to original sin, it is the sinful choice or action that is scrutinized. Recently, however, the prominent Catholic virtue and natural law ethicist Jean Porter has explored how "acts are freely chosen, and yet in some way they are not fully free, because the sinner him- or herself is not altogether free."[59] Indeed, she taps into the work of Anselm of Laon to glean possibilities for a more "comprehensive account of sin," which may "capture deep intuitions, and reflect our experiences of ourselves as struggling and unfree."[60]

This seems to get at what is happening, we think, with moral injury. The returning soldier feels guilt or remorse, even though he may believe that he did the right thing.[61] Or perhaps more so if he has doubts, as may be the case for some soldiers involved in recent wars that lacked moral clarity, from Vietnam to Afghanistan to Iraq. Their "gut" sense that something is wrong, even if they cannot articulate it with just war language, should be respectfully heard. As Admiral Iasiello puts it, warriors "sometimes return from combat with mixed emotions, and oftentimes with a spirit of regret and sadness. . . . Few feel they may now return to life as usual."[62] In his, and our, view the *jus ad bellum* criterion of right intent, which Michel emphasized, requires a *post bellum* duty to try to promote a just and lasting peace for all involved in and affected by war, including the defeated but also the returning soldiers. Iasiello suggests that the instilling of "humility, regret, and perhaps contrition acknowledge this ambivalence and may actually ease a warrior's transition to peacetime existence."[63] As LeMasters puts it, because of "involvement in warfare, the taking of human life, or other endeavors that damage the soul, the church provides spiritual therapy for healing and guidance for growth in holiness."[64] Such language of virtues and holiness reminds us of the church's

---

58. LeMasters, "Orthodox Perspectives on Peace, War and Violence," 59; Philip LeMasters, "Justifiable War: Response #4," *St. Vladimir's Theological Quarterly* 47, no. 1 (2003): 80.

59. Jean Porter, "Sin, Sickness, and Transgression: Medieval Perspectives on Sin and Their Significance Today," in *Virtue and the Moral Life: Theological and Philosophical Perspectives*, ed. William Werpehowski and Kathryn Getek Soltis (Lanham, MD: Lexington Books, 2014), 118.

60. Ibid.

61. Wilson, "Moral Grief and Reflective Virtue," 58.

62. Iasiello, "*Jus post bellum*," 41.

63. Ibid.

64. LeMasters, "Orthodox Perspectives on Peace, War and Violence," 59-60.

ancient practice of requiring penance and other rituals for returning soldiers. If, as Papanikolaou claims (we think rightly), war fighting involves "unsacramental" practices, it will take sacramental or liturgical practices to counter them, to instill virtues, to reinstate character, and to restore a just and lasting peace, which is the right intent of just war, even for the sake of the warrior.

The Recovery of Virtue: Penance, Ritual, and Just War

In *After the Smoke Clears: The Just War Tradition and Post War Justice*, Mark Allman and one of us (Tobias Winright) advocate social rehabilitation as a component of the restoration phase of *jus post bellum*, including for returning warriors.[65] Admiral Iasiello likewise calls attention not only to the need for social rehabilitation and restoration for children, the elderly, the sick, refugees, and others affected by war, especially the weakest and most vulnerable, but also for the reintegration of military personnel back into society after war.[66] Right intent requires the establishment of a just and lasting peace for all. We believe that if Catholicism and other Christian denominations are going to continue to hold that war is sometimes morally justified, even if rarely, then the church should lead the way in helping combat veterans suffering from moral injury.

Historically, such care was provided by the church for returning warriors. In his book *The Moral Treatment of Returning Warriors in Early Medieval and Modern Times*, Bernard Verkamp notes the "Christian community of the first millennium generally assumed that warriors returning from battle would or should be feeling guilty and ashamed for all the wartime killing they had done."[67] If warriors violated just war rules, they for sure should feel guilty, and even if they fought justly, they still needed reconciliation. So, rituals were put into practice providing healing and reconciliation for these soldiers. Depending on the bishop or the penitential, variation existed as to the penances imposed, with some stricter than others; nevertheless, all are evidence of an effort to address a perceived need on the part of these soldiers.

In general, the appropriate penance corresponded with "the kind of war they had been engaged in, the number of their killings, and the intention

---

65. Mark J. Allman and Tobias L. Winright, *After the Smoke Clears: The Just War Tradition and Post War Justice* (Maryknoll, NY: Orbis Books, 2010), 163–65.

66. Iasiello, "*Jus post bellum*," 39.

67. Verkamp, *Moral Treatment*, 11. He also notes how rituals of purification, expiation, and reconciliation for warriors existed prior to Christianity.

with which they had been carried out."[68] In the fourth century, for example, Saint Basil of Caesarea held that although "homicide in war is not reckoned by our Fathers as homicide," warriors returning from battle should still be made to "abstain from communion for three years."[69] Centuries later, after the Battle of Hastings in 1066, the synod of Norman bishops imposed a set of penances on *all* soldiers who fought under William the Conqueror: anyone who knowingly killed a man during the battle had to do penance for one year for each person he killed; anyone who wounded a man and did not know whether he died later had to do penance for forty days for each man he struck; anyone who did not know the number of either of these had to do penance for one day each week for the rest of his life; and archers who killed and wounded but, due to distance, did not know how many, had to do penance for three Lents.[70] For a variety of possible reasons, which Verkamp carefully considers, by the late medieval and Renaissance periods this practice waned, though a few echoes of it lingered as long as the sixteenth century. An important factor he highlights is secularization, and this also occurred in connection with developments in just war theory at that time, when it came to have less to do with character and the virtues, as well as a theological emphasis on right intention, and became more like what Daniel Bell refers to as a "public policy checklist."[71]

Still, just as Bell and other ethicists are reviving a more theological and virtue-oriented approach to just war, so too should penance and other rituals, such as pilgrimage and performing the spiritual (e.g., admonishing the sinner, counseling the doubtful, forgiving all injuries, etc.) and corporal (e.g., feeding the hungry, sheltering the homeless, visiting the imprisoned, etc.) works of mercy, be reinstated as important practices for returning warriors.[72] Of course, given the religious pluralism, along with the separation of church and state, of many modern societies such as the United States, Verkamp recognizes that simply reviving the imposition of penances is not possible. Nevertheless, he suggests that "certain aspects" could be "accommodated to modern times," including examination of conscience, the expression of contrition, and practices such as lament, confession, absolution, and penance.[73] For example, perhaps combat veterans could spend a month on a

---

68. Ibid.

69. Basil, *Letters*, 188.13; cited also in Meagher, *Killing from the Inside Out*, 84.

70. Verkamp, *Moral Treatment*, 17, 21-22.

71. Ibid., 57, 59; Bell, 53-58, 74.

72. For more on the works of mercy past and present, see James F. Keenan, S.J., *The Works of Mercy: The Heart of Catholicism*, 2nd ed. (Lanham, MD: Rowman & Littlefield, 2007).

73. Verkamp, *Moral Treatment*, 103-12.

communal retreat with fellow returning warriors, led by dedicated, experienced spiritual advisors, perhaps out in a natural setting such as the mountains. We think that the church should definitely reinstate such practices for Christians who are in the military, but for the wider society, including governmental institutions, we hope analogs or functional equivalents will be explored and implemented, even if these, from a theological perspective, only approximate these Christian practices.

Meagher is correct that the first step is listening to veterans.[74] Penance begins with the warrior's narrative being heard. Even those combat veterans who find it difficult to articulate their experience deserve a hearing. At least they feel that something is amiss, and from a just war perspective, all of us should. That many combat veterans cannot articulate why they feel this way is an indication that the JWT should be taught better and more clearly by the church, if not by the military. Indeed, improved teaching of the criteria of just war should be done for all who are considering the military as a career or vocation. Doing so might be considered an expectation of *jus ante bellum*, or justice before war. That way warriors and the church are better prepared for not only *jus ad bellum* and *jus in bello*, but also for *jus post bellum*'s expectation of restoration, which is directed toward establishing a just and lasting peace for all.

Stanley Hauerwas provocatively writes, "War is a counter church. It is the most determinative moral experience many people have."[75] Indeed, he seeks "to show that the Christian 'dis-ease' with war is liturgical. The sacrifices of war are a counter-liturgy to the sacrifice at the altar made possible by Christ."[76] Hauerwas's student, William T. Cavanaugh, makes a similar claim about how the "anti-liturgy" of the state organizes bodies and bodily actions into a "collective performance" that habituates them into "the imagination of the state."[77] According to Cavanaugh, it takes a counterliturgy, with another, more real imagination to reverse the antiliturgy and the imagination of the state.[78] As he puts it in connection with the Christian ritual that is the sacrament of the Eucharist which we celebrate at Mass, "To participate in the Eucharist is to live inside God's imagination. It is to be caught up into what is really real, the body of Christ. As human persons, body and soul, are

---

74. Meagher, *Killing from the Inside Out*, xiii, 141.

75. Stanley Hauerwas, *War and the American Difference: Theological Reflections on Violence and National Identity* (Grand Rapids, MI: Baker Academic, 2011), 34.

76. Ibid., 56.

77. William T. Cavanaugh, *Torture and Eucharist: Theology, Politics, and the Body of Christ* (Oxford: Blackwell, 1998), 12, 31.

78. Ibid., 275-76.

incorporated into the performance of Christ's *corpus verum*, they resist the state's ability to define what is real" through mechanisms such as, for Cavanaugh, torture, and, for us in this essay, unjust war.[79] Even when war might be morally justified and fought justly, we think there is need of restoration and reconciliation for returning warriors. Doing so requires more than what the state or clinical medicine offers at present. The church, with its serious approach to the JWT along with its embodied penitential practices, should witness to the possibility of another, better, maybe even more realistic way for returning warriors to deal with moral injury.

---

79. Ibid., 279.

Contributors

Lisa Sowle Cahill is the J. Donald Monan Professor in the Department of Theology at Boston College. She received her M.A. and Ph.D. from the University of Chicago. A past president of the Society of Christian Ethics and the Catholic Theological Society of America, her research interests include method in theological ethics, New Testament and ethics, Christology and ethics, social ethics, the ethics of war and peacemaking, and theological bioethics. She is the author of several books, including *Global Justice, Christology, and Christian Ethics* (Cambridge University Press, 2013), *Theological Bioethics: Participation, Justice and Change* (Georgetown University Press, 2005), *Sex, Gender, and Christian Ethics* (Cambridge University Press, 1996), and *"Love Your Enemies": Discipleship, Pacifism, and Just War Theory* (Fortress, 1994).

Stanley Hauerwas is the Gilbert T. Rowe Professor Emeritus of Divinity and Law at Duke University. Originally from Texas, he received his B.A. from Southwest University before going to Yale University, where he earned the B.D., M.A., M.Phil., and Ph.D. degrees. He also taught theological ethics at Augustana College and at the University of Notre Dame. He is internationally known for his contributions to the recovery of the importance of the virtues for the Christian moral life, his emphasis on the centrality of the church, his highlighting of the narrative character of Christian existence, as well as his commitment to Christian nonviolence. Among his many books are *The Peaceable Kingdom: A Primer in Christian Ethics* and *War and the American Difference: Theological Reflections on Violence and National Identity*. In 2001 he delivered the prestigious Gifford Lectures at the University of Edinburgh, published as *With the Grain of the Universe: The Church's Witness and Natural Theology*.

Kenneth R. Himes, O.F.M., is Associate Professor of Theological Ethics in the Department of Theology at Boston College. He received his Ph.D. from Duke University in religion and public policy. He has a special interest in the area of Catholic social teaching and how it relates to the domestic and international policies of the United States. A past president of the Catholic Theological Society of America, Fr. Himes is author of three books and coeditor of two others. His 2013 volume, *Christianity and the Political Order*, received first prize in the area of social teaching from the Catholic Press Association. His most recent book, *The Ethics of Targeted Killing and Drones*, will be published in the fall of 2015.

E. Ann Jeschke (M.T.S., Ph.D.) is currently a postdoctoral fellow at the Uniformed Services University of the Health Sciences (USUHS) in Bethesda, Maryland. She completed her doctoral dissertation, entitled "The Body Beatific: Total Force Fitness and the Social Reintegration/Rehabilitation of America's Warriors," in May 2015 at Saint Louis University. Her research investigated combat veterans' embodied experience of reintegration into civilian society as an aspect of *post bellum* ethics.

Laurie Johnston is Associate Professor of Theology at Emmanuel College in Boston, where she also serves as Director of Fellowships and coordinator of the Peace Studies program. Her teaching and research focus on social ethics and particularly the theological roots of Christian approaches to war and peace. She has published a number of chapters in books as well as articles in *Political Theology*, the *Journal of Moral Theology*, and the *Journal of Catholic Social Thought*. She received her M.Div. from Harvard Divinity School and her Ph.D. from Boston College.

John Kiess is Assistant Professor of Theology at Loyola University Maryland. He received his Ph.D. in Theology and Ethics from Duke University in 2011. As a George J. Mitchell Scholar, he earned his M.A. in Comparative Ethnic Conflict from Queen's University Belfast and M.Phil. in Theology from Cambridge University. His research interests include moral theology, political philosophy, and peace studies. He is the author of *Hannah Arendt and Theology* (London: T. & T. Clark, 2015) and has published articles in *Modern Theology*, the *Christian Century*, and other journals.

Elias Omondi Opongo, S.J., is the Director of Hekima Institute of Peace Studies and International Relations (HIPSIR), Nairobi. A Jesuit priest from Kenya, he holds a Ph.D. in Peace and Conflict Studies from the University of Bradford, UK, and an M.A. in International Peace Studies from the University of Notre Dame. His research focus is in the areas of transitional justice and postconflict reconstruction, state building, and community peacebuilding. He has published a number of books, book chapters, and articles on conflict resolution, transitional justice, peacebuilding, and Catholic social teaching.

Gerard F. Powers is Director of Catholic Peacebuilding Studies at the Joan B. Kroc Institute for International Peace Studies. He is also Coordinator of the Catholic Peacebuilding Network, which links scholars and Catholic leaders from countries torn by war in an effort to enhance the study and practice of conflict prevention, conflict management, and postconflict reconciliation. From 1998 to 2004, he was Director of the Office of International Justice and Peace of the US Conference of Catholic Bishops, and from 1987 to 1998 was a foreign policy advisor in the same office. He specializes in the ethics of the use of force; religion, conflict, and peacebuilding; and ethics and US foreign policy. He is coeditor (with R. Schreiter and S. Appleby) of *Peacebuilding: Catholic Theology, Ethics, and Praxis* (Orbis Books, 2010); coeditor (with D. Philpott) of *Strategies of Peace: Transforming Conflict in a Violent World* (Oxford University Press, 2010); and coeditor (with D. Christiansen and R. Hennemeyer) of *Peacemaking: Moral and Policy Challenges for a New World* (United States Catholic Conference, 1994).

Cristina Richie (M.Div., Th.M.) is currently Adjunct Faculty of Health Care Ethics at Massachusetts College of Pharmacy and Health Sciences (Boston). She has previously been an Adjunct Lecturer at Tufts University (Medford, MA) and Visiting Professor of Medical Ethics at Zaporozhye Bible College and Seminary (Zaporozhye, Ukraine). She has published over two dozen articles, book reviews, or book chapters, and her work has appeared in *Journal of Medical Ethics, Feminist Theology, Hastings Center Report*, and the *Heythrop Journal,* among others. In 2013 she won the Catholic Health Association's annual theology and ethics colloquium contest for her essay "Building a Framework for Green Bioethics: Integrating Ecology into the Medical Industry," which is the topic of her Ph.D. dissertation at Boston College.

Anna Floerke Scheid is Assistant Professor of Theology at Duquesne University in Pittsburgh, Pennsylvania. She completed her doctoral studies in Theological Ethics at Boston College in 2009 and earned an M.A. from Catholic Theological Union in 2004. Presently, she teaches and researches in the area of Christian social ethics with special attention to the ethics of conflict, peacebuilding, and postconflict reconciliation. She is the author of *Just Revolution: A Christian Ethic of Political Resistance and Social Transformation* (Lexington Books, Rowman & Littlefield, 2015). Her articles appear in *Horizons,* the *Journal of the Society of Christian Ethics, Teaching Theology and Religion,* and the *Bulletin of Ecumenical Theology.*

Brian Stiltner is Professor and Chair of Philosophy, Theology, and Religious Studies at Sacred Heart University in Fairfield, Connecticut. His teaching and research focus on virtue ethics, religion and politics, the ethics of war and peace, and moral issues within Catholicism. He formerly directed Sacred Heart's Institute for Applied Ethics and founded its Catholic Studies program. He is the author of *Religion and the Common Good* (1999); *Faith and Force: A Christian Debate about War* (with David L. Clough, Georgetown University Press, 2007); and *Character and Community: Virtue Ethics and the Pursuit of Personal and Social Flourishing* (forthcoming in 2016). He received his M.A.R. from Yale Divinity School, his Ph.D. from Yale University.

Tobias Winright is the Hubert Mäder Endowed Chair of Health Care Ethics in the Gnaegi Center for Health Care Ethics at Saint Louis University, where he is also Associate Professor of Theological Ethics in the Department of Theological Studies. His teaching and research focus on fundamental moral theology and applied ethical issues concerning bioethics, war and peace, criminal justice, and the environment. He coauthored *After the Smoke Clears: The Just War Tradition and Post War Justice* (Orbis Books, 2010); edited *Green Discipleship: Catholic Theological Ethics and the Environment* (Anselm Academic, 2011); coedited *Violence, Transformation, and the Sacred: "They Shall Be Called Children of God"* (Orbis Books, 2012); and coedited *Environmental Justice and Climate Change: Assessing Pope Benedict XVI's Ecological Vision for the Catholic Church in the United States* (Lexington, 2013). He is also coeditor of the *Journal of the Society of Christian Ethics*. He received his Ph.D. from the University of Notre Dame and his M.Div. from Duke Divinity School.

Rachel Hart Winter is the Director of the St. Catherine of Siena Center and Adjunct Professor of Theology at Dominican University in River Forest, Illinois. The Siena Center offers public lectures and classes that explore the intersection of church and society. Her teaching focuses on the intersection of ecology and theology, health care ethics, and Catholic social thought. She is currently collaborating with a team of international scholars on an interdisciplinary textbook that integrates ecology, ethics, and spirituality called *Healing Earth* through the International Jesuit Ecology Project. She served as a Jesuit volunteer in the Marshall Islands from 2000 to 2002. She received her M.A. and Ph.D. from Loyola University in Chicago.

Index